T0294504

THE TWO-STATE DILEMMA

THE TWO-STATE DILEMMA

A GAME THEORY PERSPECTIVE ON THE ISRAELI-PALESTINIAN CONFLICT

MICHAEL DAN

BARLOW BOOKS
fine books for enterprising authors

Library and Archives Canada Cataloguing in Publication data available upon request.

ISBN 978-1-988025-45-2 (hardcover)

Printed in Canada

TO ORDER IN CANADA:
  Georgetown Publications
  34 Armstrong Avenue, Georgetown, ON L7G 4R9

Publisher: Sarah Scott
For more information, visit
www.barlowbooks.com

Barlow Book Publishing Inc.
96 Elm Avenue, Toronto, ON
Canada M4W 1P2

To Amira, with love and with gratitude
for your wisdom and support

"But the Jews, once settled in their own State,
 would probably have no more enemies."
— THEODOR HERZL, 1896

"We and they want the same thing:
 We both want Palestine. And that is the fundamental conflict."
— DAVID BEN-GURION, 1936

CONTENTS

Preface

A NEW GAME

The three-thousand year presence of the Jewish people in the Land of Israel (*Eretz Yisrael* in Hebrew) is beyond any doubt. The future existence of a Zionist state in Eretz Yisrael is far from certain, however.

In the late nineteenth century, the Zionist movement dreamed of establishing a sovereign Jewish state, with a Jewish majority, in the whole of Palestine—a territory that in biblical times straddled both banks of the Jordan River. Jewish nationalists often refer to this territory as *Eretz Yisrael HaShlema* (the whole, or complete, Land of Israel). After 1921, however, efforts shifted to establishing a Jewish state in only the western portion of Eretz Yisrael HaShlema—in the territory of British Mandatory Palestine—or as it's called today, *historic Palestine* (see figure P.1).

It took a while for the Zionist dream to be realized, but between 1967 and 1994, the state of Israel was fully sovereign over the entire territory of historic Palestine *and* the majority of the inhabitants of historic Palestine were Jewish. Today the situation is different. Although Israel continues to exercise indirect control over all of historic Palestine, the territory under *direct* Israeli control has gotten smaller and the demographic picture has become more precarious for the Jews. The Zionist dream has begun to unravel.

With the signing of the Oslo II Accord in 1995, the Palestinian Authority gained civilian control over a series of scattered enclaves in the West Bank (Areas A and B), as well as the Gaza Strip. This represents a form of partial sovereignty for the Palestinians. (See figure P.2.) Entry into Area A is now forbidden to Israeli civilians. Construction of Jewish settlements in Areas A and B is likewise precluded. The Israel Defense

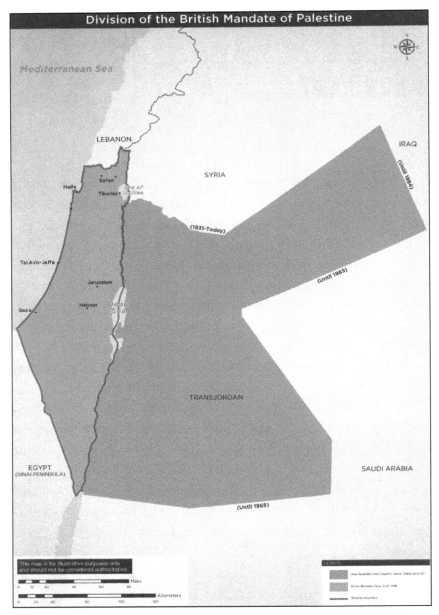

[light grey] Under direct British control [dark grey] Emirate of Transjordania

FIGURE P.1 DIVISION OF THE BRITISH MANDATE FOR PALESTINE (1921)

SOURCE: Israel Ministry of Foreign Affairs. https://mfa.gov.il/mfa/aboutisrael/maps/pages/the%20league%20of%20nations%20mandate%20for%20palestine%20-%201920.aspx. Public domain, Israel Ministry of Foreign Affairs.

MICHAEL DAN

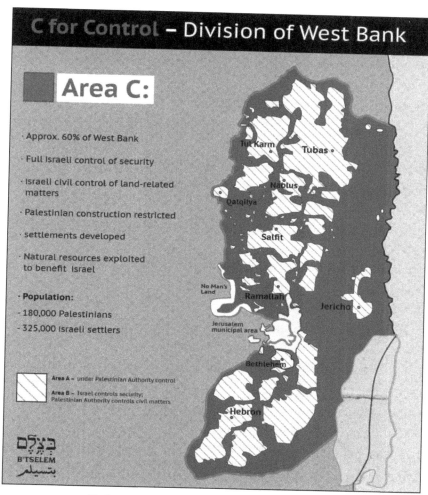

C for Control – Division of West Bank

Area C:

- Approx. 60% of West Bank

- Full Israeli control of security

- Israeli civil control of land-related matters

- Palestinian construction restricted

- settlements developed

- Natural resources exploited to benefit Israel

- **Population:**

- 180,000 Palestinians

- 325,000 Israeli settlers

Tul Karm
Tubas
Nablus
Qalqilya
Salfit
No Man's Land
Ramallah
Jericho
Jerusalem municipal area
Bethlehem
Hebron

Area A – under Palestinian Authority control

Area B – Israel controls security;
Palestinian Authority controls civil matters

צלם
B'TSELEM
بتسيلم

[dark grey] Area C [white with hatches] Areas A and B

FIGURE P.2 MAP OF DIVISION OF THE WEST BANK. AREA C IS UNDER FULL ISRAELI CONTROL, FOR BOTH CIVIL AND SECURITY MATTERS. AREAS A AND B ARE AREAS OF PARTIAL PALESTINIAN SOVEREIGNTY

SOURCE: B'Tselem. https://www.palestineportal.org/learn-teach/israelpalestine-the-basics/maps/maps-1967-to-present/. Used with permission of B'Tselem—The Israeli Information Center for Human Rights in the Occupied Territories.

Forces (IDF), however, enter Areas A and B on a regular basis for purposes of conducting anti-terrorist raids (typically at night, and typically in coordination with the Palestinian Security Services). Following Hamas's takeover of the Gaza Strip in 2007, any Israeli civilian caught visiting without the proper entry and exit permits may have their citizenship revoked.

The era of Zionist territorial maximalism is now well behind us, and at some point in the not too distant future, the number of non-Jews living in historic Palestine will exceed the number of Jews. This will mark a long-dreaded turning point for the Zionist project—perhaps even a point of no return.

What kind of state does Israel wish to become on the day that Jews constitute a minority in Eretz Yisrael? Can one even pose such a question and still be considered a good Zionist? Clearly, there's an elephant in Zionism's living room.

For decades now, demographic forces in historic Palestine have been pulling the Jewish state towards two very different political horizons. In one direction lies a state of all its citizens (the majority of whom won't be Jewish), and in the other direction, an undemocratic, apartheid-like state dominated by Jewish ultranationalists. And neither of these are Zionist choices—at least not the kind of Zionism that's envisioned in Israel's Declaration of Independence (which, if you read it carefully, embraces a two-state solution with economic union, and complete equality of social and political rights for all inhabitants).

Under the Westphalian system of government (which forms the basis for the modern international system), a sovereign state should have well-defined borders, a permanent population, a single government, and the capacity to enter into normal relations with other sovereign states. And above all else, a sovereign state should not interfere in the affairs of other sovereign states. Such a system was imposed on the defeated Ottoman Empire at the conclusion of the First World War; for a variety of reasons, it never really caught on.

Neither the state of Israel nor the state of Palestine conforms well to the Westphalian model. If we accept for a moment that Palestine is already a de facto state in international law (which isn't a particularly controversial position to take), then it's abundantly clear that the state of Israel is constantly interfering in the affairs of the state of Palestine (allegedly for security reasons). The state of Israel has no international border with the state of Palestine (or Syria or Lebanon for that matter). And the state of Palestine, for its part, no longer has a single government.

None of these details seems to matter very much to most Israelis. But to a generation of Palestinians raised on the dream of full sovereignty over just 22 per cent of their historic homeland (the maximum area now claimed by the state of Palestine), there's nothing left but the misery of colonization.

The two-state game has ended; a new game is now underway.

WHY NOW?

Like two lost travellers wandering through the desert, Israel and the Palestinian Authority have spent more than a quarter century chasing a mirage called the two-state solution. But instead of two states for two peoples between the river and the sea, there's at best perhaps one and a half. And instead of peace, there's the most intractable conflict in modern history: the Israeli-Palestinian conflict. Why is it that Israel and Egypt, Israel and Jordan, or even the Irish and the British were able to patch things up and accomplish the previously unthinkable, but not Israel and Palestine? Is the so-called peace process for real, or only a game? And if it's a game, then is it a game that can even be 'won'?

As I write these words, Israelis are heading to the polling stations for the third time in less than a year following two failed attempts by Benjamin Netanyahu to form a coalition government. Along the way, his efforts were aided (but obviously not sufficiently so) by his political twin from across the ocean, Donald Trump. For American presidents going back five decades, the opportunity to leave their mark on the Middle East has become a veritable rite of passage.

In 1970, US president Richard Nixon waded into the pool when he endorsed a plan that was presented to the world by his secretary of state, William Rogers. The so-called Rogers Plan essentially attempted to compel both sides into accepting the basic framework for peace as outlined by UN Resolution 242. The latter had been cobbled together following the Six-Day War, and formed the basis for at least a partial withdrawal from the territories recently occupied by Israel. In a rejection that exquisitely captured the uniquely absolutist flavour of the conflict, the Rogers Plan was dismissed as too pro-Israel by one side and not pro-Israel enough by the other.

Following the Yom Kippur War of October 1973 and a fresh outbreak of calls for a permanent peace between Arabs and Israelis in the Middle East, President Jimmy Carter served as the grinning master of ceremonies between Egyptian president Anwar Sadat and Israeli prime minister Menachem Begin at the Camp David summit in 1978. The two parties appeared to create traction for meaningful implementation of UN Resolution 242 (a "land for peace" swap that conspicuously made no mention of the Palestinians), and a second accord a year later seemed to signal that peace between Israel and her Middle East neighbours might be at hand.

Begin and Sadat shared the Nobel Peace Prize in 1978, and the world celebrated the achievement as an historic step on the road to a lasting regional peace. Unfortunately, sentiment among hardline Arabs was less than enthusiastic, and when President Sadat was assassinated in October 1981 by a Jihadi cell in the military, it exposed—once again—the powerful and recalcitrant ideological undercurrents at play.

A decade later, in 1991, the United States and the Soviet Union co-sponsored a summit in Madrid between Israel and the Palestinians (as well as a number of other Arab countries). Although the accomplishments of this conference were thin, its symbolic value was significant.

Optimism for peace was renewed in 1993 when—for the first time—Palestinians and Israelis met face to face (privately and in secret) in Oslo, Norway. Among many firsts, Palestinian Liberation Organization (PLO) chairman Yasser Arafat acknowledged the right of Israel to exist "in peace and security." Israeli prime minister Yitzhak Rabin astonished the world by being the first to recognize the PLO as "the legitimate representative of the Palestinian people." It was also—most significantly—the first time since the declaration of independence by Israel in 1948 that both parties hinted at the possibility of the creation of a separate Palestinian state alongside the state of Israel. In a celebration on the White House lawn (which included former US presidents Jimmy Carter and George H.W.

Bush), Arafat and Rabin stood on either side of President Bill Clinton to cement the deal. When Arafat and Rabin shook hands, the crowd erupted in applause. A year later Arafat, Rabin, and Shimon Peres (Israel's minister of foreign affairs) would have their turn to share a Nobel Peace Prize.

The euphoria didn't last very long. Two years later, while attending a peace rally in Tel Aviv, Rabin was assassinated by an ultranationalist Israeli university student. More than twenty-five years after the Oslo peace process began, virtually none of its historic agenda has been implemented.

Israel and the Palestinian Authority met in Hebron in January 1997 as part of the Oslo peace process, and again a year later in Wye Valley, Maryland, with President Bill Clinton moderating. Once again, an American president attempted to jump-start a stalled peace process, and once again there was very little traction. The two sides were brought together at Camp David in 2000, where Israeli prime minister Ehud Barak made what he believed was an incredibly generous offer to Palestinian chairman Yasser Arafat, an offer that touched on all the core issues of the conflict, but which was ultimately turned down because of a disagreement over the Temple Mount/Haram al-Sharif. Arafat left the conference without even making a counter-offer.

The following year, an undaunted Bill Clinton improvised a new approach he called a "bridging proposal" in an attempt to make headway. In conferences in Washington, DC, Cairo, and Taba, Egypt, the two parties continued to negotiate, but to no avail.

In 2002, Republican president George W. Bush broke precedent with a series of announcements sketching out a new route to resolving the conflict, and he became the first US president to formally call for the establishment of a Palestinian state. The following year the UN, the European Union, Russia, and the United States presented what became known as the Roadmap for peace. As the name implies, the approach bypassed a direct resolution of the Palestinian-Israeli conflict and focused instead on a series of conditions that would need to be resolved in order to achieve peace. By 2005—the deadline for the Roadmap—nothing had been agreed upon.

Bush tried again in 2007 at Annapolis in a summit between Israeli prime minister Ehud Olmert and Palestinian Authority president Mahmoud Abbas. Negotiations got off to a stumbling and inauspicious start, and the newly empowered organization Hamas (now in control of the Gaza Strip) flatly refused to abide by any agreement reached in the conference. Nevertheless, in 2008 Israel made for the second time what it believed to be an extremely generous offer to the Palestinians, only to be rebuffed once again. With Prime Minister Olmert facing corruption charges, the deadline for Israel's offer came and went. Olmert's successor, Benjamin Netanyahu, refused to engage in further peace talks with the Palestinians. The Roadmap seemed further away from its destination than ever.

The negotiating door was pried open an inch in 2009 when incoming US president Barack Obama authorized secretary of state George Mitchell to test the waters in an attempt to kick-start the peace process. When the Obama administration successfully convinced Netanyahu to commit to a ten-month partial freeze on new settlements in the West Bank, the door seemed suddenly to swing wide open. Mahmoud Abbas, however, immediately cold-shouldered the overture as duplicitous and insufficient. Negotiations resumed in 2010 but expectations were so low that failure was essentially a foregone conclusion.

United States secretary of state John Kerry made a last-ditch effort in 2013 and 2014 to revive the peace talks, but with the passing of Shimon Peres in 2016, the Oslo peace process itself seemed to have departed forever from this earth.

Today, the prospects for a two-state solution in historic Palestine have all but evaporated. As the hard-right long ago pointed out, there's simply no room for two states between the river and the sea.

President Donald Trump took office in 2017 and almost immediately assigned his son-in-law the task of definitively solving the Israeli-Palestinian conflict. "I am looking at two states and one state, and I like the one that both parties like," he said. "If the Israelis and the Palestinians want one state, that's okay with me. If they want two states, that's okay with me. I'm happy if they're happy." This marked the first time that the

United States had publicly floated the idea of a one-state solution. But what exactly did President Trump mean by "one state?" Did he mean joint Israeli/Palestinian co-sovereignty over the territory of historic Palestine, or something else?

Meanwhile, against this backdrop of alleged support for both sides, the Trump administration relocated the American embassy from Tel Aviv to Jerusalem, shuttered Palestinian diplomatic offices in Washington, cut back hundreds of millions of dollars in humanitarian aid to the Palestinians, recognized Israeli sovereignty over the Golan Heights, and reversed decades of American policy that held that Israeli settlements were a violation of international law.

On January 28, 2020, Trump (while in the midst of an impeachment trial in the Senate) finally announced his long-awaited "deal of the century" to a room packed with Jewish and Christian Zionist supporters. Netanyahu (recently indicted on bribery, fraud, and breach of trust) was at his side, and the Palestinians, conspicuously absent.

Trump's plan (optimistically dubbed "Peace to Prosperity") amounts to a Hobson's Choice ("take it or leave it") that has already been rejected out of hand by the Palestinians. The plan green lights Israeli annexation of the Jordan Valley and the "seam zone" (the area between the separation barrier and the 1967 border), and sets impossible conditions on the Palestinians that essentially amount to a demand for regime change as a prerequisite for very limited, very conditional, semi-autonomy. Trump went out of his way to remind the Palestinians that this was the best deal they were ever going to get, thereby confirming, once and for all, that the dream of Palestinian sovereignty had all but evaporated. It was a total victory for the Israelis. Or was it? Wishful thinking aside, the back story behind the conflict never changes and the numbers behind it don't lie.

For more than a century now, the Zionist movement has worried and fretted over three unresolved dilemmas: Jewish demographics, Palestinian national legitimacy, and partition. Yet despite all the musings and angst, it went ahead and built a Jewish state in nearly the whole of historic Palestine. So why are these triple dilemmas so important today?

Why now? Why change anything when it's clear that Israel is winning the zero-sum game according to what Israeli author Avi Shlaim calls the "doctrine of perpetual conflict" (i.e., living by the sword forever)?

The answer is that the biggest threat to Israel today is not the doctrine of perpetual conflict, but the doctrine of perpetual *growth*. Simply stated, the latter holds that whatever Israel's current difficulties, they can always be overcome by adding more Jews to Eretz Yisrael. But if we are to believe the numbers, then there are already over thirteen million people living in historic Palestine, which makes it more densely populated than India. The Gaza Strip now boasts a whopping five thousand people per square kilometre—all of whom are Palestinian.

Already, Israel is heavily dependent on desalination technology for much of her fresh water, and she grows less than half the calories she needs to feed herself. Her electrical grid is not connected to any regional partners. The *Haredim* (ultra-Orthodox community), now a million strong, have one of the highest fertility rates in the world—an average of seven children per woman of child-bearing age—comparable to any Third World country. What will be the quality of life of the average Israeli in thirty years' time? The name Thomas Malthus springs to mind.

As the number of Israelis and Palestinians increases, so too does the friction between everyone. Even the words that we use to describe the conflict manage, both intentionally and unintentionally, to reinforce its intractability. Take, for example, the term "Arab-Israeli." It's an invention of history. An epithet that didn't exist prior to 1948, and it delegitimizes and degrades the Palestinian people by lumping them together with all other Arab people. Yet Arab-Israeli is entirely consistent with both Zionist theory and Israeli domestic law, which maintains that Arabs are a legitimate national group but that Palestinians are not. Perhaps it would make more sense to replace the term Arab-Israeli with the less politically charged term "Palestinian Israeli" (without the hyphen), or better yet, "Palestinian citizen of Israel."

The term "occupation" is equally problematic. It's a technical term, plucked from the lexicon of international law, and it grossly under-represents the indelible physical transformations that have taken place in the territories that Israel captured in 1967 (in particular, in and around the Old City of Jerusalem). Occupations are theoretically temporary—not fifty years long and still counting. What's happening today in the Palestinian Territories isn't occupation—it's colonization. And this should come as no surprise because Jews have been systematically colonizing historic Palestine since the days of the *Yishuv* (the pre-state Jewish community in Palestine). Everything that's happened since 1967 is merely the continuation of a pre-existing colonization program. So, instead of "occupation," perhaps it would make more sense to use the term "colonization."

Most challenging of all is the idea of Zionism itself. As originally formulated in the late nineteenth century, political Zionism regarded the Jewish people as members of a stateless nation in desperate need of a home. Today, that's obviously no longer the case. The state of Israel exists, and has existed, for over seven decades now (and is, by definition, a Jewish state). So, mission accomplished: the Jews have a state. What further use do we have for Zionism? Why bother clinging to an ideological relic from the nineteenth century and, in particular, the antiquated *ethnonational theory* that forms its 'moral' foundation?

The answer is that ideas and ideologies persist because they take on a life of their own. Most non-Israelis have probably never heard of the Population Registry Law (1965), which takes the odd view that there's no such thing as an "Israeli" nationality (this has been challenged several times before the Israeli Supreme Court and has always been upheld, most recently in 2013[1]).

The Population Registry Law is the direct result of tenacious and anachronistic Zionist thinking. Whereas the international community may regard citizens of Israel as Israeli nationals, *there are no Israeli nationals according to Israeli domestic law.* Instead, citizens of Israel are classified according to the following national groups: Jewish, Arab, Druze, Circassian, etc., and *only Jewish nationals have collective rights in Israel* (e.g., the right to buy, mortgage, or lease land held by the Jewish National Fund—about 13 per cent of the total land base in Israel).

In the Hebrew language, the word *l'om* (לְאוֹם), which once appeared on every Israeli ID card, translates into English as either ethnicity or nationality; and for many in the world today, these are essentially the same concepts (indeed, the Greek word for nation is *ethnos* [ἔθνος]).

Tragically, it took Europeans hundreds of years of bloody internecine warfare before they finally became comfortable with the idea that ethnicity and nationality could mean two different things. The results today are a number of reasonably successful, multi-ethnic European countries, mostly in the western half of the continent (Eastern Europe, as always, continues to struggle with its identity politics).

But Zionist theory (which originated in Eastern Europe) holds that Israeli citizens may possess either Jewish nationality (*l'om yehudi*) or Arab nationality (*l'om aravi*), but not both because Jews and Arabs are separate 'nations.' An Arab-Jew, or a Jew-Arab, or even an ethnic Israeli are all technically impossible and illegal under Israeli domestic law. This point seems to be lost on most members of the so-called progressive Zionist camp.

At the heart of Zionist theory, therefore, lies a monstrous error of deductive reasoning. Although it's true that Israel is a nation according to international law, and that Israel is a Jewish state according to its own domestic laws, it's a mistake to conclude that the Jewish people are also a nation according to international law. If this were the case, then the *Jewish nation* would have been recognized by the UN Security Council in 1948, and the *Jewish nation* would have signed peace treaties with Egypt in 1979 and Jordan in 1994. But the Jewish nation has no standing in international law. It only exists as a form of collective and historical memory.

In the Middle East, however, collective memory *is* reality, just as demographics *are* politics. Which means that the Israeli Central Bureau of Statistics doesn't just tally up the country's various ethnoreligious communities—it also keeps score in an *inter*-national battle—a battle that the Jewish 'nation' may one day lose.

The Two-State Dilemma aims to shed light on the Israeli-Palestinian conflict by examining it from a game theory perspective. It's an approach that asks: Who are the players? What game(s) are they playing? And what does co-operation or winning look like? The focus is analytical rather than prescriptive. This book doesn't propose solutions to the conflict so much as draw our attention to *non*-solutions, such as apartheid (obviously) or the two-state 'solution.'

The mathematical concepts presented in this book are relatively simple and don't exceed anything beyond the grade ten level. Each chapter builds on material presented in the previous chapters. Chapter 1 is a necessarily brief, but (I hope) sufficient, introduction to game theory in order to show how it can illuminate our understanding of the two-state solution and its ultimate non-viability in the context of historic Palestine. Chapter 2 explores the three core dilemmas that confront (and have always confronted) the Zionist project. Chapter 3 is an exploration of the history of pre-state Israel as viewed from a game theory perspective. In chapter 4 we switch gears a bit and digress into evolutionary biology. We examine concepts such as replicators, vehicles, and the evolutionarily stable strategy to show us how tenaciously we cling to our beliefs and how those beliefs colour our politics. Chapter 5 examines some of the social dilemmas facing contemporary Israeli society. Chapter 6 attempts to understand the Gaza wars in terms of game theory. Chapter 7 traces the history of eight decades of effort at imposing the two-state solution on historic Palestine (and why such efforts ultimately failed). Chapter 8 examines the consequences and implications of the 'doctrine of perpetual growth,' and finally, chapter 9 explores some of the systemic and structural factors that undermine the prospects for peace between Israel and Palestine.

This book strives to be as objective and dispassionate as possible. And it's not an anti-Israeli book. Israel is a dynamic, democratic, and pluralistic country that exists, and that has every right to exist, as a full-fledged member of the international community. Nor is it an anti-Palestinian or anti-Zionist book. The state of Palestine, too, has every right to exist and to flourish, free to shape its own destiny without any outside interference.

Critics of Israel should note that for over a century, Zionism has given hope to millions of people, including generations of Palestinian Israelis. And not just hope, but also a degree of tangible material prosperity.

But respect for minority rights has always been a bedrock value of the Zionist movement (if you disagree with me, go read Herzl). And minority rights in Israel have been steadily deteriorating over the past decade—as objectively demonstrated by the legislative track record of the Netanyahu government. Many years from now, when we look back on the Oslo era, we will continue to be amazed at how viciously and mercilessly Jewish nationalists and ultranationalists swept aside all progress that was being made towards social equality and a two-state solution (the names Baruch Goldstein and Yigal Amir come to mind).

In any event, one of the most important conclusions reached in this book is that the two-state solution is simply no longer viable. Although such an arrangement was once acceptable to the founders of the state of Israel, it's now clear (some seventy years later) that 'two states for two peoples' has stuck around way past its expiry date.

Of course it's always possible to come up with even *less* palatable solutions for historic Palestine, but let's not even think about a full-blown apartheid state (which would be completely beyond the pale). So, that eliminates two very popular choices: two states for two peoples, or a single apartheid state. But as they say in the psychoanalysis business, there are *always* choices.

Will historic Palestine—after many years of struggle—end up as yet another autocratic Arab state, or will it blossom into the Belgium of the Middle East (a profoundly binational country, capable of functioning for 589 consecutive days without a sitting prime minister)? Perhaps the only thing that's certain is that whichever way Israel turns, either as a partner for peace or as a colonizer, there's no way to separate completely from the Palestinians. As much as Jewish ultranationalists would like to sequester every Palestinian man, woman, and child behind an 'iron wall' (or maybe a concrete separation barrier), Jews and Palestinians are forever destined to share the same land—one way or another.

Chapter 1

THE GAME THEORY PERSPECTIVE

The Book of Genesis opens with the familiar verse, "In the beginning, God created the heavens and the earth." In his commentary on Genesis 1:1, the great medieval Torah scholar Rashi explains that Eretz Yisrael is the possession of the Jewish people by virtue of it having been given to them by the Creator of the world. In the *Tanakh* (which consists of the *Torah, Nevi'im*, and *Ketuvim*—basically the Christian Old Testament), we encounter the United Monarchy of David and Solomon, the boundaries of which extended from Dan in the north to Beersheba in the south, and eastward across the Jordan River (see figure 1.1). No other geography has been so deeply imprinted on the Jewish soul.

Recent archeological discoveries have cast serious doubt on the veracity of the Exodus from Egypt as well as the existence of the United Monarchy of David and Solomon. And the Babylonian exile of 586 BCE only affected the political and intellectual elite. But even if we discount the United Kingdom of David and Solomon as a myth, there is little doubt about the existence of a Roman province called Iudea (Judea).

First established in 6 CE through the amalgamation of Judea, Samaria, and Idumea (Edom), Judea reached its final size in 44 CE with the addition of the Galilee (to the north) and Perea (on the east bank of the Jordan River). Judea was the site of much unrest against Rome. During the Great Revolt, which lasted from 66–73 CE, Rome destroyed the Jewish Temple in Jerusalem and confronted the last survivors of the rebellion at Masada— zealots who would rather commit suicide than endure Roman captivity. All of this was carefully documented by Flavius Josephus, who witnessed these events first-hand.

FIGURE 1.1 PALESTINE UNDER DAVID AND SOLOMON (ABOUT 1015–930 BCE)

SOURCE: *Smith Bible Atlas*, London, 1905. Public domain.

MICHAEL DAN

In 135 CE, Simon Bar Kokhba led the final Jewish rebellion against Rome. It was mercilessly crushed by Emperor Hadrian, who subsequently changed the name of Judea to Syria Palestina, and that of Jerusalem to Aelia Capitolina, in order to obliterate all memory of Jewish sovereignty. But regardless of whether our historical reference point is the United Kingdom of David and Solomon, or the Roman province of Judea, or Syria Palestina, or simply Palestine, it's all the same geography—a geography for which the Jewish people have yearned for nearly two millennia.

APPLYING A NEW LENS TO AN ANCIENT CONFLICT

Since biblical times, every major conflict in the Middle East has been framed as an "us versus them" trade-off: a zero-sum game in which one side's gains represent the other side's losses. Such a worldview dates back to the conquest of Canaan, and continues—with modest and short-lived interruptions—to today.

But there are other types of conflicts, which mathematicians refer to as *non-zero-sum* games, in which there is an opportunity for rational co-operation between two opponents. Rational co-operation was the goal of the Palestine Royal Commission (1937), the UN Partition Plan for Palestine (1947), and the Oslo peace process (1993–2014). Sadly, all of these modern efforts at creating two states for two peoples ended in failure.

Why? Is failure an inevitable feature of the Israeli-Palestinian conflict, or is the conflict so deeply entrenched that the parties lack all capacity for rational co-operation?

As a conceptual tool, the importance of game theory in conflict resolution—especially the simple elegance of what is known as the 2×2 matrix—is that it forces us to think about a solution that is mutually beneficial rather than one forced into simplistic win/lose terms. Game theory tells us how co-operation could 'look' in real life, and the Prisoner's Dilemma is the mother of all non-zero-sum games.

THE PRISONER'S DILEMMA

The Prisoner's Dilemma (PD) was formulated in 1950 by Melvin Dresher and Merrill Flood, two mathematicians working at the RAND Corporation, in California. In a PD, two opponents play a game in which they must choose between co-operation and betrayal (sometimes represented as a choice between co-operation and defection). In Dresher and Flood's original example,[1] two suspected burglars are arrested and brought to the police station. Each is placed in solitary confinement and has no means of communicating with the other. Here's the problem: the district attorney (DA) doesn't have enough evidence to convict either prisoner of all possible charges, but neither prisoner knows this. This is the key to the dilemma. So what does each prisoner do?

The dilemma is illustrated in figure 1.2.

| | | Prisoner B | |
		mum	snitch
Prisoner A	mum	A and B keep mum	A keeps mum and B snitches
	snitch	A snitches and B keeps mum	A and B "sing like canaries"

FIGURE 1.2

There are four possible scenarios as represented by a simple 2×2 matrix. Prisoner A is on the left and prisoner B is at the top. Each has the opportunity to either co-operate with or betray the other prisoner.

What is the matrix telling us?

Hoping to receive a lighter sentence, a prisoner might decide to inform on his partner. This is called snitching, finking, ratting, singing, spilling the beans, etc. On the other hand, a prisoner might just as easily decide *not* to inform on his partner in the hope that his partner would do the same. This is called keeping mum, remaining tight-lipped, staying close-mouthed, playing dumb, etc. From the individual prisoner's perspective, however, the 'hands down' best choice is to always snitch on a partner who decides to keep mum. That way your partner gets stuck with most of the blame. But what are the chances of having a partner who plays dumb? To snitch or not to snitch, that is the question.

Now, let's flip things around and look at the situation from the DA's perspective. Without at least one of the two prisoners snitching, there isn't enough evidence to convict either of them on all possible charges. So, the DA decides to offer a deal to each prisoner, and each prisoner is informed that the deal is the same for both (of course, it is still true that neither knows what the other will choose). We can assume that each prisoner—being sensible—will rank his respective choices in the same order (versus secretly wishing for more jail time, for example).

Here's the deal: if both prisoners keep mum, each will receive a one-year sentence. If one prisoner snitches and the other keeps mum, the snitcher will go free and the prisoner who keeps mum will receive a three-year sentence. Finally, if both prisoners "sing like a couple of canaries" (to use a favourite expression from old gangster movies), each will receive a two-year sentence because their individual confessions are of very little value once they've both confessed to the same crime.

OK so far? Now, let's assign numbers (values) to the choices presented. This can be represented by a *payout matrix*; basically, it quantifies the consequence of each combination of choices made (see figure 1.3).

Prisoner B

		mum	snitch
Prisoner A	mum	A and B receive a 1-year jail sentence	B goes free; A receives a 3-year jail sentence
	snitch	A goes free; B receives a 3-year jail sentence	A and B receive a 2-year jail sentence

FIGURE 1.3

For the sake of consistency, we will only use negative numbers, which represent years spent in jail (see figure 1.4). The number zero means a prisoner goes free. There are no positive numbers in this particular example but that doesn't matter. Only the relative ranking of the numbers is important. Also, we need to be careful here about what we mean by "co-operate" and "betray." Co-operating with the district attorney doesn't count as co-operation. What we mean by co-operation and betrayal is limited to behaviour that impacts the other prisoner. Keeping mum is a form of co-operation. Denouncing your partner to the police is the ultimate betrayal.

		B	
		C	D
A	C	-1, -1	-3, 0
	D	0, -3	-2, -2

C = co-operate, D = defect/betray; A in bold text, B in regular text

FIGURE 1.4

If we add four points to each number in each cell in the matrix, we can get rid of the negative numbers. This is purely for cosmetic purposes. This now gives us the traditional numbering system for a PD (see figure 1.5). The numbers represent the relative values (or utility) of each choice (co-operate or betray) to each player (A or B). For instance, if both A and B choose to co-operate, then the relative value to each is 3 and the collective value is 6. If both A and B choose to betray, then the relative value to each is 2 and the collective value is 4.

		B	
		C	D
A	C	3, 3	1, 4
	D	4, 1	2, 2

C = co-operate, D = defect/betray; A in bold text, B in regular text

FIGURE 1.5

Where is the dilemma?

So, where is the dilemma in a Prisoner's Dilemma? It's important to remember that a dilemma is not simply a difficult choice. Properly, a dilemma exists when a player must choose between two equally undesirable alternatives.

Think of our two hapless prisoners. Let's assume each believes the worst of the other. In that case, snitching—regardless of what the other does—makes the most sense, and both will end up snitching in what amounts to a double betrayal. The consequences of a double betrayal will be two years of jail time each (for a total of four years). On the other hand, what about the principle of honour among thieves? Perhaps both prisoners take this principle seriously, in which case they will conclude, both individually and collectively, that keeping mum is the best possible choice (we call this double co-operation). In this case, the consequences of a double co-operation will be only one year of jail time each (for a total of two years).

Seems simple, right? Okay, maybe not. What is really important to understand is what happens in the case where one prisoner extends a hand in co-operation, but the other betrays them (it doesn't matter if it's prisoner A or B because the matrix is symmetrical). In such a case, the betraying prisoner receives a payoff of 4 (we call this the temptation payoff), and the co-operative prisoner receives a payoff of only 1 (we call this the sucker's payoff). Obviously, the sucker's payoff is something to be avoided at all costs.

If you have been following along, you will now see that the PD neatly crystallizes a timeless question: is it better to co-operate with a stranger in the hope that they will also be co-operative, or is it better to always mistrust them because the price of betrayal is always dear? The answer, I think, is that there isn't a simple answer. That's why the Prisoner's Dilemma is a dilemma. Ultimately, it doesn't really matter if the combinatorial logic is clear yet. What makes the PD so useful in our story is that it helps us to think about the *cost* of co-operation versus betrayal, both individually and collectively.

Another example of a Prisoner's Dilemma

If you are confused by the classic story of the Prisoner's Dilemma, you're not alone. It's difficult to keep track of what is meant by co-operation (Is it co-operation with the police or the other prisoner? Answer: with the other prisoner.) and also the significance of three vs. two vs. one year in jail (All are negative numbers, but some are more negative than others.). So here is another example of a PD that I hesitate to use except for its illustrative value (personal disclaimer: I have no direct experience with the following illustration!).

The open marriage dilemma: Colin and Rose met in college and got married in their early twenties. They have been faithful to each other during thirty long, boring years of marriage. Now in their early fifties and with the kids all grown up and living independently in another city, Colin and Rose have begun to weigh the pros and cons of continuing with their long-standing monogamous relationship.

One summer evening, after a particularly good bottle of Chardonnay, they both decide to invigorate their marriage by playing a daring and dangerous game: they will each give the other an opportunity to cheat—no consequences and no questions asked. There are only two rules: (1) you can only cheat once, and (2) each spouse mustn't tell the other whether or not they've cheated. Will they both cheat, or is the *idea* of cheating enough for them? Figure 1.6 represents the payout matrix (Rose is for rows and Colin is for columns). Their choices are ranked from 1 to 4, with 4 being the most desirable.

		Colin	
		faithful	cheat
Rose	faithful	**3**, 3	**1**, 4
	cheat	**4**, 1	**2**, 2

Rose in bold text, Colin in regular text

FIGURE 1.6

From Rose's perspective, she would like to be the one who cheats while Colin remains faithful. And from Colin's perspective, it's the opposite. But if neither one cheats, their sex life will probably remain just as boring as it is now. Clearly, if both end up cheating, it could put the marriage at risk (how sure can either be that they will "cheat" only once?). A divorce at this stage in life would be financially catastrophic and their kids would never forgive them. So the dilemma comes down to cheating because you think your spouse will cheat, or *not* cheating because you think your spouse *won't* cheat!

Fortunately for Colin and Rose, they both studied introductory game theory in college and realized the next morning that the collective utility of maintaining a monogamous relationship is the highest-valued of all possible choices. They agree to call off their foolish game, and visit a sex shop instead.

I like this story because it exemplifies the motivational logic of a 2×2 game matrix, as opposed to the threat of death by stoning, which is the biblical punishment for adultery.

IS THE ISRAELI-PALESTINIAN CONFLICT A PRISONER'S DILEMMA?

How do Colin and Rose help us? Well, during the Oslo peace process (which lasted from 1993 to 2014), Israel and the Palestinian Authority had the opportunity to either co-operate or undermine each other. What happened? If we represent the conflict as a Prisoner's Dilemma, then we get a payout matrix (see figure 1.7).

		Palestine	
		co-operation	autonomy
Israel	co-operation	one-state solution (3,3)	Arab state (1,4)
	autonomy	Zionist state (4,1)	two-state solution (2,2)

FIGURE 1.7

In the upper left-hand quadrant is the so-called one-state solution (also known as one state for two peoples). Such an idealistic situation would necessitate a high degree of rational co-operation between Jewish and Palestinian citizens, but the potential benefits to both would be enormous.

For one thing, it wouldn't be necessary to divide the Land. Everybody would have the freedom to live and work wherever they wanted and to vote in free and fair elections. Palestinians would receive the same individual and collective rights as Jews. Both cultures would be protected, and so would the democratic nature of the state—but with a minimum of identity politics. The relative value to each side of such a utopian scenario, on a scale of 1 to 4 (with 4 being the highest), is a 3. Collectively speaking, the one-state solution *should* be the best solution for everyone because 3 + 3 = 6. Another name for the one-state solution is "Hand in Hand."

In the bottom right-hand quadrant of the matrix is the so-called two-state solution (also known as two states for two peoples). From a political perspective, this should represent a very stable, long-term solution to the conflict provided that the two sides can *completely* separate from each other and go their respective ways. From a mathematical perspective, it's also a compelling case. Interestingly, the relative value of the two-state solution to each side is a 2, and collectively it would be a 4, which makes it 33 per cent *worse* for everyone than the one-state solution. This intuitively makes sense: under such an arrangement, Palestinians wouldn't be able to live in Israel and vice versa. The main advantage of a two-state solution over a one-state solution is that each nation would have autonomy and sovereignty over their own affairs and would be free to pursue their own agenda. Another name for the two-state solution is the "Happy Divorce."

In the bottom left-hand quadrant of the matrix is the option of continued colonization of the Palestinian Territories. This represents a scenario in which Israel exercises strict control over the Palestinian population, with the latter reluctantly complying and co-operating. To Israel, the relative value of colonization is a 4, but to Palestine it's a 1. To put it bluntly, after decades of failed peace talks and two intifadas, colonization has become Israel's *number one choice*. Let's call this solution the "Zionist state," although once Jews become a minority in Eretz Yisrael, it would be more appropriately described as a "Jewish ultranationalist state" since such a state would by definition be undemocratic and probably apartheid-like.

In the top right-hand quadrant of the matrix is the option of governing strictly by the numbers. In the very near future, there will be a non-Jewish majority in historic Palestine, so according to the principles of democracy, Palestinians should eventually achieve the upper hand, with the Jews having to reluctantly comply and co-operate. Let's call this solution the "Arab state." This isn't the same as the one-state solution. In a one-state solution, there is co-operation between Jews and Palestinians regardless of demographics (analogous to the co-operation between English and French Canadians at the federal level—both have equal rights). In an Arab state, a 49 per cent Jewish minority would have to comply with the wishes of a 51 per cent Arab majority. This is obviously a scenario which Jews, for reasons of power and privilege, would like to avoid at all costs.

To summarize, framing the Israeli-Palestinian conflict as a Prisoner's Dilemma yields four possible scenarios: a one-state solution, a two-state solution, a Zionist state, and an Arab state. In the coming years, it will be up to the people of historic Palestine to decide which of these four scenarios will ultimately prevail.

To many outside observers, the conflict remains completely irrational. But to the people of historic Palestine, there's nothing irrational about it. Each side believes they will prevail—and there's nothing irrational about wanting to win.

NASH EQUILIBRIUM AND THE PARETO PRINCIPLE

Let's now delve deeper into the game theory behind the two-state solution. The two-state solution is what mathematicians refer to as a Nash equilibrium (or "no regrets" choice): the "optimal outcome of a game where there is no incentive to deviate from an initial strategy."[2] In other words, even when a player has an opportunity to consider an opponent's choice, he sticks with his script.

Some readers may be familiar with the 2001 movie *A Beautiful Mind*, which dealt with the life of the mathematician John Nash. The PD is an example of what mathematicians refer to as a 2×2 symmetrical game with a *single* Nash equilibrium. Some 2×2 games have two Nash equilibria, some have one, and some have none. A Nash equilibrium occurs when all players are simultaneously making a no regrets best-choice response to the strategic choices of all the other players. It functions like a mathematical magnet, and marks the most likely resting spot for both players. (Think of a situation where player A knows that player B knows that player A knows that player B knows, etc. *That's* the Nash equilibrium.)

No regrets also means the best possible choice under the worst possible circumstances. For example, if both Israel and Palestine set out to co-operate by pursuing a one-state solution, but one side secretly decides to undermine the other, then the no regrets choice would be to betray the other side before they have a chance to betray you.

Almost there. We have one more very important concept to introduce.

Around 1900, the Italian engineer and economist Vilfredo Pareto proposed a simple rule of thumb that's known today as the Pareto principle. According to the Pareto principle, we should not accept any economic system if there is an alternative system available that would make everyone better off. From this flows the concept of Pareto-superior and Pareto-inferior solutions.

In a PD, the double co-operation strategy leads to a higher *collective* outcome than the double betrayal strategy. Double co-operation is therefore the Pareto-superior choice. Recall that in our original example, the two prisoners spent a total of two years in jail if both co-operated and kept silent. But if both snitched on each other, the collective jail time was four years, which is obviously worse than two years in jail. But double betrayal is the Nash equilibrium in a PD. So, which combination should we choose? The Pareto-superior double co-operation or the Nash equilibrium double betrayal? The answer is that there is no clear answer, which is why it's called a dilemma.

From a game theory perspective, the Israeli-Palestinian conflict may be reduced to a dilemma between co-operating with the other side (be it Israeli or Palestinian) in the hope that they will co-operate with you, or betraying the other side because you're almost certain that they will betray you. It all comes down to trust.

Israel and Palestine are not unique. As we will see in chapter 7, the 1946 partition of the British Raj into two states (India and Pakistan) was a politically stable—albeit Pareto-inferior—resolution to the conflict between Hindu and Muslim nationals in the Indian subcontinent. Sadly, like their counterparts in India and Pakistan, Jews and Palestinians seem equally determined to follow a Pareto-inferior path. Why is Israel (one of only two democracies in the Middle East—the other one being Tunisia) so stubborn? To the dismay of many of her friends and supporters, the Jewish state's deliberate embrace of a Pareto-inferior sociopolitical trajectory makes no rational sense. The answer is that Israel is not, and has never been, a liberal democracy. It's an *ethnocracy*, which means that according to its own constitution, Israel is not a "state of all its citizens." The legal sovereign of the state of Israel is the Jewish people—regardless of their citizenship status or place of residence in the world. Most liberal Jews in the Diaspora don't understand these fine distinctions, or how they impact the democratic rights of the 26% of Israeli citizens who are not Jewish.

In any event, game theory analysis of the Israeli-Palestinian conflict will not resolve the conflict, but it might help us to think about it in original and counter-intuitive ways—which is the primary purpose of this book.

Chapter 2

THREE ZIONIST DILEMMAS

It would be fantastic if the Israeli-Palestinian conflict could be reduced to a simple Prisoner's Dilemma. Alas, if it were only so easy, any graduate student in the social sciences would have a shot at winning the next Nobel Peace Prize. In reality, the current conflict consists of a whole series of dilemmas, each layered on top of the other like the seven layers of a Hungarian dobos torte (the kind that Theodor Herzl was well acquainted with). But fear not, because we can slice through the whole mess by dialing back our time machine to mid-nineteenth century Europe, and then moving slowly forward, frame by frame.

THE BIRTH OF POLITICAL ZIONISM

The year 1848 marked a series of bourgeois revolutions throughout Europe. These, in turn, set the stage for Jewish national consciousness to flourish. Within fifty years (in 1897), the First Zionist Congress was held in the concert hall of the Stadtcasino Basel, Switzerland. Its objective was to function as a quasi-parliament of the Zionist Organization, and to adopt a series of resolutions in support of the Zionist movement.

All proceedings were conducted in German, and delegates were requested to appear in formal dress (i.e., white tie) for the festive opening. The idea behind the aristocratic dress code was to project the image of the Jew as a successful and confident member of the community of nations, as opposed to a passive and cowering victim of the ghetto.

On the second day of the congress, the Zionist Organization adopted a resolution that later become known as the Basel Program (see figure 2.1). Handwritten in German, its opening sentence proclaimed: *"Die Zionismus*

*erstrebt für das jüdische Volk die Schaffung einer öffentlich [und] recht-
lich gesicherten Heimstätte in Palästina.*" This transliterates into English
as, "Zionism strives for the Jewish people, the creation of a publicly [and]
legally secured homestead in Palestine."

The German word "*Heimstätte*" is often mistranslated into English
as "home" or "homeland" in order to make the language of the Basel
Program consistent with the language of the Balfour Declaration (1917).
But a *homestead* is not the same as a *homeland*, much less a *national home*
(the expression used by Lord Balfour in his famous sixty-seven-word-long
letter to Lord Rothschild). *Heimat*, or *Heimatland*, is the German word for
homeland, and *Heimstätte* was deliberately chosen by the drafters of the
Basel Program for its political minimalism. The word evokes the image
of a simple, rustic dwelling surrounded perhaps by a white picket fence
and plenty of space for the cattle to roam.

**FIGURE 2.1 THE BASEL PROGRAM, HANDWRITTEN IN GERMAN, AS PROCLAIMED AT THE
FIRST ZIONIST CONGRESS, BASEL, 1897**

SOURCE: Public domain.

MICHAEL DAN

In his testimony before the Palestine Royal Commission some four decades later (1937), Ze'ev Jabotinsky, the founder of Revisionist Zionism and a self-proclaimed territorial maximalist, stated that when he was "a boy they [the drafters of the Basel Program] certainly wanted the whole of Palestine, yet the Basle programme of Zionism, published in 1897 speaks of 'Heimstätte in Palästina.' They never thought there was any difference [between homestead and sovereign state]."

The drafting committee of the Basel Program consisted of Max Nordau, Nathan Birnbaum, Alexander Mintz, Siegmund Rosenberg, Saul Rafael Landau, Hermann Schapira, and Max Bodenheimer—all early Zionist thinkers. It's not clear if any of these gentlemen had even *visited* Palestine prior to the First Zionist Congress, let alone lived there for any length of time or gotten to know the natives (Bodenheimer and Herzl visited Palestine for the first time a year later, in 1898; see figure 2.2). In retrospect, their lack of proper due diligence seems rather astonishing. Their naively formed ideas about Arabs in general, and Palestinian Arabs in particular, tended to stick, however.

Thirty years before the First Zionist Congress, Samuel Clemens (known familiarly as Mark Twain) toured Palestine as part of a multi-month pleasure trip to southern Europe, the Middle East, and Egypt. His travel diaries were eventually compiled into a best-selling book, *The Innocents Abroad, or The New Pilgrims' Progress*, in which he summarized Palestine as a

> desolate country whose soil is rich enough, but is given over wholly to weeds—a silent mournful expanse ... A desolation is here that not even imagination can grace with the pomp of life and action ... We never saw a human being on the whole route ... There was hardly a tree or shrub anywhere. Even the olive and the cactus, those fast friends of the worthless soil, had almost deserted the country.

Clemens devoted many chapters of his sixty-one-chapter book to the topic of Palestine's mostly arid, unforgiving, and unproductive terrain. But in other chapters, Palestine is described as rich and fertile. Today, it's

FIGURE 2.2 ZIONIST DELEGATION TO JERUSALEM, 1898
From left to right: Max Bodenheimer, David Wolffsohn, Theodor Herzl, Moses
Schnirer, and Joseph Zeidner. All five gentlemen are dressed in white tie, but
with dark waistcoats. Each is holding a pair of white gloves and a top hat.
SOURCE: Public domain.

the goal of Jewish nationalists to portray nineteenth-century Palestine
as a quasi *terra nullius*—or "empty land"—the legal term used by the
British when they arrived in Australia and decided that the Indigenous
Australians, whose ancestors had been living there for some fifty thousand years, were not quite human beings.

We sometimes forget that nineteenth-century Zionism was just as
colonial and Eurocentric as the rest of nineteenth-century Europe—neither one taking much interest in the Palestinian Arabs and their wishes.

In 1901, the British-born journalist Israel Zangwill, who was a close
associate of Herzl, wrote an article for the *New Liberal Review* in which
he used the phrase, "Palestine is a country without a people; the Jews

MICHAEL DAN

are a people without a country." The Christian Restoration Movement of Britain, which sought to create a purer form of Christianity, had been using variations of this phrase since the mid-nineteenth century. A few years later, Zangwill acknowledged the existence of the Palestinian community, but the phrase stuck in people's minds because political Zionism only makes sense if one maintains a certain willful blindness to the Palestinians.

POLITICAL ZIONISM DEFINED

For political Zionism, the common theme has always been the creation of a sovereign and democratic state, with a Jewish national majority, in the whole of Palestine. To this we might add that such a state must also respect the rights of minorities and have enough absorptive capacity for all the Jews in the world, should they ever need to, or choose to, resettle there.

But now, as in the past, the Zionist project is confronted by three core dilemmas: the dilemma of demographics, the dilemma of Palestinian national legitimacy, and the dilemma of partition.

Demographics pose a dilemma because it's now doubtful that there will ever be a sustainable Jewish majority in historic Palestine. Palestinian national legitimacy poses a dilemma because as a de facto nation in international law, Palestinians have the right to national self-determination in their homeland of Palestine. And partition poses a dilemma because any partition of historic Palestine would preclude the possibility of a sovereign Jewish state in the *whole* of historic Palestine.

RESOLVING DILEMMAS

Not all dilemmas are Prisoner's Dilemmas. Broadly speaking, the nature of any dilemma is the requirement to make a choice between two or more equally difficult (or impossible) alternatives. The game of Basic Dilemma is illustrated by the following story.

Susie and Janet are sisters. Both wish to play with the Barbie doll but not the Ken doll. Figure 2.3 shows the payout matrix for the game of Basic Dilemma.

		Ken doll	Barbie doll
Susie	Ken doll	Nobody plays with the Ken doll (1, 1)	Janet plays with the Barbie doll (1, 4)
	Barbie doll	Susie plays with the Barbie doll (4, 1)	***Nobody plays with the Barbie doll*** ***(1, 1)***

Nash equilibrium in bold italics text

FIGURE 2.3

The Nash equilibrium for this particular game is for nobody to play with the Barbie doll. By this point you're probably wondering: what possible use is game theory to the social sciences? But wait—instead of pulling the arms and the legs off the Barbie doll, there's a novel and creative way of resolving this particular dilemma. It's called *taking turns* (please note, I could have just as easily picked two brothers fighting over a scooter and a bicycle, but that would have introduced the additional complexity of one brother bashing the other over the head with a bicycle, which is how boys tend to resolve conflicts). *Taking turns* is a novel and creative solution to the Basic Dilemma of two sisters wanting to play with the same toy at the same time. Humans have no doubt been using this approach for over 200,000 years (i.e., since we first walked the earth).

In general, I can think of only three different approaches to resolving dilemmas (regardless of the nature of the dilemma):

1. *Come up with new facts and arguments in order to tip the scales in favour of one side or the other.* In this scenario, Susie gets to play with the Barbie doll because her mother gave it to her for her previous birthday (this is analogous to the Talmudic rule for reconciling two contradictory verses by referencing a third verse).
2. *Arbitrarily pick one side and then find ways to rationalize your choice.* In this scenario, Janet gets to play with the Barbie doll because her mother says that she can play with it, and to heck with Susie.

3. *Transcend the dilemma altogether by means of some novel and creative solution.* In this scenario, each girl takes five-minute turns playing with the Barbie doll until they get bored of it and decide to fight over something else.

The first approach may fail if the new facts and arguments are 'thin.' The second approach is inherently weak, which means that the same dilemma may present itself repeatedly over time without ever being fully resolved. And the third approach may never materialize. Different approaches, therefore, may be applied to the same dilemma at different times until the dilemma is finally resolved (or not resolved).

The dilemma of counting a minyan

As an aside, I find Jewish dilemmas to be particularly fascinating. For example, in Judaism there's a prohibition against counting individual Jews or the Jewish people as a whole (as in taking a census). The basis for this prohibition can be found in Exodus 30:12. According to Rashi, the reason is that "the evil eye can affect that which has been counted, and pestilence can come upon them, as we have found in the days of David." But Jews are also commanded to pray three times a day, and in order to conduct proper religious services there's a requirement for a *minyan* (a quorum of ten Jews). But how do you count a quorum if you're prohibited from counting? The creative and transcendent solution to this dilemma is to count the *hats* worn by individual Jews and not the Jews themselves (in some synagogues, I'm told, a minyan is counted as follows: "not one, not two, etc."). To many this is just splitting hairs, but to Orthodox Jews, the only way to function is to sometimes split hairs.

Some basic terms

Before delving any deeper into Zionism's three core dilemmas, we must first clarify the following political, geographic, and demographic terms: (1) Israel, (2) Palestine, (3) the Palestinian Territories, (4) the original Palestine Mandate, and (5) historic Palestine.

Israel is a de jure (legally recognized) state in the Middle East, bordered by the Mediterranean Sea to the west, by an international border with Egypt and the pre-1967 border with the Gaza Strip to the south, by an international border with Jordan and the pre-1967 border with the West Bank to the east, by the 1967 ceasefire line with Syria to the northeast, and by the 1949 armistice line with Lebanon to the north. In addition, Israel includes the territory of East Jerusalem and the Golan Heights (both of which were annexed after 1967). The demographics of Israel include all persons, both Jewish and non-Jewish, living within the pre-1967 borders of Israel, plus all Jews living in East Jerusalem, the Golan Heights, and the West Bank settlements. Palestinian residents of East Jerusalem or the Golan Heights are not included in the demographics of Israel. All Jews throughout the world are potential citizens of Israel via the Law of Return, but less than half the world's Jews hold Israeli citizenship.

Palestine is often used in reference to a geographic region of the Middle East, and this is of course correct. But Palestine is also a de facto (recognized in fact)—and many would say de jure—state in the Middle East, recognized by 136 out of 193 UN-member countries, including Russia and China (both permanent members of the UN Security Council). Palestine has no internationally recognized borders, but for practical purposes, is relatively sovereign over Areas A and B of the West Bank (as defined by the 1995 Oslo II Accord), and also the Gaza Strip. The demographics of Palestine include the non-Jewish residents of the West Bank, all the residents of the Gaza Strip, the Palestinian permanent residents of East Jerusalem and the Golan Heights, the Palestinian refugees of the 1948 Arab-Israeli conflict living in refugee camps in the Middle East, and the Palestinian refugees of the 1948 Arab-Israeli conflict living in other countries throughout the world. All these individuals are considered to be Palestinian. The state of Palestine claims the territory of East Jerusalem, including the Haram al-Sharif (Temple Mount) and the Gaza Strip, but not the Golan Heights.

The *Palestinian Territories* consist of the West Bank and the Gaza Strip and are controlled, either directly or indirectly, by Israel. The Golan Heights are not part of the Palestinian Territories (even though they are home to a population of Palestinian refugees). They are part of Syria. They were seized by Israel in 1967 and annexed in 1981 (allegedly for security reasons). The latter was recognized by the United States in 2019.

The *original Palestine Mandate*, as agreed upon at the San Remo Conference of 1920, corresponds to the territory of modern Jordan and Israel plus the Palestinian Territories, but not the Golan Heights. This is the territory that Jabotinsky and the Revisionists believed they were entitled to settle.

Historic Palestine is the territory of the original Palestine Mandate that lies to the west of the Jordan River. It is frequently referred to as Mandatory Palestine, Eretz Yisrael, or the land "between the river and the sea." All of these terms refer to the same geography.

With all of these confusing and overlapping definitions, it's easy to see why the Zionist project is fraught with so many dilemmas.

THE DILEMMA OF DEMOGRAPHICS

Today, Israel controls the whole of historic Palestine (either directly or indirectly). This represents the fulfillment of a hundred-year-old Zionist dream. Other aspects of the Zionist dream, however, remain unfulfilled. Demographics, in particular, pose a problem because very soon Jews won't constitute the majority in historic Palestine. For instance, figure 2.4 charts the percentage of Jewish nationals living in historic Palestine from 1920 to 2017.

Figure 2.5 shows the percentage of Jewish nationals living in the state of Israel since it was founded (in 1948) to 2017.

From these two graphs we can instantly grasp why demographics pose a dilemma for the Zionist project. From a peak of 63.52 per cent in 1973, the percentage of Jewish nationals living in historic Palestine has declined steadily to the point where it was barely above 50 per cent in 2017. Today (in 2020), Jews barely constitute a majority in the territory that Israel controls.

These facts carry heavy political weight. Were historic Palestine ever to become a single state, there would be no clear Jewish majority. Even

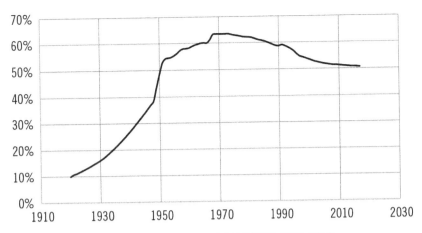

FIGURE 2.4 PERCENTAGE OF JEWS IN HISTORIC PALESTINE, 1920–2017

SOURCE: Data from the British Census of Palestine (1922 and 1931), the Israeli Central Bureau of Statistics, and the United States Census Bureau (International Programs).

within pre-1967 Israel (which for census purposes includes more than 600,000 settlers living in East Jerusalem, the Golan Heights, and West Bank settlements), the percentage of Jewish nationals continues to decline, having topped out at 89.16 per cent in 1957. Today (in 2020), it's below 75 per cent.

The demographic dilemma is something that every Israeli citizen, whether Jewish or non-Jewish, is consciously or subconsciously aware of. And in recent years it has provided Jewish nationalists with the necessary political 'fuel' to enact a series of racist laws, including the Admissions Committee Law (2011), that threaten one of the most sacred values of Zionism: respect for minority rights.

Briefly, even though Palestinian citizens of Israel may sit as Members of the Knesset or on the Israeli Supreme Court, the Admissions Committee Law effectively bars them from living in 43 per cent of all residential areas in Israel.[1] The only way to describe this law is 'apartheid-like' (all that's missing from full-blown apartheid is the formal disenfranchisement of Palestinian Israelis; 'soft' disenfranchisement is already a state-sanctioned reality). What would be the reaction if the tables were turned and Jews

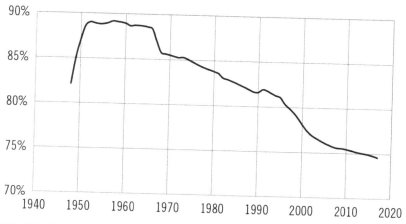

FIGURE 2.5 PERCENTAGE OF JEWS IN ISRAEL, 1948–2017

SOURCE: Data from the Israeli Central Bureau of Statistics.

were barred from living in 43 per cent of all residential communities in Canada or the United States? Signs from the 1930s that proclaimed "No Dogs or Jews Allowed" are probably an urban myth—at least in Canada[2]—but not signs marked "Christians Only—Jews Not Allowed" and "Jews Not Wanted."

THE DILEMMA OF PALESTINIAN NATIONAL LEGITIMACY

As far back as 1922, David Ben-Gurion, head of the Labor Zionist movement and socialist founding–prime minister of Israel, recognized the existence of a separate Palestinian Arab nation. Commenting at the time in his diary, he noted: "The success of the Arabs in organizing the closure of shops shows that we are dealing here with a national movement."[3] To this day, many Israelis and supporters of Israel are in frank denial of the existence of a distinct Palestinian nation. In 1969, Israeli prime minister Golda Meir was infamously quoted in the *Sunday Times* saying that "there were no such thing as Palestinians."

But this was not how Ben-Gurion saw things, according to historian Shabtai Teveth:

[As] part of a great Arab people, the Arabs of Palestine could be granted civil rights in a Jewish state and regard the independence of neighboring Arab states as their own political fulfillment. But if there existed a separate Palestinian people, was it not entitled to self-determination in its own country, Palestine? As a just movement, Labor Zionism would have to appeal for the equal division of both civil and political rights between Jews and Arabs. That pointed to possible partition.[4]

Teveth further comments:

In linking his Zionism to socialism, Ben-Gurion entered a labyrinth of contradictions. Socialism demanded an equal division of all resources, without regard for religion, nationality, or race; and did not the needs of hundreds of thousands of Arabs come before those of the few Jewish immigrants? Yet Zionism was sworn to devote most if not all of its energies to the immigration and absorption of Jews. How could the socialist vision of peace among nations be realized, when Zionism stood for separate Jewish status and claimed the lion's share of the country's resources? If the aim of socialism was peace among nations, did Jewish immigration not represent a stumbling block, since it aggravated relations between Jews and Arabs?[5]

It took until 1993 for Israel to finally recognize the existence of the Palestinian nation. As part of the Oslo Accords, Prime Minister Yitzhak Rabin exchanged letters of recognition with Chairman Yasser Arafat as head of the PLO, the legitimate representative of the Palestinian people. This should have settled the dilemma of Palestinian national legitimacy once and for all, but Rabin's assassin, Yigal Amir, and his entourage of rabbis thought otherwise. Palestinian national legitimacy, after all, is not a dilemma for Palestinians. It's simply a fact of life.

THE DILEMMA OF PARTITION

Ben-Gurion believed that the original Palestine Mandate could be partitioned into separate Jewish and Arab spheres of activity. Quoting again from historian Shabtai Teveth:

Ben-Gurion … told a visiting delegation in 1920 that the possibilities for massive settlement of Jews lay in the abandoned or uninhabited reaches—including, of course, those across the Jordan—on land that had no owners, and on partially utilized tracts owned privately or by the government. He estimated that four fifths of the country's territory was available for new settlement. Six million persons using modern methods could earn their livelihoods from farming these lands; an untold number could prosper from industry. None of this activity would impinge on the Arabs, who would continue to live in their established areas, while Jews lived in new settlements and worked new fields. Contact, and friction, between the two peoples would thus be reduced to a minimum.[6]

To Ben-Gurion, partition had both a physical as well as a functional dimension.

Jews and Arabs, separated by religion and culture, would live in separate settlements and work in separate economies. Only in one field would there be mixed labor: in public works and government service. By this division into two national entities, Ben-Gurion sought to lay the foundation of a partition of the country into two autonomous frameworks, Jewish and Arab. The idea of *partition* had struck him even before his arrival in the country [in 1906].[7] (emphasis added)

THE PALESTINIAN RESPONSE

The Palestinian Arabs didn't view Jewish immigration in mutually beneficial terms—partition or no partition—and anti-Jewish riots broke out in the original Palestine Mandate in 1920 and again in 1921, after which Great Britain split the Mandate in two and Jews were forbidden from settling "across the Jordan." To Ze'ev Jabotinsky and his Revisionist Zionists, such an act of "treason" constituted a violation of the spirit—if not the letter—of the League of Nations Mandate for Palestine, and they would tolerate no further partitioning (or re-partitioning) in the future. The Irgun, for instance, founded in 1931 as the military wing of the Revisionist

Zionist movement, underscored the hardline Revisionist approach by incorporating into its emblem a map of the original Mandate for Palestine, including both the east and west banks of the Jordan River (see figure 2.6). Revisionist thinking about the geography of Palestine has always reflected the historical reality of the Roman province of Judea, and for this we must give the Revisionists full credit.

Riots broke out again in Mandatory Palestine in 1929—more widespread than previously, and more destructive in scope. Sixty-nine members of the ancient Jewish community of Hebron—the second-holiest city in Judaism after Jerusalem—were massacred, even as 435 Jews from Hebron were sheltered by their Palestinian neighbours. Afterwards, the British established the Shaw Commission, followed by the Hope-Simpson Commission (1930), and finally the Passfield White Paper (1930), which

FIGURE 2.6 **IRGUN EMBLEM.** The map in the background shows both Mandatory Palestine and the Emirate of Transjordania, which the Irgun claimed in its entirety for a future Jewish state (at a time when Jews constituted only 11 per cent of Mandatory Palestine). In Hebrew, the acronym "Etzel" is written above the map and "raq kach" ("only thus," implying through force of arms) is written below.

SOURCE: Public domain.

MICHAEL DAN

recommended curtailing Jewish immigration to Mandatory Palestine in order to appease Arab fears of a socio-demographic takeover by the Jews. Then in 1931, British policy reversed course, shifting once more in favour of the Zionists. Prime Minister Ramsay MacDonald sent a letter to Chaim Weizmann, chairman of the World Zionist Organization, reaffirming Britain's support for a Jewish national home in Palestine.

The situation remained calm for half a decade; however, in 1935 the British killed Arab resistance fighter Sheikh Izz al-Din al-Qassam in a shootout in the mountains near Nablus. Riots subsequently broke out in 1936, followed by an Arab general strike. Afterwards, Britain convened the Palestine Royal Commission (also known as the Peel Commission) in 1937, followed by the Woodhead Commission in 1938, and for the first time it looked like the only viable long-term solution would be a partition of Mandatory Palestine. But after months of careful study, the Woodhead Commission concluded that a two-state solution was impossible, thereby contradicting the view held by the Peel Commission.

The two-state 'solution' for historic Palestine is an idea that was pronounced dead over eight decades ago. It has literally been on life support ever since.

The diagram in figure 2.7 summarizes the three core dilemmas that have confronted and confounded the Zionist project from the outset.

Starting in the top right-hand corner is the Zionist ideal of a sovereign Jewish state in the whole of historic Palestine (light grey box). The first question to ask is: Does Israel control the territory of the whole of historic Palestine? Prior to 1967, the answer to this question was "not yet," but since 1967, the answer has been clearly "yes." The second question to ask is: Does Israel have a Jewish majority? If the answers to our first and second questions are "yes," we can form a feedback loop that reinforces the Zionist ideal of a Jewish state in the whole of historic Palestine; there are no dilemmas and no need to proceed any further along the decision tree.

Returning now to the box labelled "Israel has a Jewish majority," if the answer to this question is "no," we have our first dilemma: the Jewish demographic dilemma. This then begs the question: Are Palestinian

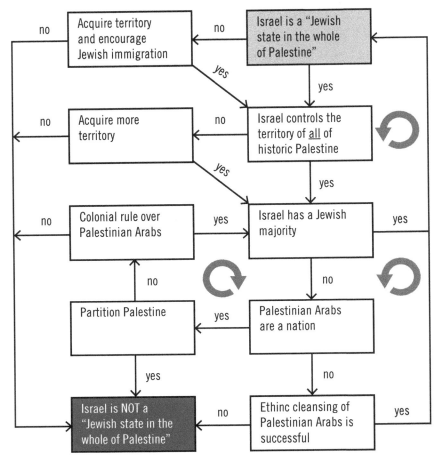

FIGURE 2.7 SUMMARY OF THREE CORE DILEMMAS FACING THE ZIONIST PROJECT

SOURCE: Michael Dan, 2020.

Arabs a distinct nation? If we conclude that they are not—the position of the Israeli right and, increasingly, the Israeli centre—it becomes morally acceptable to "transfer" Palestinian Arabs to neighbouring countries. Once enough Arabs have been "transferred" from Palestine, we can revisit the question of Jewish demographics, thereby closing another feedback loop in our decision tree.

If we conclude that Palestinian Arabs do indeed constitute a distinct nation (the current consensus of the international community), then we have our second dilemma: the dilemma of Palestinian national legitimacy. This then raises a third dilemma, the partition dilemma, because if you partition historic Palestine, then Israel will no longer be a Jewish state in "all" of Palestine.

The alternative is to impose colonial rule over the Palestinian nation (some would call it occupation, but occupations typically don't last five decades), and then to revisit the question of Jewish demographics a few years later in hopes that the balance has shifted in favour of the Jews. This creates a third feedback loop in our decision tree, and this particular feedback loop is now the dominant one in Israeli society: colonization of the Palestinians continues while Israel waits for the dilemma of Jewish demographics to resolve itself.

If Israel were to (1) partition Palestine and/or (2) accept the reality of Palestinian national legitimacy and/or (3) cease colonial rule over the Palestinians, it would then run the risk of heading down the left-hand side of our decision tree, into the dark grey box marked "Israel is NOT a Jewish state in the whole of historic Palestine." Likewise, if the ethnic cleansing or population transfer of Palestinians failed to outpace their natural growth rate, Israel could also run the risk of heading for the dark grey box in the bottom left-hand corner of the decision tree.

ZIONISM AS SETTLER COLONIALISM

A few years ago, I picked up a French newspaper and began reading an article about "les colonies de la Cisjordanie." At first, I didn't understand what the article was about, but then I realized that the French word for settlement is *une colonie* and that "Cisjordanie" is on the opposite side of the Jordan River from "Transjordania"—now called the Hashemite Kingdom of Jordan.

In the English language, a settlement can mean an outpost, village, or group of houses in a *thinly populated place*. Today, the West Bank is about as thinly populated as South Korea—one of the most densely populated countries in the OECD. Therefore, the Zionist project is not just a settler project; it's a settler *colonial* project, and settler colonialism is something completely different—something that I understood from my interactions with Indigenous people in Canada. It's odd, but perhaps not surprising, that as a Jewish Canadian, I first had to understand what the Canadian government had done to Indigenous people before I could understand what Israel is doing to the Palestinians.

Some academics would argue that Zionism isn't a settler colonial movement, but a national liberation movement—although liberation from what isn't exactly clear since Jews living in western countries now experience unparalleled freedoms (not to mention that we were allegedly liberated from Egyptian bondage over three thousand years ago).

Setting aside Jabotinsky's prolific use of colonial language and metaphors in his speeches and his writings, in a settler colonial movement there's typically a distant motherland. But to the Jews, Israel *is* the motherland, and Jews are her indigenous people. But if our understanding of population history and genetics is correct, then the Palestinians are also indigenous to Palestine. There is little merit, therefore, in trying to figure out who is more indigenous than whom: Jews or Palestinians.

But the term "national liberation" can also be interpreted to mean national redemption, as in "the Land of Israel is the legal property of the Jewish people, who have now come to reclaim it after an absence of some two thousand years." From this perspective, Zionism may also be regarded as an irredentist movement (from the Italian word, *irredento*, for unredeemed).

Indigeneity and prior legal claims notwithstanding, the *methodology* of the Zionist project is clearly a settler colonial methodology. Zionism is guilty of ethnic cleansing, theft of land, intentional destruction of "native" settlements (to use Jabotinsky's word), intentional destruction or appropriation of native culture, and systemic and structural impoverishment of the native population. This is analogous to what Canada did to Indigenous nations, including Indigenous nations with whom Canada had previously signed treaties.

Equally challenging is the use of the term "occupation," which suggests a temporary settlement or encampment. What Israel has done—and continues to do in the territories captured during the Six-Day War—is not occupation but outright colonization. So, rather than speak of occupation, it would make more sense to use the expression "colonization of Palestinian territories acquired during the Six-Day War," or simply, "colonization of Palestinian Territories."

Think of it this way: If I move into your backyard, pitch a tent, and live in it for a month, then I've *occupied* your backyard for a month. But if I move into your backyard and build a permanent home complete with municipal services, a garage, and a swimming pool—and don't move out for fifty years—then that's no longer occupation, that's colonization.

ZIONISM GIVES WAY TO POST-ZIONISM

What then, should we call today's reality in historic Palestine if after more than a century of effort, the Zionist project is barely able to achieve a Jewish majority in that geographic space? Does it even make any sense to talk about political Zionism, or should we switch the conversation to post-Zionism? And sporadic incidents aside, is state-sponsored genocidal antisemitism on a continental or global scale (e.g., Nazism) really a threat today? And if not, then do we even need a sovereign state, or safe haven, where all the Jewish people of the world might seek refuge from future genocides?

The truth is that during the last quarter century, we have seen the emergence of a post-Zionist reality in Israel. Not only is the Labor Zionism of Ben-Gurion gone forever, so too is the Revisionist Zionism of Jabotinsky and Begin because of threats from demographics, Palestinian national legitimacy, and international pressure to partition.

Zionism, like communism, is a nineteenth-century socio-political ideology that has had a long life but has otherwise run its course. In order to move forward, we need to loosen Zionism's grip on our thinking and stop pretending that it continues in good health, or even exists in its original form. Zionism was never intended to be a zero-sum game; the real zero-sum game is Jewish ultranationalism.

Chapter 3

AN UNFINISHED COUNTRY

Tsar Alexander II of Russia must have wondered if he was the luckiest sovereign who ever lived. Between April 1866 and April 1879, he survived three assassination attempts. In December 1879, a fourth attempt was made on his life—which he also survived. The radical revolutionary group, Narodnaya Volya (the People's Will), tried to blow up the Czar's train, but their timing was off, and the train rolled along to its destination unharmed.

There was even a fifth attempt: on February 5, 1880, a time bomb exploded under the Czar's dining room at the Winter Palace, killing eleven people and wounding thirty. The Czar, however, was late for dinner that evening and—once more—his life was spared.

But on Sunday, March 13, 1881, the Czar's luck ran out.

As he was riding across the Pevchesky Bridge towards the Mikhailovsky Manège, Nikolai Rysakov, a member of Narodnaya Volya, chucked a dynamite bomb under the team of horses pulling the Czar's bulletproof carriage. A member of the Czar's Cossack guard was instantly killed, and the driver and several bystanders were also wounded. But the Czar was unharmed!

Moments later he emerged from his carriage, but instead of dashing for safety, he lingered just long enough for a second member of Narodnaya Volya, Ignaty Grinevitsky, to approach him with a second dynamite bomb. Grinevitsky detonated the bomb and was killed instantly. The Czar—badly injured—was rushed to the Winter Palace where he died that evening in what would prove to be the world's first suicide attack involving TNT.

And in a sense, this set the stage for the Zionist movement to really take off.

In a moment of exquisite irony, when the Czar died later that evening in his study in the Winter Palace, it was in the same room where twenty years earlier he had signed the Emancipation Edict that freed the serfs. In the weeks before he died, the Czar had been working on plans for an elected parliament. Had he lived another forty-eight hours, it's possible that Russia would have embarked down the road towards a constitutional monarchy. Instead, the new Czar, his son Alexander III, suppressed all civil liberties in Russia, unleashed a campaign of police brutality, and enacted antisemitic legislation (the May Laws), which facilitated a series of pogroms that lasted for three years.

In fact, it was only after the first pogroms that large-scale immigration of Jews to Ottoman Palestine began; the First Zionist Congress would be convened some fifteen years later (in 1897). These earliest immigrants, most of whom were either Russian or Moldovan, called themselves Hovevei Zion (Lovers of Zion), and they had a cultural, rather than political, agenda. They weren't interested in building all the organs of a Jewish state; their main goal was merely to settle the Land of Israel.

In 1891, one of the most profound early Zionist thinkers, Ahad Ha'am (born Asher Ginsberg, and whose Hebrew name means "One of the People"), visited Palestine. "The Arab," he observed, "like all the Semites, is sharp minded and shrewd." He noted that Arab merchants were no different from their European counterparts. "All the townships of Syria and Eretz Yisrael are full of Arab merchants who know how to exploit the masses and keep track of everyone with whom they deal—the same as in Europe."

Ahad Ha'am seemed guardedly optimistic that the Jews and Arabs could live and work together co-operatively and in relative peace. But then he introduced a note of caution: "The Arabs, especially the urban elite," he wrote, "see and understand what we are doing and what we wish to do on the land, but they keep quiet and pretend not to notice anything. For now, they do not consider our actions as presenting a future danger to them."

He concluded with a warning that was sadly prophetic: "But, if the time comes that our people's life in Eretz Yisrael will develop to a point where we are taking their place, either slightly or significantly, the natives are not going to just step aside so easily."

Without the benefit of game theory, Ahad Ha'am understood that Jewish immigration to Ottoman Palestine could end up as a zero-sum game.

THE ZERO-SUM GAME AHAD HA'AM FEARED

In a zero-sum game, for every strategic move, one player's gains are another player's losses. The Prisoner's Dilemma (PD), introduced in chapter 1, is not a zero-sum game because strategic choices exist in a PD that are mutually beneficial. In a zero-sum game, there are no mutually beneficial strategies.

The simplest example of a two-person zero-sum game is the game of cutting a cake. Two children must share a cake; one child cuts and the other child gets to choose the first slice. Under ideal circumstances, this shouldn't make any difference because both slices will be equal.

Ahad Ha'am feared that Jewish immigration to Palestine could reach a tipping point, and that the Palestinian Arabs might one day be reluctant to share even a crumb of Palestine with the Jews. The Jews, on the other hand, might reach a point where they would not want to share a crumb of Palestine with the Palestinian Arabs. Another name that game theorists use to describe a two-person zero-sum game is "total war."

THEODOR HERZL AND THE JEWISH NATION-STATE

Theodor Herzl was born in 1860 into a family of German-speaking assimilated Jews. His childhood home in Budapest was immediately adjacent to the Dohány Street Synagogue, which today is still the largest in Europe. Along with numerous other prominent figures in early Zionism, he considered himself to be an atheist.

At age eighteen and following the death of his younger sister to typhus, Herzl moved with his family to Vienna, where he studied law and launched his literary and journalistic career. The latter eventually took him to Paris, where he witnessed first-hand the unravelling of civil society during the Dreyfus Affair, a political and antisemitic scandal that shook the Third French Republic. The message that Herzl internalized was that if a secular society such as France couldn't protect Jews from institutional antisemitism, then no country could.

Under Napoléon, France began emancipating Jews in 1791. Social and political equality eventually led to a flourishing of Jewish culture beginning in the mid-nineteenth century, known as the Haskalah (Enlightenment). As the Jews gradually emerged from the poverty of the *shtetl* (the small, predominantly Jewish towns of Eastern Europe; plural: *shtetlech*), there was a parallel resurgence of antisemitism because the successful Jewish merchant class began to compete with the established non-Jewish middle class. The situation was further aggravated by the emergence of the pseudoscience of social Darwinism and the development of racial antisemitism, both of which regarded Jews as "inferior" human beings.

Herzl understood the paradoxical connection between emancipation and antisemitism: emancipation led to economic success, and economic success led to jealousy and resentment. He viewed the relationship as a form of class struggle. "In the principal countries where antisemitism prevails," he wrote in 1896 in the pamphlet *Der Judenstaat* (The Jewish State), "it does so as a result of the emancipation of the Jews." In other words, emancipation—rather than eliminating antisemitism—actually created conditions for it to flourish. According to Herzl,

by the time the Jew was emancipated, it was too late: he had become a direct threat to the existing economic and social order …When civilized nations awoke to the inhumanity of discriminatory legislation and enfranchised us, our enfranchisement came too late. It was no longer possible to remove our disabilities in our old homes. For we had, curiously enough, developed while in the Ghetto into a bourgeois people, and we stepped out of it only to enter into fierce competition with the middle class.

MICHAEL DAN

Herzl maintained that the rule of law, in terms of guaranteeing equality, was—for the Jew—"a dead letter." It meant nothing. The situation for the Jew, he warned, was dire. "No one can deny the gravity of the situation of the Jews. Wherever they live in perceptible numbers, they are more or less persecuted." When it came to equality before the law, the Jews "are debarred from filling even moderately high positions, either in the army, or in any public or private capacity. And attempts are made to thrust them out of business also: 'Don't buy from Jews!'"

Herzl regarded the fate of European Jewry as a zero-sum game. For him, there could be no mutually beneficial co-operation between Jews and Europeans on European soil, and the only solution to The Jewish Question was the creation of a sovereign Jewish nation-state somewhere else in the world (preferably Palestine, although Argentina and Uganda were also contenders at one time).

In certain aspects, Herzl was unerringly prescient. Argentina and Palestine, for instance, he regarded as "neutral piece[s] of land" where "experiments in colonization" had been attempted, "though on the mistaken principle of a gradual infiltration of Jews."

"An infiltration," he cautioned, "is bound to end badly." Echoing Ahad Ha'am's words, Herzl warned: "As soon as the non-native [i.e., Jewish] population rises to the point where it is seen as a threat to the native [i.e., Palestinian Arab] population further immigration is halted." Immigration is "futile" he concluded, "unless we have the sovereign right to continue such immigration."

The Jewish state that Herzl envisioned was to be a secular one, recognized by a Great Power, with strong cultural ties to Europe and financial ties to Great Britain. Ironically, he frowned upon Hebrew as a language for everyday use. "It might be suggested that our want of a common current language would present difficulties," he wrote. "We cannot converse with one another in Hebrew. Who amongst us," he asked, "has a sufficient acquaintance with Hebrew to ask for a railway ticket in that language! Such a thing cannot be done." It seems that Herzl was unaware that the Hebrew language was undergoing a modernization and revival at the time.

In advocating for a secular state, Herzl worried openly about the power of the rabbinate and its claims on Jewish identity. He advocated for a clear separation of religion and state, and tellingly compared the power implicit in a priesthood with that of a military force.

We shall keep our priests within the confines of their temples in the same way as we shall keep our professional army within the confines of their barracks. Army and priesthood shall receive honors high as their valuable functions deserve. But they must not interfere in the administration of the State, which confers distinction upon them, else they will conjure up difficulties without and within.

His conclusions were blunt. "Shall we end up by having a theocracy? No, indeed … Faith," he conceived famously, "unites us, knowledge gives us freedom." The former should not suppress or restrain the latter.

When it came to the relationship between Jewish sovereignty and antisemitism, however, Herzl got it spectacularly wrong. "But the Jews, once settled in their own state, would probably have no more enemies." Apparently unable to imagine (as were most Europeans at the time) something as horrific as Nazism or the "final solution," Herzl made the worst prediction in all of Jewish history when he opined that "action may be taken against individuals or even against groups of the most powerful of Jews, but Governments will never take action against all Jews."

Herzl never gave much thought to the idea of binational governance for Palestine (i.e., Jewish/Arab co-sovereignty). According to Herzl, a co-sovereign state would be incompatible with Zionism's vision of a Jewish state. The rights of minorities would of course be protected in any Jewish state—on this point Herzl could not have been more emphatically clear. But to Herzl and most other Zionist thinkers, a Jewish state had to have a Jewish majority because the Jewish people were not just a religious community or an ethnic group, but a stateless nation in need of "normalizing" (in other words, a physical home).

Every man will be as free and undisturbed in his faith or his disbelief as he is in his nationality. And if it should occur that men of other creeds and different nationalities come to live amongst us, we should accord them honorable protection and equality before the law.

I suspect that Herzl's understanding of Jewish identity was influenced by his understanding of his native Hungarian identity. Hungarian identity is also a zero-sum game: you either are or you aren't. The Hungarian language, which is unrelated to any other language of Central Europe, is either your mother tongue or it isn't. If it's your mother tongue, then your ancestors either entered the Carpathian Basin in 895 CE as part of a single founder Magyar population, or they didn't. If they didn't, then you're not an authentic Hungarian even if your family has lived in Hungary for a thousand years (as many Hungarian Jews discovered during the Holocaust, when their ethnically Hungarian neighbours gladly turned them over to the Arrow Cross fascists).

Reading Herzl, one is left with the impression that "gathering in the Exiles" was going to be as straightforward as bringing all the Hungarians back to Budapest.

As the philosopher Immanuel Kant observed, "out of the crooked timber of humanity, no straight thing was ever made." Jewish identity, in particular, isn't nearly as straightforward as Hungarian identity. In fact, at no point in the last two thousand years were the Jews of Europe, the Middle East, and North Africa as ethnically or culturally homogeneous as the Hungarians.

Herzl was an assimilated Ashkenazi Jew whose vision of a Jewish state favoured a citizen who was modern, secular, democratic, and German-speaking—exactly like himself.

THE REALITY OF OTTOMAN PALESTINE

One popular myth about life in the Ottoman Empire is that it was terminally sclerotic and moribund. This was clearly not the case. Important social changes, in the form of the Tanzimat reforms, began in the early nineteenth century. In 1839, Jews in the Ottoman Empire were granted the right to vote, nineteen years before they received full emancipation in Great Britain. By 1856, all Ottoman citizens were guaranteed equality in education, government appointments, and administration of justice, regardless of creed. Under late Ottoman rule, Jews had more collective protection than in most European countries: the Jewish community was led by a *Haham Başi* (chief rabbi) and Jewish law in personal matters was guaranteed by the millet system. The primary identity of many Jews in the late Ottoman Empire was overwhelmingly Ottoman rather than Zionist. Zionism originated in Europe and was mostly an Ashkenazi affair (to this day, all Israeli prime ministers have been Ashkenazi Jews).

According to Menachem Klein in his *Lives in Common: Arabs and Jews in Jerusalem, Jaffa, and Hebron*, up until the 1880s the majority of Jerusalem's Jews were Sephardim. By 1905, Klein writes, "Jerusalem was a mosaic of communities" where Jews

> made up more than half the population, but were subdivided into Ashkenazi, Sephardi, Moroccan, Yemenite, Kurdish, Georgian, and Aleppo Communities. The Muslims consisted of Jerusalem natives, blacks, Romany, and Mughrabis. The Christian community included Armenians, Armenian Catholics, Armenian Orthodox, Greeks, Catholics, Protestants, Maronites, Russian Orthodox, and Chaldeans-Syrians.
>
> And it wasn't merely a question of mosaics. Religious, cultural, and other forms of ritual and practice mixed and mingled across boundaries. For instance, in late Ottoman Palestine and even during the British Mandate prior to 1936, Klein emphasizes that Muslims took part in Jewish religious celebrations and vice versa; believers from both faiths prayed together for rain at *Nebi Samwil*, the tomb of the prophet Samuel, north of Jerusalem. Businessmen from both nations conducted transactions, Jewish and Arab families shared backyards, Jews and Arabs attended the same schools and sometimes also intermarried.[1]

THE FIRST THREE ALIYOT: WAVES OF JEWISH MASS IMMIGRATION

Following the assassination of Czar Alexander II, about two million Jews left the Russian Empire, with most of them ending up in the United States, the United Kingdom, Australia, and Canada (my maternal grandparents and great-grandparents among them). The first wave of Jewish immigration to Palestine (*Aliyah*, from the Hebrew verb to ascend; plural: *Aliyot*) occurred between 1882 and 1903. Only about twenty-five thousand Russian and Romanian Jews settled in previously sparsely populated areas, taking up farming. Credit goes to this group for founding Rishon LeZion, the first Jewish settlement in Palestine. Previously, there were only about twelve thousand Jews living in all of Palestine.[2]

The Second Aliyah occurred between 1904 and 1914, when a further forty thousand Russian Jews arrived in Ottoman Palestine. Unlike their predecessors, who farmed the land with the assistance of Palestinian labour, members of the Second Aliyah were socialist and collectivist, and insisted on using only Jewish labour. These Labor Zionists established the first kibbutz in Palestine, Degania aleph, in 1909, and laid the foundations for the first Jewish city in the Middle East, Tel Aviv. It was during this time (in 1906), that a twenty-year-old from Płońsk, Poland, by the name of David Grün immigrated to Palestine. In 1912 he donned a fez and moved to Constantinople to study Ottoman law because he believed that the future of Palestine belonged to the Ottoman Empire.[3] He later changed his name to David Ben-Gurion.

In the decade before the First World War, the Zionist movement in the British Empire was led by a brilliant biochemist—Chaim Weizmann—the father of industrial fermentation. Born in 1874 in the village of Motal, near Pinsk, Belarus, Weizmann was one of fifteen children. At age eighteen, he left for Germany and Switzerland to study chemistry. In 1904, with a PhD in organic chemistry in hand, he immigrated to England to take up a position as senior lecturer at the University of Manchester.

When the First World War broke out in 1914, Great Britain found herself at a military disadvantage; Germany had acquired practically all the available acetone in Europe—a chemical necessary for the production of cordite (a smokeless ballistic propellant). Weizmann, however, had developed a novel method of producing acetone using a fermentation process based on corn. This eventually played a critical role in the British war effort, allowing Weizmann access to senior British cabinet ministers,[4] whom he eventually rallied in support of the Zionist cause.

The Third Aliyah occurred between 1914 and 1923, when forty thousand Jews of diverse Eastern European origin arrived in Palestine, just as it was transitioning from Ottoman to British rule. Notable accomplishments by this group included the draining of the malaria-infested swamps of the Jezreel Valley, and the establishment of the *Histadrut*, the trade union that dominated the Israeli economy for decades, as well as the *Haganah*, the forerunner of the Israel Defense Forces.

THE MANY FACES OF ZIONISM

Far from being a uniform movement, by the early 1920s there were at least seven different Zionist streams. The one thing they all had in common was the desire to re-invigorate the Jewish community of Palestine. What distinguished one from the other were their politics and methodologies.

Cultural Zionism was an apolitical movement that attempted to create a cultural centre in Palestine for all Jews, including those in the Diaspora. Cultural Zionists were willing to exist as a Jewish minority within a binational state. An example is Hovevei Zion, led by Ahad Ha'am.

Political Zionism, led by Theodor Herzl in Austria and Max Nordau in Russia, espoused high-level diplomacy and formal political recognition as prerequisites for the creation of a Jewish state with a Jewish majority. *Practical Zionism*, on the other hand, emphasized settlement in Palestine as soon as possible, regardless of whether or not there was any formal political recognition or a charter. Its leaders were Moshe Leib Lilienblum and Leon Pinsker. Chaim Weizmann, Leo Motzkin, and Nahum Sokolow were leaders of what came to be known as *Synthetic Zionism*, which combined elements of both political and practical Zionism.

Labor Zionism held that a Jewish state could only be built through the efforts of a Jewish agricultural proletarian class, working the soil in a collective fashion. Nachman Syrkin, Ber Borochov, Haim Arlosoroff, Berl Katznelson, and later David Ben-Gurion believed that it was morally acceptable to settle in areas of Palestine that had been rejected by the Arab population, thereby reclaiming unwanted land through Jewish labour.

Revisionist Zionism opposed the doctrines of socialism and sought to build an economically liberal Jewish state with a Jewish majority in the territory of Greater Israel—by use of force if necessary. Ze'ev Jabotinsky, the first Revisionist leader, proposed (figuratively speaking) building an 'iron wall' around the Jews of Palestine.

Religious Zionism, led by Yitzchak Yaakov Reines and Abraham Isaac Kook, viewed the entire Zionist struggle through a religious lens. They believed secular Jews, by redeeming the Land of Israel, could hasten the arrival of the Messiah. They also supported the concept of a Greater Israel, and their ideas eventually gave rise to today's settler movement.

GAME THEORY AND OTTOMAN PALESTINE

If ever there was a time of peaceful coexistence between the Zionist new-comers and the Palestinian Arabs, it was during the final years of the Ottoman Empire. In 1908, the Young Turk Revolution loosened the grip of absolute rule, but Jews and Arabs continued to work side by side in an atmosphere of 'live and let live,' as they had done for centuries. From a game theory perspective, the situation resembled an iterated Prisoner's Dilemma of indefinite duration.

When a Prisoner's Dilemma is played more than once between the same two players, it's called an Iterated Prisoner's Dilemma (IPD). Using a simple, two-player model, each player has the choice of either co-oper-ating (C) or defecting (D) in a number of successive rounds. If the IPD is of a finite duration, then it makes sense for a player to betray in the final round since the temptation payoff is always greater than the co-operation payoff (4 versus 3 in the game matrix). But if it makes sense to betray in the final round, then it would also make sense to betray in the one before that, and so on. So, if we know that we are in an IPD of finite duration, it always pays to betray on the first round.

In an IPD of an undetermined duration, it would make more sense to co-operate most of the time than to betray because you never know when the last round is going to be. One strategy might be to always co-operate regardless of what the other player does (all C). Another strategy might be to always defect (all D). Different strategies aside, the most robust strategy of all is called TIT FOR TAT.

TIT FOR TAT always begins by co-operating with an opponent. If the opponent co-operates, then TIT FOR TAT will co-operate on the next round. If the opponent defects, then TIT FOR TAT will defect on the next round. If the opponent then co-operates again, then TIT FOR TAT will revert to co-operating. TIT FOR TAT does not bear grudges. It simply responds, measure for measure, to whatever its opponent did in the previous round.

Another IPD strategy is called GRUDGER, which always co-operates with a co-operative opponent, but never co-operates after a single defection no matter how many times the opponent subsequently co-operates. Then there's the strategy known as TIT FOR TWO TATS, which lets an unco-operative get away with two consecutive episodes of defection before also defecting.

In his seminal book *The Evolution of Co-operation*, Robert Axelrod describes a contest in which game theorists from a number of academic disciplines (and even a few amateurs) were invited to submit IPD strategies that could be played against each other in a contest of undetermined duration. Two contests were eventually held, and the winning strategy in both cases was TIT FOR TAT.

TIT FOR TAT was developed by Anatol Rapoport of the University of Toronto, and it's a winning strategy because it can play co-operatively against a range of other strategies, yet never scores more points than any of its opponents. In a system populated by "mean" IPD strategies (strategies whose opening move is to always defect), just a few TIT FOR TAT players will eventually prevail because they can always play "nicely" against each other ("nice" refers to IPD strategies whose opening move is to always co-operate).

These purely mathematical results help to illuminate some of the more paradoxical aspects of human co-operation. For example, during the First World War, peace would occasionally break out between British and German troops who were otherwise supposed to be engaged in trench warfare. During these spontaneous lulls in the fighting, both sides would refrain from firing directly at each other, much to the frustration of their commanding officers.

Typically, these informal truces would happen around mealtime. Sometimes during a lull, one side or the other would fire off a series of shots with pinpoint accuracy aimed at some neutral target, such as the side of a barn, just to show that they were capable of hitting the enemy if they so wished. If somebody either accidentally or deliberately broke the quiet by firing off an unexpected shot or two, then the response would often be a brief volley in return, typically a multiple of the shots received, but nothing fatal.

The best-known example of spontaneous co-operation between British and German troops during the First World War was the famous Christmas truce, when both sides ceased fire and entered no man's land to exchange small gifts in a spirit of camaraderie. Eventually, their commanding officers devised methods of disrupting the live-and-let-live mindset that infected their troops, usually by ordering them to raid the enemy's trenches and return with trophies to prove that they had indeed conducted the raid.

All of this has bearing on our understanding of the Israeli-Palestinian conflict because prior to the mass immigration of European Jews to the Middle East, which began in the late nineteenth century, the relationship between the various ethnoreligious communities can best be described as live and let live. This is our sociological baseline.

SYKES-PICOT: SOWING THE SEEDS OF FUTURE CONFLICTS
In 1916 Great Britain and France (with the assent of Russia) signed the secret Sykes-Picot Agreement. The agreement (formally Sykes-Picot-Sazanov) dictated how the Middle East would be carved up into mutually exclusive British and French spheres of influence following the presumed defeat of the Ottoman Empire by the Triple Entente.

The French were assigned control over Syria, Lebanon, and northern Mesopotamia; the British were assigned Palestine, Transjordan, and southern Mesopotamia.

The existence of the Sykes-Picot Agreement was not disclosed publicly until three years after it was signed (in 1919), and only because a disgruntled Lenin and his new Bolshevik regime decided to discredit Russia's former allies. By this time, however, Britain and France had already abandoned the colonial framework of Sykes-Picot in favour of the idea of national self-determination, as proposed by American president Woodrow Wilson.

According to author Christopher Simon Sykes (the grandson of Sir Mark Sykes), after the fall of Damascus to British forces, a meeting took place in which it was pointed out that Britain had just entered the French sector as defined by Sykes-Picot. When Prime Minister Lloyd George was informed of this, he demurred, stating that he "had been refreshing his memory about the Sykes-Picot Agreement and had come to the conclusion that it was quite inapplicable to present circumstance, and was altogether a most undesirable agreement from the British point of view."[5]

Sykes was Britain's expert on Ottoman affairs. A Tory MP from a wealthy family in Yorkshire, he derived most of his expertise from extensive travels throughout the Middle East in his earlier life. An extrovert by nature, Sykes attended but never graduated from Cambridge University and in 1917 had had no serious practical experience in government. He was, as Christopher Sykes writes, "a novice in government—in 1917 he had held executive office for only two years—and was a mercurial personality who remained subject to sudden enthusiasms."

The inexperienced diplomat was, according to his grandson, "quick to take up a cause or to put it down. But though inconsistent, he was not dishonest: he did not dissemble."

Sykes was only thirty-seven years old when he negotiated the now-infamous agreement that bears his name. Two years later he died in Paris of the Spanish flu—a global pandemic that killed more people than the First World War.

McMAHON-HUSSEIN AND BALFOUR

About a year before the Sykes-Picot Agreement was signed, Great Britain made a series of promises to the al-Hashemi family of the Hejaz in exchange for their assistance in mounting a rebellion against the Turks. The promises were crystallized in the 1915 McMahon-Hussein correspondence.

Then, on November 2, 1917, while actively backing the efforts of T. E. Lawrence and the Arab Revolt against the Ottomans, Great Britain issued the sixty-seven-word Balfour Declaration in support of the establishment of a Jewish homeland in Palestine, thus laying the foundation for a major social and demographic change in a territory that it didn't yet control. All of this was done without any consultation or consent from the Palestinian Arabs, many of whom had been living there since the time of the Islamic Conquest (637 CE), if not earlier.

"His Majesty's government" reads a key section of the Declaration,

> view with favour the establishment in Palestine of a national home for the Jewish people, and will use their best endeavours to facilitate the achievement of this object, it being clearly understood that nothing shall be done which may prejudice the civil and religious rights of existing non-Jewish communities in Palestine, or the rights and political status enjoyed by Jews in any other country.

The Balfour Declaration made no attempt at clarifying the terms "national home," "Jewish people," or "Jews." Arabs are not even mentioned by name (even though they made up the vast majority of the population of Palestine at the time), and as far as what was understood by the term "Palestine," we can only assume that this referred to the geographic region of Palestine since there was never an Ottoman administrative district or province called Palestine.

There were at least two good reasons why Britain issued the Balfour Declaration. On June 4, 1917, Jules Cambon, secretary-general to the French Foreign Ministry, had already signed a formal document accepting the principle of Jewish colonization in Palestine, which created a rationale for Britain issuing a pro-Zionist statement that fall in 1917. And second, Britain wanted to ensure the loyalty of the Empire's Jewish community. Sykes "was also genuinely worried that if the Allies failed to offer the Jews a place in Palestine, then this might tip the scales in favour of [them supporting] the Turks and Germany, wherein lay the possibility of Allied defeat."[6]

Following the signing of the Armistice of Mudros on October 30, 1918, the Ottoman Empire ceased all hostilities and Palestine briefly fell under joint British and French control. At the Paris Peace Conference of 1919, Chaim Weizmann (as president of the World Zionist Organization) and Emir Faisal I bin Hussein bin Ali al-Hashemi, third son of Hussein bin Ali al-Hashemi, King of the Hejaz, signed an agreement (subsequently referred to as the Faisal-Weizmann Agreement) promising "the most cordial goodwill and understanding" in all their relations. At the Conference, the World Zionist Organization presented a map of the proposed Jewish homeland (see figure 3.1), which today would include portions of modern Lebanon, Syria, Jordan, and Egypt. Although mostly aspirational in nature, the map provides some insight into Zionist thinking at the time, including the desire to colonize the east bank of the Jordan River.

The Palestinian Arabs who attended the Paris Peace Conference flatly rejected the idea of a separate Palestinian state (either Jewish or Arab). Instead, they adopted the following resolution: "We consider Palestine as part of Arab Syria, as it has never been separated from it at any time. We are connected with it by national, religious, linguistic, natural, economic and geographical bonds."[7]

In other words, by 1919 we essentially had agreements all around: between Great Britain and France, between Great Britain and the Zionists, between Great Britain and the al-Hashemi family, and between the Zionists and the al-Hashemi family. The only ones left out of the equation were the Palestinian Arabs—the very people whose land had been carved up and pre-assigned without their knowledge or consent. Neither Great Britain, the Zionists, nor the al-Hashemi family seemed to care very much for them.

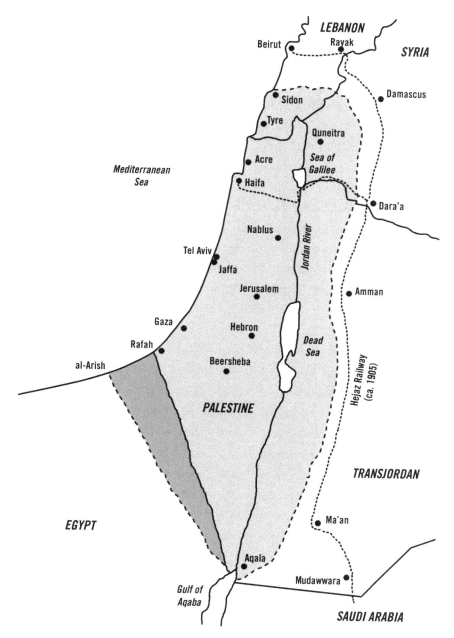

FIGURE 3.1   ZIONIST STATE AS CLAIMED AT THE PARIS PEACE CONFERENCE, 1919
SOURCE: Public domain.

THE TWO-STATE DILEMMA

With the end of the First World War, as anticipated, the entire Levant fell under joint British and French administration (also referred to as Occupied Enemy Territory Administration, or OETA). This transitional administration ended in April 1920 at the San Remo Conference, with the formulation of a British Mandate for Palestine and a French Mandate for Syria and Lebanon. Palestinian Arab identity had finally been severed from any connections with Syria. That same month, the Palestinian Arabs took their anger to the streets.

SCHELLING'S DILEMMA AND THE NEBI MUSA RIOTS

The Nebi Musa riots of April 1920 are regarded by many as the birth of the Palestinian resistance movement. What sparked the riots isn't exactly clear, but only a month earlier, the Battle of Tel Hai had taken place (in which Joseph Trumpeldor gave his life as one of Zionism's earliest heroes), and there was a lingering atmosphere of tension between Jews and Palestinian Arabs.

In game theory, a Schelling's Dilemma (also called a Hobbesian Trap) refers to a situation in which fear of a conflict precipitates an arms race that leads to even more fear. A common example is the dilemma faced by the armed burglar confronted by the armed homeowner. Neither wants to shoot, but one may end up shooting pre-emptively in order to avoid being shot (even though the more favourable outcome would be for neither to shoot). Schelling's Dilemma explains why pre-emptive strikes occur, and why riots may break out without much in the way of provocation.

The Nebi Musa riots took place in and around the Old City of Jerusalem. Five Jews and four Arabs were killed, but several hundred were injured. For reasons unclear, the British were slow to respond, and so trust between Jews, Arabs, and the British began to erode. This initiated a cycle of fear in which the Jews, at the urging of the Revisionist Zionist leader Ze'ev Jabotinsky, decided to arm themselves. Subsequent riots in Jaffa in 1921 only reinforced this negative cycle, eventually prompting the British to reconsider their position vis-à-vis Transjordania (which was part of the original Palestine Mandate).

THE ORIGINAL PALESTINE MANDATE IS DIVIDED

The area of Transjordania (known today as the Hashemite Kingdom of Jordan) was a political no man's land following the defeat of the Arab Kingdom of Syria by French forces in July 1920 (the Arab Kingdom of Syria was a self-proclaimed, unrecognized state that existed for only four months). In 1921 Winston Churchill convened the Cairo Conference to resolve the many conflicting promises between the McMahon-Hussein letters (1915), the Sykes-Picot Agreement (1916), and the Balfour Declaration (1917). At the conference, the area of Transjordania was assigned to Abdullah bin Hussein al-Hashemi, in keeping with promises contained in the McMahon-Hussein letters. This angered Revisionist Zionist leader Ze'ev Jabotinsky, who felt deeply betrayed by the loss of Transjordania (the area of Transjordania constitutes roughly 75 per cent of the territory of the original Palestine Mandate, and Jabotinsky wanted all of it to be set aside for Jewish colonization).

In the early twentieth century, much of Palestine was infested with malaria. A 1920 British Department of Health map (see figure 3.2) shows an astonishing prevalence of spleen enlargement from malaria in the Coastal Plain, Jordan Valley, Hula Valley, and Upper Galilee. Not surprisingly, these were among the first areas to be sold to Zionist settlers by Palestinian absentee landlords, who were only too happy to receive above-market prices for what they regarded as nearly worthless land.[8] The first kibbutz ever built, Degania aleph, was situated right smack in the middle of a malaria-infested swamp on the south shore of the Sea of Galilee.

In July 1922, almost five years after it was issued, the Balfour Declaration was incorporated into the text of the Palestine Mandate, and formalized by the League of Nations. This gave international legitimacy to the concept of a homeland for the Jewish People. It was the political formula that Herzl and Weizmann had explicitly sought: a publicly and legally secured home in Palestine.

The 1922 Palestine Mandate can best be thought of as a legal instrument that empowered Great Britain to provide 'tutelage' to the people of Palestine (Jewish and non-Jewish alike—Arabs are not specifically

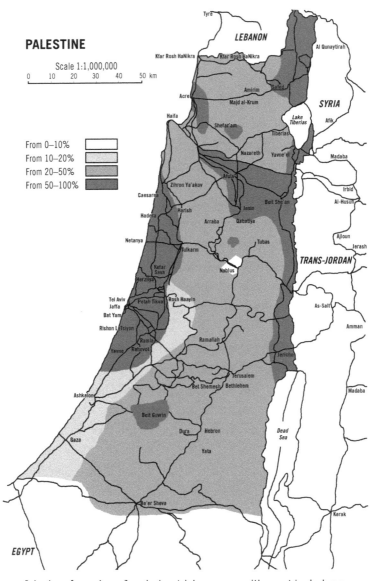

PALESTINE

Scale 1:1,000,000

0   10   20   30   40   50 km

From 0–10%
From 10–20%
From 20–50%
From 50–100%

[shades of grey boxes] malaria-stricken areas, with worst in dark grey

FIGURE 3.2 PREVALENCE OF SPLEEN ENLARGEMENT IN PALESTINE, 1920

SOURCE: Palestine Dept. of Health, "A Review of the Control of Malaria in Palestine (1918–1941)."

MICHAEL DAN

mentioned by name even though they made up 89 per cent of the population) until such time as they were deemed capable of managing their own affairs (the same system of paternalistic administration was also applied to the French Mandate for Syria and Lebanon).

The 1922 Palestine Mandate enabled the "close settlement by Jews on the land." In practice, however, this amounted to an internationally sanctioned population transfer from Eastern Europe to the Middle East, with the nominally Christian rulers of France and Great Britain effectively double-crossing the Arab Christian population of Palestine—one of the oldest such populations in the world. Once again, all of this was done without the consent of the Palestinian Arabs, whose wishes were basically ignored until race riots eventually broke out.

In 1922 the British conducted a very thorough census of Palestine, and Jews constituted only 11.07 per cent of the population. In other words, non-Jews outnumbered Jews by a hefty ratio of 9:1. According to the census, 757,182 people were living in Mandatory Palestine, of whom 83,794 were Jews and 590,890 were Mohammedans (the remainder were classified as either Christians or Others).

From a perspective of pure numbers, Jabotinsky's dream of colonizing the whole of Palestine and Transjordania with millions and millions of Jewish immigrants comes across as an example of extreme chutzpah. Jabotinsky, however, was undaunted and undeterred. Following Churchill's 1921 order prohibiting Jewish settlement on the east bank of the Jordan River, Jabotinsky defiantly and boldly challenged the prime minister's authority. "There is only one thing the Zionists want," he declared in his famous essay *The Iron Wall*.

> [It] is that one thing that the Arabs do not want, for that is the way by which the Jews would gradually become the majority, and then a Jewish Government would follow automatically, and the future of the Arab minority would depend on the goodwill of the Jews; and a minority status is not a good thing, as the Jews themselves are never tired of pointing out.

He concluded his manifesto with an emphatic, stark and uncompromising choice: *"Zionist colonisation must either stop, or else proceed regardless of the native population."* What that meant, Jabotinsky said, was that colonization could "proceed and develop only under the protection of a power that is independent of the native population—behind an iron wall, which the native population cannot breach."

According to historian David Fromkin in *A Peace to End All Peace: The Fall of the Ottoman Empire and the Creation of the Modern Middle East*, Jabotinsky felt betrayed by Great Britain over the loss of Transjordania to Zionist colonization, whereas the al-Hashemi family was twice betrayed. First, they couldn't have found out until 1919 that Lebanon and Syria had already been assigned to the French under the Sykes-Picot Agreement; and second, they weren't told until 1920 that by helping Britain to defeat the Ottomans, they had also helped Britain to keep her promises to the Zionists per the Balfour Declaration (the Balfour Declaration was publicly disseminated in London in 1917, but it wasn't until 1920 that news of it reached the average Palestinian).

It is likewise doubtful that Jabotinsky understood—not having been privy to the McMahon-Hussein correspondence—that his Zion Mule Corps (which fought with distinction in the Battle of Gallipoli, and for which he was made a Member of the Order of the British Empire) was indirectly assisting Great Britain to keep her promises to the al-Hashemi family.

Great Britain treated Arabs, Jews, Armenians, and Kurds—in fact, all the people of the Middle East—with colonial disdain, wrestling control of the Middle East from the Ottomans without carefully thinking through how they planned to govern it afterwards. "The Mesopotamian provinces were the first to be captured from the Ottoman by Britain during the war," writes Fromkin.

Whitehall's failure to think through in practical detail how to fulfill the promises gratuitously made to a section of the local inhabitants was revealing and boded ill for the provinces that were next to be invaded: Palestine, Syria, and Lebanon. It showed that Sykes and his colleagues had adopted policies for the Middle East without first considering whether they could feasibly be implemented in existing conditions and, if so, whether British officers on the spot would actually allow them to be implemented.

A hundred years ago, the strategic value of the Middle East lay primarily in its geography and not its hydrocarbons. During the First World War, Britain controlled the Suez Canal and the port of Aden in Yemen. Oil had been discovered in Iran in 1908, but not yet in Iraq, Saudi Arabia, or any of the Gulf States. The British navy, under Winston Churchill, had recently converted from coal to oil (in 1914), and Britain needed to secure her transportation and logistical supply networks for India, her most valuable colony. Britain also controlled the oil resources of Iran via the Anglo-Persian Oil Company, which later became known as British Petroleum, and then BP. Most of the oil that Britain relied on during the First World War, however, came from the United States, and not the Middle East.

Britain's main concern upon entering the Middle Eastern theatre of war was that her ally, Russia, would end up encroaching on India. Following the Russian Revolution, Britain shifted her concerns towards potential German hegemony in the Middle East. Zionism, therefore, was of important strategic value to Great Britain, with Palestine being regarded as a vital land link between the crescent of British colonies stretching from Africa to Asia, and to the Pacific. The simple truth is that both Zionism and Arab nationalism were in part moulded by Whitehall, in keeping with Britain's overall military strategy during the First World War.

Zionist thinking about Palestine, from Herzl to Jabotinsky, had always been irredentist and colonial. The foundational texts of Zionism make liberal use of colonial vocabulary. The Hovevei Zion movement, which predated Political Zionism, was acutely aware of the delicate balance between the Jewish minority and the Arab majority in Ottoman Palestine. But the Political Zionists and their descendants (Practical Zionists, Labor Zionists, Revisionist Zionists, etc.) only understood the colonial zero-sum game.

THE ALIYOT CONTINUE

The Fourth Aliyah, comprising eighty-two thousand Jews mainly from Poland and Hungary, arrived in Mandatory Palestine between 1923 and 1929. Many of the new arrivals were middle-class families who, preferring the life and amenities of the growing towns, established small businesses and light industry. These were not the same rugged pioneers as previous Aliyot, and approximately twenty-three thousand eventually returned to their home countries.

The Fifth Aliyah was larger than all previous Aliyot combined. In the decade between 1929 and 1939, a quarter of a million Jews fleeing Nazi persecution arrived in Mandatory Palestine and completely overwhelmed its British administrators. Comprised of many urban professionals, this newest influx of settler added to the infrastructure and cultural life of pre-state Israel. It was during this phase, however, that Palestinian Arab resentment reached a boiling point. Despite all the challenges, by 1940 the Jewish population of Palestine had reached four hundred and fifty thousand.

One little-known chapter from the 1933–39 era involved a Transfer (*Ha'avara*) Agreement between Nazi Germany and Mandatory Palestine. According to the agreement, some fifty thousand German Jews and $100 million of their assets were quietly moved to Palestine prior to the outbreak of the Second World War.[9]

THE 1936 RIOTS AND THEIR AFTERMATH

In November 1935, Sheikh Izz al-Din al-Qassam, a popular Syrian Muslim preacher and Palestinian revolutionary leader who fought against British, French, and Zionist forces in the Levant, and Italian forces in Libya, was killed in a shootout with the British, in retaliation for the assassination of a British policeman. Al-Qassam's death precipitated the 1936–39 Arab general strike and riots. These, in turn, prompted the British government to convene the Peel Commission of 1937 to investigate the cause of the riots. Eventually, the Peel Commission proposed a two-state solution for Palestine, which, in turn, necessitated the convening of the Woodhead

Commission of 1938 to find a way of implementing the recommendations of the Peel Commission. After the recommendations of the Woodhead Commission were rejected by Whitehall, Britain ended up issuing the infamous 1939 White Paper that limited Jewish immigration to Palestine on the very eve of the Second World War.

Whereas Ahad Ha'am had predicted a backlash by the natives against a Jewish influx, Zionist leaders like Ze'ev Jabotinsky seemed to almost welcome the challenge. He boldly testified before the Peel Commission in 1937, stating:

> What I do not deny is that in the process [of creating a Jewish state] the Arabs of Palestine will necessarily become a minority in the country of Palestine. What I do deny is that this is a hardship. This is not a hardship on any race, any nation, possessing so many national states now and so many more national states in the future. One fraction, one branch of that race, and not a big one, will have to live in someone else's state. Well, that is the case of all the mightiest nations of the world.

Not only is it an astonishingly arrogant statement, it introduces into the Zionist discourse several fallacies that continue to be used by many right-wing groups to this day. First, it takes the racist view that the Jewish claim to Palestine is morally or perhaps legally superior to the Palestinian claim. Second, it assumes that the territory of Palestine can be easily filled with as many Jews as necessary in order to ensure a Jewish majority. Third, and rather naively, it supposes that a Jewish majority would always behave magnanimously towards a Palestinian minority so long as the latter would be prepared to live under Jewish rule of law.

The 1939 White Paper (that limited Jewish immigration to seventy-five thousand in total over the next five years) didn't stop Jews from making their way to Palestine. A wave of illegal immigration, known as *Aliyah Bet*, was organized by the Mossad and the Irgun. It continued until the founding of the state in 1948. A total of one hundred and ten thousand Jews, mostly from Europe, arrived in this way (in particular after 1945).

In retrospect, the 1939 White Paper seems particularly indefensible given the climate of genocidal antisemitism that prevailed in Germany at the time. Britain, however, was very much caught in a bind between her obligations to the Jews (by virtue of the 1922 Palestine Mandate) and her need to appease her Arab partners and clients. Having publicly stated her support for a two-state solution, it was no longer possible for Britain to get the two sides to co-operate. All interactions between Jews and Palestinian Arabs were now zero-sum.

THE QUEST FOR JEWISH SOVEREIGNTY

With the exception of Jabotinsky, the Zionist movement was outwardly content with a national home in Palestine, while quietly hoping for a sovereign state. The explicit demand for a sovereign state only became mainstream Zionist policy at the Biltmore Conference, which was held in May 1942 in New York. The shift came about as a reaction to the 1939 White Paper and was seen as a virtual coup d'état against the more moderate senior Zionist leadership. Weizmann, observes one historian,

> was pushed aside by a younger generation of pioneering Zionists, led by David Ben-Gurion. They believed that ultimately, only by building Jewish settlements on the ground, establishing a Zionist economy and embryo government-in-waiting, with or more likely without British blessing, would that Jewish state become a reality. And they were right.[10]

The Biltmore Conference also marked an important shift in the centre of gravity of the Zionist movement away from Great Britain, towards the United States.

Other Zionist intellectuals flatly rejected the call for a Jewish state with a Jewish majority. Henrietta Szold (the founder of Hadassah, the Women's Zionist Organization of America), Judah L. Magnes (an American-born Reform Jewish rabbi, and the first chancellor of Hebrew University), both of whom lived at the time in the Sheikh Jarrah neighbourhood of East Jerusalem,[11] and the philosopher Martin Buber, attempted to form a political party, Ichud (Unification), which called for a binational Arab-Jewish state. Their efforts to find a Pareto-superior solution to the Zionist's dilemma were quickly isolated by mainstream Zionists.

The small Haredi community of pre-state Palestine was also notoriously anti-Zionist, but in June 1947, they cut a deal (known as the "status quo" arrangement) with Ben-Gurion in order to present a united front to the United Nations Special Committee on Palestine. The net result was the exemption from military service of some thirty-five hundred Torah scholars, in exchange for the neutrality of the Haredi political wing, the Agudat Yisrael (Union of Israel). Today, the Haredi community is the fastest growing and economically poorest Jewish community in Israel, and numbers over a million.

But it wasn't quite the end of Jewish anti-Zionism. In the United States, the American Council for Judaism took the view that Jews are a religious—and not a national—group (the exact same view was adopted years later by the PLO). The same view was also favoured by the Reform Jewish movement (which had ties with the American Council for Judaism). Thus, it's not difficult to understand why to this day the state of Israel continues to look down on the Reform Jewish movement (for example, by denying their request for an egalitarian prayer space at the Western Wall).

At face value, a Jewish "national home" can be anywhere in the world. In the past, serious consideration had been given to creating one in Uganda, Argentina, and under Stalin, as an autonomous oblast in the Russian Far East region of Birobidzhan. A sovereign Jewish state, according to the Biltmore Conference of 1942, can only exist in the territory of historic Palestine. By the same thinking, a sovereign Jewish state must also have a Jewish majority—something that had to be reverse engineered after two thousand years of exile, through mass immigration to historic Palestine. Thus, the formula for Jewish nationalist zero-sum thinking was finally set in stone by 1942.

In 1944, the central leadership of the Zionist movement adopted what became known as the One Million Plan. This was an effort to absorb one million Jews from Europe, the Middle East, and North Africa into Mandatory Palestine.

While Gandhi was busy applying non-violent pressure on the British in India, Zionist terrorism against the British flourished. Bloody attacks by the Jewish terrorist organization, Lehi, included the assassination of the British minister of state for the Middle East, Lord Moyne, in Cairo in November 1944; the bombing of the King David Hotel in July 1946; and the bombing of the British embassy in Rome in October 1946. Two future prime ministers of Israel, Menachem Begin and Yitzhak Shamir, were intimately connected with these events.

AN UNFINISHED COUNTRY IS BORN

On November 29, 1947, the UN General Assembly passed UN Resolution 181 recommending the partition of Mandatory Palestine into two states— one with a Jewish majority and one with an Arab majority. As a convenient shorthand, most people use the terms "Jewish state" and "Arab state," but we must remember that there is no universally accepted definition of who is a Jew or who is an Arab. Jews and Arabs, however, know who they are, and so the best that the international community could offer was to recognize a state with a self-identified Jewish majority and a state with a self-identified Arab majority.

Britain abstained from voting on UN Resolution 181 for fear of undermining her important relationships with Jordan, Egypt, and the rest of the Arab world (Britain still controlled the Suez Canal at the time). The UN partition plan also included very specific borders for the two states, but these were never enshrined in international law because the very next day (November 30, 1947), civil war broke out in Mandatory Palestine. During the course of the war, Jewish military and paramilitary forces substantially increased their territory beyond what had been proposed for the Jewish state. This set the dangerous precedent of enlarging territory by means of armed conflict, something that Israel did once again some twenty years later, in 1967. The mixed message here is that if it was acceptable to do so in 1947, then it would also be acceptable in 1967.

In any case, on April 13, 1948, a convoy of seventy-eight Jewish doctors, nurses, students, patients, *Haganah* escorts, and one British soldier were ambushed and massacred by Arab forces near Mount Scopus, in Jerusalem. The convoy was bringing both medical and military supplies and personnel to Hadassah Hospital, which formed part of the Hebrew University campus and was accessible only via a narrow road that passed through the Sheikh Jarrah neighbourhood of Jerusalem. Following the Hadassah massacre, even Judah L. Magnes (the eternal pacifist) abandoned his dream of a binational state.

Britain unilaterally withdrew from Palestine on May 14, 1948, ending her Mandate without ever attaining the goal of governing Palestine "until such time that the country was able to stand on its own." Thus, over a span of thirty years, two great empires—Ottoman and British—relinquished control of Palestine. At midnight on May 15, 1948, the state of Israel issued a Declaration of Independence, and two days later (on May 17, 1948), the Soviet Union offered de jure recognition (i.e., recognized Israel as a legally sovereign state). The United States, although offering de facto recognition of the state of Israel some fourteen minutes after she declared her independence, chose not to offer de jure recognition until January 31, 1949, after Israel's first general elections.

On the day that Israel declared her independence, the country was in the midst of an existential war on four fronts, and with borders that hadn't yet been finalized. Israel was an unfinished country—without diplomatic relations with any of her Arab neighbours, her population in flux, an embryonic judiciary, and tenuous sovereignty in parts of her territory.

Twenty-four hours previously, the Arab League had massacred 129 residents and Haganah militia of the Kfar Etzion kibbutz, 15 of whom were murdered after they had surrendered. About a month earlier, on April 9, 1948, irregular troops from Irgun and Lehi carried out a massacre of 107 Arabs in the village of Deir Yassin (the events played a key role in the eventual displacement of 710,000 Arabs from Palestine). Lehi, led by Menachem Begin, continued to act as an independent paramilitary organization for a month after Israel was recognized by the UN.

On June 15, 1948, David Ben-Gurion ordered the Israeli Defense Forces to fire on the Lehi-commanded ship, *Altalena*, which refused to comply with a previously agreed-upon ceasefire order. The picture of Jews firing twentieth-century ordnance at other Jews was a new low point in their three-thousand-year-long history.

Recognition by a Great Power of an unfinished country is highly unusual but not without precedent. The previous year (1947), the British parliament had passed the Indian Independence Act, about a month before the borders of India and Pakistan were actually finalized. The partition of the British Raj into two self-governing countries based on a two-nation theory most likely influenced Whitehall's thinking towards Mandatory Palestine.

Immediately following independence, and in stark contrast to the generous promises enshrined in the Israeli Declaration of Independence, Palestinian citizens of Israel were placed under martial law. Travel permits, curfews, administrative detentions, and expulsions became part of daily life. These practices continued until May 1966—exactly a year before the Six-Day War. It was a dangerous precedent of security trumping minority rights—one that continues to this day.

Israel's Declaration of Independence promises that

> the state of israel ... will foster the development of the country for the benefit of all its inhabitants; it will be based on freedom, justice and peace as envisaged by the prophets of Israel; it will ensure complete equality of social and political rights to all its inhabitants irrespective of religion, race or sex; it will guarantee freedom of religion, conscience, language, education and culture; it will safeguard the Holy Places of all religions; and it will be faithful to the principles of the Charter of the United Nations.

This is Herzlian Zionism at its best—a Zionism that explicitly respects the rights of minorities.

Regarding a two-state solution for historic Palestine, the Declaration of Independence is crystal clear:

> the state of israel is prepared to co-operate with the agencies and representatives of the United Nations in implementing the resolution

of the General Assembly of November, 1947 [i.e., Resolution 181, in favour of a two-state solution], and will take steps to bring about the economic union of the whole of Eretz-Israel [i.e., the exact same formula as proposed by the Peel Commission in 1937 and the 1947 UN Partition Plan for Palestine].

There's no ambiguity here. Support for a two-state solution was 'on the table' from the outset.

The Declaration continues:

we appeal—in the very midst of the onslaught launched against us now for months—to the Arab inhabitants of the State of Israel to preserve peace and participate in the upbuilding of the State on the basis of full and equal citizenship and due representation in all its provisional and permanent institutions.

This can be regarded as a form of social contract between Jews and Palestinian citizens of Israel: preserve the peace and help build the state in exchange for full and equal participation in all its institutions. There's very little room for other interpretations.

An Israeli constitution (which was promised by October 1948) never materialized and probably never will because of objections from religious parties (who hold that only the Almighty may act as the supreme authority in Israel). Instead of a constitution, Israel has a series of Basic Laws that serve as a skeleton constitution and that can only be amended or overturned by a two-thirds majority in the Knesset.

Taken in its broader historical context, the Israeli Declaration of Independence stands as one of the most uplifting documents of the twentieth century. But not all Zionists endorsed it. Notably absent from the document itself is the signature of Menachem Begin, Jabotinsky's political successor and future prime minister of Israel.

In Israeli politics, then as now, the fundamental divide is not so much between left and right, as it is between Universalists and Nationalists (both of whom proclaim themselves to be Zionists). Over the years, the term "Zionism" has been diluted to the point of near irrelevance—much like Israel's promise of complete social and political equality for all inhabitants, or endorsement of a two-state solution.

Chapter 4

THE EPISTEMOLOGY OF IDENTITY

Anyone who has watched the Netflix series *Fauda* (which tells the story of a fictitious IDF unit tasked with pursuing a fictitious Hamas operative in the West Bank) must surely ask themselves: how do they know which side they're on? The IDF unit depicted in *Fauda* is comprised of *Mistaravim*. The word "Mistaravim" loosely translates as "those who live among the Arabs." A couple of *Fauda* episodes later, there's a group of Palestinian terrorists taking Hebrew classes at Bir Zeit University in order to disguise themselves as Jews. In the Middle East, belonging—or appearing to belong—to the right group can sometimes be the difference between life and death. But how do you really know if you belong to *l'om yehudi* (the Jewish nation) or *l'om aravi* (the Arab nation)?

Epistemology is the branch of philosophy that attempts to answer the question: how do we know that we know? This has direct bearing on the Israeli-Palestinian conflict because in order to reduce it to a game between two players, each player must first know which side they're on—and why.

In this chapter, we'll unearth the deepest roots of the Israeli-Palestinian conflict; we'll explore the intersection between sacred texts, game theory, and evolutionary biology; and we'll seek answers to questions such as: Why has the conflict persisted for so long? And why is it so inefficient from the perspective of human lives and scarce resources?

THE DEAD SEA SCROLLS: A TIME CAPSULE OF SACRED TEXTS

In November 1946, a group of teenage Bedouin shepherds took turns tossing small stones into a cave near Khirbet Qumran, in what is now the West Bank. But instead of hearing the familiar *thunk* of stones landing on dirt, what echoed back from inside the cave was a sharp shattering sound.[1] When the boys investigated, they found several cylindrical clay jars containing ancient parchments and papyrus scrolls. Similar caves were later discovered nearby, and between 1949 and 1956, a total of 981 scrolls dating from between the third century BCE to the first century CE were recovered from eleven different caves near Qumran. Because of Qumran's location near the Dead Sea, the scrolls eventually became known as the Dead Sea Scrolls (DSS)—a veritable time capsule of sacred texts dating back to at least 68 CE (the date that the cave was sealed off from the outside world), two years before Rome captured Jerusalem and destroyed the Second Temple.

What archaeologists and linguists have been able to confirm is that most of the texts are composed in Hebrew; a smaller number are in Greek, Aramaic, and Nabatean-Aramaic. The texts fall into three broad categories: (1) copies of texts from the Hebrew Scriptures, (2) texts from the Second Temple period that were never canonized in the Hebrew Scriptures, and (3) previously unknown texts that may have been unique to the community that hid the scrolls in the caves in the first place. Exactly who these people were isn't entirely clear, however; they appear to have belonged to an ascetic sect, most likely the Essenes or an offshoot of the Sadducees. Even less clear is the origin of the Qumran scrolls themselves; some may have been written in the Qumran caves, while others most likely originated elsewhere and were placed in the caves for safekeeping.

In his *Jewish War* (the most important chronicle of the insurrection of the Jews against Rome between 66 and 70 CE), Flavius Josephus describes the four major Jewish sects that existed during the time of the Second Temple: (1) the Pharisees, (2) the Sadducees, (3) the Essenes, and (4) the Zealots. The Pharisees evolved into mainstream rabbinic Judaism; the other three sects eventually died off (the Essenes were an ascetic and eschatological group who practised celibacy, which meant that they faced a practical problem and a steep uphill battle when it came to passing on their DNA and cultural practices!).

Today, all major branches of rabbinic Judaism (Orthodox, Conservative, Reform, and Reconstructionist) use something called the Masoretic Text

(MT)—a version of the Hebrew Scriptures that hasn't changed by so much as a letter in the last thousand years. A thousand years may seem like an eternity to some, but *two* thousand years ago there was still a degree of fluidity surrounding the Hebrew Scriptures.

Except for the Book of Esther (a copy of which was never found in the caves of Qumran), the text of the DSS, when compared word for word and letter for letter with the MT, appears to be remarkably similar. No doubt, this is a testimony to the immense dedication of countless generations of scribes whose job it was to faithfully and diligently copy out sacred texts without introducing any errors whatsoever. Nevertheless, there are small differences between the DSS and the MT. And for a text that's supposed to be divinely authored, even the slightest inconsistencies demand a full explanation.

SACRED TEXTS, LIKE THE DNA OF LIVING CELLS, MUST REPLICATE FAITHFULLY

According to Orthodox Jewish tradition, the Torah was dictated in Hebrew (and not Aramaic, Yiddish, King James English, or any other language), word for word, letter for letter, by God Himself directly to Moses on Mount Sinai—including the passage in Deuteronomy that describes Moses's own death. Setting aside the problem of Moses writing about future events, including the passage in Numbers 20:11 when he loses his temper and strikes a rock with his staff instead of merely speaking to it nicely (thereby forfeiting his chance to enter the Promised Land), there's an even bigger issue with the writing system of the Torah itself.

Archeologists have now established that the twenty-two-letter Paleo-Hebrew alphabet that Moses would have used to write the Torah is based on the much older, twenty-two-letter Phoenician alphabet, which, in turn, is based on the even older twenty-two-letter Proto-Sinaitic alphabet. Although a variety of writing systems have been invented throughout human history (including abjad, logographic, and alphasyllabary systems), *the alphabet has only been invented once*, and every subsequent alphabet ever developed (including Paleo-Hebrew, Aramaic, Hebrew, Greek, Latin,

Arabic, and Cyrillic) is modelled on the Phoenician alphabet. [Technically speaking, the Phoenician alphabet isn't a complete alphabet, but an abjad because it lacks vowels. The Greek alphabet was the first complete alphabet to be developed, but it's clearly based on the Phoenician abjad.]

Presumably, having grown up in Egypt since infancy, Moses was familiar with hieroglyphics. Why, then, didn't he use hieroglyphics to write the Torah as it was being dictated to him by God? Why use something that very closely resembled Phoenician script? Why would a Phoenician writing system be preferable to an Egyptian one? And why didn't God invent a completely novel alphabet and orthography for the Hebrew language as proof that the Torah was originally transmitted as a written text?

Many ancient texts (e.g., the Epic of Gilgamesh) have their basis in even older oral traditions. There's now compelling evidence that the *Iliad* was written not by Homer, but by an entire culture. Linguists are almost certain that unlike the *Odyssey*, the *Iliad* originated as an epic poem that was memorized and transmitted orally for hundreds of years before finally being committed to writing sometime in the eighth century BCE. Given the ubiquity of the writing system used in the Torah, it's difficult to make a strong case that at least some passages of the Torah are *not* the products of an oral tradition, analogous to the *Iliad*. (Just to round out the picture, Orthodox Jews believe that Moses received *two* Torahs on Mount Sinai: one written and one oral, with the latter forming the basis for the Mishna and Talmud. The idea that I wish to convey is that even the *written* Torah may be the product of an oral tradition by virtue of it being written using an alphabet that pre-dates the revelation at Sinai.)

In any case, today, whenever a Jewish scribe copies out a new Torah (a process that takes about a year, using the same parchment, pen, and ink technology as in ancient times), not a single letter can be added, subtracted, or changed. Borrowing a bit from the field of genetics, it's as if each letter in the Torah represents a single nucleotide in a gene. The process of copying a Torah, therefore, is analogous to the process of mitotic cell division. Ideally, the complete DNA sequence (or Torah letter and word sequence) is replicated without any errors or mutations.

Perhaps it's not by coincidence that of the 613 commandments found in the Torah, the first one involves the replication of human DNA (God's instruction to Adam and Eve to be fruitful and to multiply; Genesis 1:28), and the next to last involves the replication of the Torah itself (each Jewish male must write a Torah scroll in their lifetime; Deuteronomy 31:19).

WHY ANCIENT TEXTS MATTER TODAY

So, why all the fuss over the historical integrity of the Torah? The short answer is that to Orthodox Jews and religious Zionists, the Torah isn't merely a divinely inspired text—it's a divinely *authored* text (down to the very last letter).

Sacred texts form the basis for religious faith, and religious Zionists believe in the marrow of their bones that they have a right—today—to build settlements in Judea and Samaria (the West Bank) because a four-thousand-year-old text *commands* them to build settlements in Judea and Samaria (which formed the core of Ancient Israel). If it were feasible to do so, they would be delighted to build settlements in the western portion of the Hashemite Kingdom of Jordan, too (which also formed part of Ancient Israel).

To the settler movement, the resolutions of the UN Security Council are merely ink on paper compared to the commandments of the immutable Torah. Religious Zionists see themselves as active players in a divinely sanctioned zero-sum game, and there can be no rational co-operation or compromise when it comes to carrying out divine commandments.

But how do we know that the MT is true to the original Torah if we don't have the original Torah (assuming there even was one)? This is a matter of epistemology (How do we know that we know?), and a detailed examination of ancient texts such as the DSS sheds light on this important question.

Again, not to overstretch a point, but finding even the smallest of errors in the MT would be highly significant because it would undermine the fundamental dogma that the *entire* Torah is divinely authored. If even a single letter or word can be proven to be missing or wrong, then the Torah itself would cease to be a divine text; it would become a *human* text, containing human errors, and thus subject to much more lenient interpretation.

As a human text, the door to rational co-operation would be pried open a crack; as a divine text, it's slammed and bolted shut.

SHOW ME THE PARCHMENT

Prior to the discovery of the DSS, the oldest known physical copy of the Hebrew Scriptures was the Aleppo Codex, which dates from ca. 930 CE. Unfortunately, the Aleppo Codex is missing most of the Torah section except for the final portion of Deuteronomy. This represented a gap of some three thousand years between the putative Torah of Moses and the oldest physical copy of the Torah—and the one thing that we know for certain is that the Aleppo Codex[2] is nothing like any Torah that Moses would have ever written (or even been able to read).

For instance, the writing system used in the Aleppo Codex is known as Assyrian block script with diacritical marks, and is believed to have been developed by the Masoretes, a group of Jewish scribes and scholars based in Tiberias, Jerusalem, and Babylonia in the seventh-to-tenth centuries CE. The Masoretes are responsible for standardizing the spelling, pronunciation, cantillation (chanting), verse, and paragraph structure of the Torah.

As pointed out earlier, the writing system that Moses would have used (as the Torah was allegedly being dictated to him by God) is Paleo-Hebrew script. Assyrian block script didn't even exist at the time. Look closely at the two tablets that Charlton Heston is holding as he descends Mount Sinai in Cecil B. DeMille's *The Ten Commandments* and you will see that they're written in Paleo-Hebrew script (see figure 4.1). It's one of the few historical details that DeMille got right (even after making allowances for a pharaoh who speaks flawless English).

The Masoretes were responsible for compiling the MT, and there's a MT for all three sections of the Hebrew Scriptures (Pentateuch, Prophets, and Writings). Today, Orthodox Judaism regards only the MT as the

FIGURE 4.1 MOSES (CHARLTON HESTON) CARRYING THE TWO TABLETS INSCRIBED IN PALEO-HEBREW SCRIPT, FROM THE MOVIE *THE TEN COMMANDMENTS*, DIRECTED BY CECIL B. DEMILLE (1956).

SOURCE: Used with permission of Entertainment Pictures/Alamy Stock Photo.

definitive Torah—the one true text dictated by God directly to Moses. Any other text is regarded as inferior, degraded, and unfaithful to the original. The Orthodox logic is of course perfectly circular: if it's the MT, then it's the word of God; if it isn't the MT, then it's not the word of God.

Problematic for some, but to Orthodox Jews there's no cognitive dissonance. They merely regard the DSS as the handiwork of some minor Jewish sect that took the liberty of editing the word of God for ideological and sectarian purposes. The Essene's subsequent disappearance into oblivion is enough to explain—at least to the Orthodox—the summary merits of their misguided theological efforts.

Nevertheless, it's possible—perhaps even probable—that the Masoretes made a few copy errors along the way, and that at least some of the texts found in the Qumran caves are more "correct" than the corresponding MT.

PSALM 145 IS OBVIOUSLY MISSING A VERSE

Psalm 145 forms the major part of the Ashrei prayer, which is recited three times a day by observant Jews. It's structured as an acrostic poem, meaning that each verse begins with a successive letter of the twenty-two-letter Hebrew alphabet. In the Aleppo Codex version of Psalm 145, the verse corresponding to the Hebrew letter *nun* (which comes between the letters *mem* and *samech*) is obviously missing (see figure 4.2).[3] This is analogous to reciting the ABC mnemonic ("A is for apple, B is for ball, C is for cat," etc.) without the "N is for nose" verse. It's a glaring omission. The missing *nun* verse, however, appears in the copy of Psalm 145 that was found in the cave of Qumran (see figure 4.3). So which version is correct? The MT or the DSS?

The DSS version of Psalm 145 is at least nine hundred years older than the Aleppo Codex, and in all likelihood it's the correct version simply by virtue of being older. What probably happened is that some poor scribe made an error when copying out Psalm 145, and that error became part of the DNA of the MT—much the same way that a spontaneous DNA mutation is passed on from one generation to the next during the process of cell division (if we believe that Jewish scribes never make copy errors, then how do we explain the very slight difference between the Ashkenazi and Sephardic versions of the Torah, which differ by a single letter: an *aleph* versus a *heh*—both silent—at the end of the word *dakha* in Deuteronomy 23:2?).

One way to resolve the dilemma of scriptural authenticity is to find an even older version of the text, and then to compare texts. As luck would have it, an older version of the Hebrew Scriptures exists, although it's actually a Greek translation of the original Hebrew.

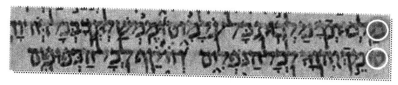

FIGURE 4.2 PSALM 145 FROM THE ALEPPO CODEX. This particular psalm is in the form of an acrostic poem. In the Hebrew alphabet, the letters *mem, nun,* and *samekh* normally follow each other. The verse beginning with *mem* is highlighted and the verse beginning with *samekh* is highlighted. There is no intervening verse beginning with *nun* in the Aleppo Codex.

SOURCE: Used with permission of Dust Off the Bible.

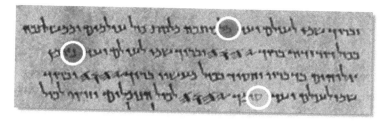

FIGURE 4.3 PSALM 145 FROM THE DEAD SEA SCROLLS. There is a verse beginning with *nun* (highlighted) between the verse beginning with *mem* (highlighted) and the verse beginning with *samekh* (highlighted). All three verses are in the correct alphabetical order. The name of God is written in Paleo-Hebrew script.

SOURCE: Used with permission of Dust Off the Bible.

The Septuagint (LXX and meaning "the seventy") is the product of seventy (or seventy-two according to Talmudic sources) bilingual rabbis who were commissioned by Ptolemy II Philadelphus of Egypt (308–246 BCE) to translate the Hebrew Scriptures into Koine Greek. According to legend, all seventy rabbis, working independently, produced identical translations, and to this day, the LXX remains the preferred text of the Eastern Orthodox Church.

There's more to the story, however. Each of the seventy rabbis deliberately incorporated thirteen small mistranslations into the text, and all thirteen mistranslations matched up exactly (which was subsequently declared to be an open miracle). Miracles notwithstanding, the translation of the Torah into Greek (which was finalized on the 8th day of Av, in 246 BCE) was regarded as a complete disaster for the Jewish people, and was followed by three days of darkness and even marked as a major fast day during Talmudic times. None of this makes much sense given that a translation of the Torah into Aramaic, which was completed around 110 CE by Onkelos (a Roman convert to Judaism), is deemed perfectly acceptable by Orthodox Judaism. Yet Targum Onkelos (the Translation of Onkelos) contains dozens of phrases and expressions that don't match up with the Hebrew text. In addition, Aramaic is the language spoken by Jesus—a fact that you would think might have troubled more than a few rabbis.

In any event, here's the problem with Psalm 145. If we compare the LXX and DSS versions of Psalm 145, both contain the identical *nun* verse ("The Lord is faithful in his words, and holy in all His works").[4] This suggests very strongly that a *nun* verse was *deleted* from the MT (which is much younger than either the LXX or the DSS) rather than *added* to both the LXX and the DSS (imagine the effort involved in adding a *nun* verse to every existing copy of the LXX, as well as re-translating Psalm 145 from the Greek of the LXX back into the Hebrew of the DSS).

It may come as no surprise that Orthodox Judaism doesn't buy the deletion hypothesis. There's a discussion in the Talmud about the missing *nun* verse (Tractate B'rachot 4b, 21). Rabbi Yochanan said: Why is there no *nun* in Ashrei? Because it would refer to the downfall of Israel, as it is written, "Fallen (*nefilah*), not to rise again, is Maiden Israel" (Amos 5:2). The discussion is interpreted as follows: King David originally included a *nun* verse, but the *nun* stood for the word "*nefilah*," which means "fallen." And because of this negative connotation, King David did not include a *nun* verse in Psalm 145.

This is yet another example of Orthodox circular logic. In the LXX and the DSS, the *nun* verse stands for the word "*ne'eman*" (faithful), which carries a very positive connotation. Instead of accepting the more parsimonious explanation for the missing *nun* verse, Orthodox Judaism has simply chosen to ignore it, or for that matter, the existence of a *nun* verse in another ancient text called the Peshitta, which is a first-century CE translation of the Hebrew Tanakh into Syriac.

Other discrepancies between the MT and the LXX may be found, including the MT of the Torah, which—again—should pose a particular dilemma for Orthodox Judaism since the MT of the Torah is *by definition* error-free (or perhaps these discrepancies represent the thirteen miraculous mistranslations of the seventy rabbis).

Deuteronomy 32:8, which forms part of the Song of Moses, is one of the few sections of the Torah that can also be found in the Aleppo Codex, and it translates into English as "When the Most High gave the nations their inheritance, when He divided all the sons of man, He set the boundaries of the people according to the number of the sons of Israel."[5] The LXX version of Deuteronomy 32:8 translates the final part of the verse as "angels of God," rather than "sons of Israel." Interestingly, the Dead Sea Scroll version of Deuteronomy 32:8 agrees with the LXX but not the MT. So, if we go with the rule of "best two out of three," the MT has probably got it wrong once again (most certainly as a result of human error).

By this point you're probably wondering: what difference does it make if the MT is off by a letter or two, or at most a few words here and there? Again, not to belabour a point, but to Orthodox Jews every letter in the Torah is sacred. A Torah with a single letter missing or out of place is unimaginably worse than an entire Mozart symphony played from start to finish with only a single false note. Both would be summarily rejected on the spot. Other ancient translations of the Hebrew Scriptures exist, each slightly different from the other. Some of these texts carry mutations forward into the next text, and they can be represented on an evolutionary tree diagram that looks a bit like the evolutionary tree of the Hominin family (see figure 4.4). This makes perfect sense because in the process of being copied and transcribed over the millennia, sacred texts undergo mutations and evolve, analogous to any living species (see figure 4.5).

As we are about to see, transcriptional errors in ancient texts are analogous to spontaneous mutations in living cells. Indeed, spontaneous mutations are a common theme linking sacred texts, evolutionary biology, and game theory.

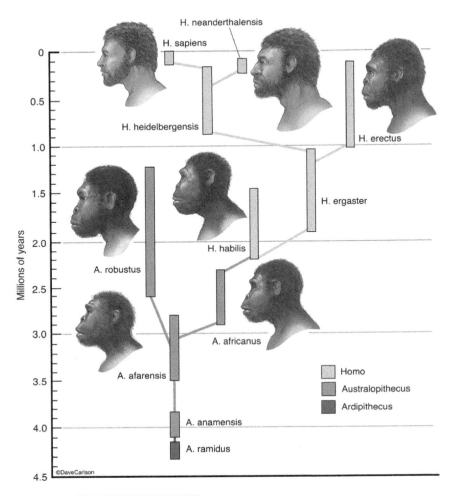

FIGURE 4.4 THE HOMININ FAMILY TREE

SOURCE: Image copyright © DaveCarlson/CarlsonStockArt.com.

MICHAEL DAN

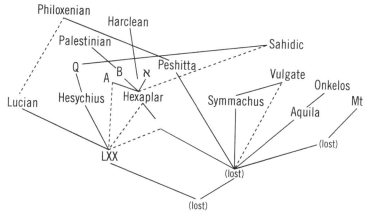

FIGURE 4.5 THE BIBLICAL FAMILY TREE

REPLICATORS, VEHICLES, AND THE SELFISH GENES

Oxford biologist Richard Dawkins introduced the concepts of "replicator" and "vehicle" in his now classic book *The Selfish Gene* (1976). "The fundamental units of natural selection," he writes, "the basic things that survive or fail to survive, that form lineages of identical copies with occasional random mutations, are called replicators." DNA molecules, he explains, are replicators. "They generally … gang together into large communal survival machines or vehicles."

Think of your body as the flexible shell in which the replicators operate. "Vehicles don't replicate themselves," writes Dawkins. "They work to propagate their replicators." It's the job of the vehicle to shield and protect the replicator until it finishes the job of replicating, and those vehicles that do a good job of shielding and protecting their replicators are, by definition, "good" vehicles. "Replicators don't behave, don't perceive the world, don't catch prey or run away from predators; they make vehicles that do all those things."

By this account a human being is simply human DNA's way of making more human DNA. There is no "purpose" to DNA other than to make more copies of itself. There's lots of DNA in our genome that just sits around and doesn't do much other than get copied from one generation to the next (e.g., humans share 50 per cent of their DNA with bananas—and in the case of one particular American president, the percentage may be even higher).

"Any gene that behaves in such a way as to increase its own survival chances in the gene pool," observes Dawkins, "will, by definition, tautologously, tend to survive. The gene is the basic unit of selfishness." Although living organisms may behave selfishly and steal resources from each other, the true locus of selfishness occurs at the level of the genes that code for the selfish behaviour.

The Victorian philosopher, biologist, and politician Herbert Spencer introduced the public to the phrase "survival of the fittest" in *Principles of Biology* (1864), which he published—interestingly—after reading Darwin's *On the Origin of Species*. By "survival of the fittest" Spencer meant "survival of the form that will leave the most copies of itself in successive generations." Dawkins turned things upside down to equate fitness with survival of the gene that codes for the *form* that leaves the most copies of itself in successive generations.

If we adopt a *gene-centred view* of Spencer's survival of the fittest, then we can begin to make sense of certain altruistic behaviours that previously baffled evolutionary biologists. Altruistic behaviour is merely a label for behaviour directed from one *vehicle* towards another, the result of which is more copies of a gene in the general population.

The classic example of altruistic behaviour is the honeybee. There are three castes (drones, workers, and queens). Worker bees can only sting once, after which they die from evisceration. From the perspective of someone observing the behaviour of individual worker bees, this would be regarded as altruistic behaviour (self-sacrifice of the individual for the sake of the collective). But the worker bees are sterile females; their deaths don't represent a loss of DNA that would otherwise be passed on to the next generation. Only the queen's DNA needs to be preserved for the next generation. From an evolutionary perspective, it's more efficient to design a queen that can replenish her supply of worker bees than it is to design a worker bee that can sting multiple times. Evolution is very parsimonious when it comes to design. (The dodo is a prime example of evolutionary parsimony. These grotesque-looking creatures originated from a population of pigeons that were blown off course and landed on the island of Mauritius. With no natural predators for thousands of miles, successive generations of pigeons wasted little energy in developing sleek wings and an aerodynamic body. The more energy-efficient flightless offspring gradually outcompeted the less energy-efficient offspring that still expressed the genes for well-developed wings.)

MEMES, LIKE GENES, REPLICATE SELFISHLY AND WITHOUT ANY PURPOSE

It is important for us to realize that culture—like DNA—can also be passed on from one person to the next, and from one generation to the next. The term that Dawkins coined to describe a self-replicating unit of culture is the "meme" (a word that he deliberately chose because, to his ear, it rhymes with gene).

A meme acts as a unit carrying cultural ideas, beliefs, symbols, or practices that can be transmitted through writing, speech, gestures, rituals, or other imitable phenomena. Memes can be relatively simple, such as the graffito "Kilroy was here" (thought to be one of the first memes to spread throughout the world, in the 1940s; see figure 4.6), or they can be quite complex and even cluster together to form a "memeplex" in the same manner that certain genes cluster together to form a chromosome (and by extension, a living cell). The alphabet, as discussed earlier, is the classic example of a highly successful and tenacious meme that needed to be invented only once in order to ensure its long-term survival.

Memes, like genes, are also capable of selfish replication—often at the expense of their human hosts. And because memes can only survive through human intermediaries (who are notoriously poor at copying things), they can undergo change and evolve—or slowly disappear over time.

As Susan Blackmore (a British psychologist and evolutionary theorist) likes to point out, both memes and genes replicate selfishly, with the former often doing so at the expense of the latter. In *The Meme Machine* she writes:

FIGURE 4.6 THE MEME "KILROY WAS HERE" SPREAD THROUGHOUT THE WORLD IN THE 1940S, TYPICALLY IN ASSOCIATION WITH AMERICAN SERVICEMEN

Nobody knows exactly who Kilroy was or where the meme originated.

SOURCE: Public domain.

The whole point of mimetics is to treat the meme as a replicator in its own right, operating entirely for the benefit of its own selfish replication. If there is no second replicator, and you are a committed Darwinian, then somehow or other everything must come back to the genes—to biological advantage. If there are two replicators (or more) then there will inevitably be conflicts of interest—circumstances in which the interests of the genes pull in one direction and those of the memes in the opposite direction.[6]

From a mimetic perspective, the Jewish religion (like any other major religion) may be regarded as a complex cultural organism—a memeplex with a tradition attached to everything: from the most mundane of actions (such as tying one's shoes, which should be done from left to right, in the same sequence as donning *tefillin*) right up to concepts about the afterlife.

Incidentally, a set of tefillin (or phylacteries) consists of two small black leather boxes containing parchment scrolls inscribed with verses from the Torah. They are worn in a ritual manner on the forehead and on the left

MICHAEL DAN

arm (if you're right-handed, otherwise the converse) by observant Jews during morning prayers, each day except for the Sabbath. Tefillin serve no purpose whatsoever other than to remind the wearer to concentrate their thoughts on their connection to God (but I can think of dozens of other ways of achieving this same goal). Reform Jews—who tend to think of themselves as more rational than some of their co-religionists—typically don't wear tefillin, and this is perhaps one of the reasons why they are looked down upon by the Orthodox.

Tefillin that date from the Middle Ages were sometimes round, instead of square. And a set of tefillin were discovered in the caves of Qumran—which came as no surprise to the Orthodox rabbinate—but the texts that they contained were different from the texts used today. Like all other memes, the tefillin meme has evolved over time.

The custom of ritual slaughter is another tenacious meme in Judaism, and I would argue that the laws of kashrut (which may be found in the books of Leviticus and Deuteronomy) evolved in order to preserve the ancient custom of ritual slaughter. To use Dawkins's terminology, the custom of ritual slaughter is the replicator, and the laws of kashrut are the vehicle that surrounds and protects the replicator. The vehicle endures because it results in social cohesion, which imparts a distinct survival advantage.

Ritual slaughter dates back to the earliest agrarian communities, and was practised in Ancient Egypt over four thousand years ago. The custom was likely transmitted to the Ancient Israelites, where it eventually became incorporated into the Temple service. As practised in ancient Judaism, ritual slaughter involves the killing of an animal with a single stroke of a knife across the jugular vein, then collecting of the blood and sprinkling of it against the base of an altar.[7] Most domestic animals in the Middle East are considered to be kosher, but not horses and camels. If there was a tradition of ritual slaughter of horses and camels, then any community that practised it would be at a disadvantage in the face of an advancing army and would not survive over the long run. Thus, the laws of kashrut evolved to exclude the ritual slaughter of horses and camels.

One plausible explanation for the pig being deemed non-kosher is that its thick and muscular neck prevents it from being killed in a ritual fashion (in more primitive cultures, pigs needed to be clubbed on the head before being killed by exsanguination—a very gruesome and unholy spectacle). So, for the sake of preserving the custom of ritual slaughter, pigs were excluded from the list of kosher animals.

Rabbits, hyraxes, dogs, and cats aren't kosher because they represent an emergency food source (Judaism allows for suspension of the laws of kashrut in a food emergency). Any community that has already killed off its emergency food sources would not be able to survive a food emergency or pass on its DNA to the next generation. So, the laws of kashrut evolved to exclude the ritual slaughter of emergency food sources.

THE BIBLICAL NARRATIVE IS ALSO A MEMEPLEX

Around 632 CE, another sacred text began to appear in the Middle East. The Qur'an, according to tradition, was dictated to the prophet Muhammad by the angel Gabriel—slowly and over the course of some twenty-three years. It was never completely redacted during the prophet's lifetime, but it was committed to memory by his companions and later fully transcribed.

It's clear that the Qur'an was heavily influenced by the narrative memes of Judaism and Christianity, without incorporating the specific texts themselves. In the Qur'an, you can find a version of the Ten Commandments, but the wording is completely different from the Torah. The replicator that carried on from Judaism to Christianity, and from Christianity to Islam, is the biblical narrative rather than the specific texts themselves. For example, Islam recognizes numerous prophets that are shared by both Judaism and Christianity, including Abraham, Isaac, Jacob, Aaron, Moses, Joshua, and Samuel. Islam also recognizes Adam, Noah, David, and Solomon as prophets, whereas Judaism does not. John the Baptist, Mary (the only woman to make the list), and Jesus are also considered to be prophets in Islam, but obviously not in Judaism.

What's perhaps unique about the sacred texts of Judaism is that they have developed an endosymbiotic relationship with the canon of Christian sacred texts, analogous to the endosymbiotic relationship between mitochondria and eukaryotic cells.

Inside every mammalian cell is a nucleus, which contains the bulk of the cell's DNA, and an organelle called a mitochondrion, which supplies the cell with energy and which contains its own DNA. When a mammalian cell divides, the nuclear DNA and the mitochondrial DNA replicate separately. It's believed that mitochondria first evolved as separate organisms, and that billions of years ago they entered an early type of cell where they established a symbiotic relationship, inside the early cell.

As a result of the endosymbiotic relationship between Jewish and Christian sacred texts, the Tanakh, which is sacred to some 14.7 million Jews worldwide, continues to survive and replicate within the canon of sacred texts of some 2.4 billion Christians. The Jewish community itself may suffer tremendous setbacks from time to time (analogous to worker bees defending the hive), but the DNA of the Jewish text lives on. It's a brilliant survival strategy—as far as the text is concerned—but such a strategy was never deliberate. No third-century rabbi ever made the conscious decision to embed the sacred texts of Judaism within the sacred texts of Christianity. It simply happened that way. But as a result, the Jewish text is able to survive (albeit in translation) without any assistance from Jewish scribes or the Jewish people themselves. (There are other ways for a text to survive over the millennia. For example, the Babylonian king Hammurabi wrote multiple copies of his code of laws on various basalt stele and clay tablets. These, too, have survived for thousands of years, but not as tenaciously as the Old Testament.)

In the case of sacred texts, what counts is the survival of the text (replicator) and not necessarily the individual or community (vehicle), whose task it is to transmit the text to the next generation. As Dawkins famously points out, the gene (or meme) has no purpose other than to make more copies of itself. Equally famously, the early Zionist thinker Ahad Ha'am has said: "More than the Jews have kept the Sabbath, the Sabbath has kept the Jews." The Sabbath with all its customs and rituals is the meme, which in this case, is beneficial to the Jewish community because it fosters social cohesion.

Not all memes are neutral or beneficial to humans, however. A good example of the harmful variety are the Crusades. From the perspective of an eleventh-century European knight, the Crusades involved a dangerous journey through malaria-infested regions of the Middle East, and violent clashes with well-seasoned and well-armed Muslims for control of neither land, nor water, nor food, nor any other resource that might impart any sort of survival advantage to someone living in Europe. The loss of life was completely pointless, other than from the perspective of the Christian memeplex. But after Jerusalem fell to the Crusaders in 1099, there were no doubt more physical copies of the New Testament to be found than copies of the Qur'an (which were probably burned). The Christian memeplex prevailed until 1187, at which point Jerusalem was retaken by Muslims led by Saladin.

ORIGINS OF THE MODERN PALESTINIAN POPULATION

Sacred texts aren't the only form of DNA to be copied from one generation to the next. The same process obviously occurs with the DNA molecule itself, including the DNA of Jews and Palestinians.

In 313 CE, Emperor Constantine I issued the Edict of Milan, which recognized the legal status of Christianity throughout the Roman Empire. Under Emperor Theodosius I, in 380 CE, Christianity became the official religion of Rome. Jews were still living in Palestine at the time, but their geographic base was now in the Galilee, in the vicinity of Yavneh. After 640 CE, which coincided with the Islamic conquest of Palestine, many Jews and Christians living in the region of Palestine converted to Islam and—essentially—founded what we know today as the modern Palestinian population. Most of the people whom we refer to today as Palestinians are in fact Arabized Jews who over the centuries converted first to Christianity and then to Islam. This is something that was recognized by many of the early Zionists, including David Ben-Gurion, but now seems to have been mostly forgotten.

By examining the history of the Jewish community in Palestine after the destruction of the Second Temple, and analyzing the Arabic names of villages, Ben-Gurion's mind was made up that the *fellahs* had preserved ancient Jewish traditions through the centuries as well as the place names cited in the Bible, Talmud, Midrash, and *The Jewish War* by Flavius Josephus. So greatly did the fellahs venerate and preserve the ancient legacy of their forefathers that Islamic law was utterly foreign to them, and they still submitted only to their sheikhs. Ben-Gurion had no doubt that the fellahs were descendants of the country folk who had inhabited the land at the time of the Arab conquest in the seventh century. In that era, wrote Ben-Gurion, there were "no fewer than a quarter of a million Jews in the country, and quite possibly more," and he believed that he had established the origins of the fellahs in this remnant.[8]

One important Palestinian clan comes from a small town near Hebron called Yatta. In 1928, research by Yitzhak Ben Zvi, a future president of Israel, suggested that three out of six extended families in Yatta belonged to the Mahamra clan (or were possibly descended from a Jewish-Arab tribe[9]). Mahamra means "wine maker" in Palestinian Arabic, which is certainly not a respectable profession among observant Muslims. A Jewish cemetery dating from the second century was found in Yatta in 1931. And in the fourth century CE, Eusebius of Caesarea described Yatta as "a very large village of Jews." The biblical city of Jutta (pronounced Yutta) is also described in the Book of Joshua 15:55 and 21:16 as a city designated for Kohanim.[10]

So, how did the Jews of Jutta become the Palestinians of Yatta? The answer is really quite simple. When the Romans sacked the Second Temple in Jerusalem in 70 CE, the Jews did not disappear altogether from Palestine; only the Temple service disappeared. When the Bar Kokhba revolt of 132–35 CE was crushed by Rome, the Jews did not disappear altogether from Palestine; only the dream of a Jewish Messiah disappeared. Following Thedosius's edict in 380 CE establishing Christianity as the official religion of the Roman Empire, the Jews did not disappear altogether from Palestine; only their numbers diminished after many of them converted to Christianity. And when the Jerusalem Talmud (also known as the Palestinian Talmud) was redacted in 425 CE by Jews living in the Galilee, *again* the Jews did not disappear altogether from Palestine; only their scholarly activity diminished as the epicentre of Rabbinic Judaism shifted eastward towards Baghdad.

Finally, after the Islamic conquest of Palestine in 640 CE, the Jews did not disappear altogether from Palestine; only their numbers continued to dwindle as many of them converted to Islam in order to avoid paying the *jizya* tax that was imposed upon Christians and Jews by their Muslim conquerors.

Fewer and fewer, but never quite disappearing. All throughout Palestine's complex history, Jews have been a part of Palestine. And today, Ancient Israelite DNA makes up much of the core of modern Palestinian DNA.

JEWISH AND PALESTINIAN DNA ARE VIRTUALLY IDENTICAL

In 2000, two researchers, Michael Hammer at the University of Arizona and Almut Nebel at Hebrew University in Jerusalem, made separate but related—and startling—discoveries.[11] The Y-chromosomes of Arabs and Jews, Hammer's group concluded, were essentially a single population. In fact, DNA from the Palestinian population occupies a position right in the middle of DNA from the different Jewish populations. Nebel's group, meanwhile, was able to show that Jewish lineages essentially bracket Muslim Kurds,[12] but that they are also very closely related to Palestinians.

These findings, taken together, flatly contradict the notion that the Jewish people should be regarded, first and foremost, as a religious community (which happens to be the position of the PLO). For most Jews of Middle Eastern origin (i.e., Mizrahi Jews), there's an obvious *ethnic* component to their Jewishness—one that's shared with Palestinians (the Ashkenazi Jewish community, which arose in Europe approximately fifteen hundred years ago, also has Middle Eastern roots).[13]

In other words, Jews and Palestinians are closely linked by blood. And not just blood—by history and by culture, too.

Palestinians celebrate pilgrimage festivals that interest few other Muslims, such as Nebi Musa, Nebi Samwil, and Nebi Rubin. These festivals are named after the Jewish prophets Moses, Samuel, and Reuben (the oldest son of the patriarch Jacob), respectively. Ironically, it was during the Nebi Musa pilgrimage festival of 1920 that the first stirrings of Palestinian national resistance emerged. If only we knew back then how closely Palestinians and Jews are related by history and by genetics!

As recently as a couple of generations ago, members of the Mahamra clan of Hebron practised the Jewish customs of sitting *shiva* for seven days (instead of the usual three, as is common among Muslims), ripping clothing when hearing of a death, lighting candles on Friday night, and levirate marriage. Some Palestinians have been known to put on tefillin or pray at the graves of famous rabbis whenever they got sick. Many homes in Palestinian villages have doorpost indentations for a mezuzah, with a scroll placed in some of them. And by one account, up to 85 per cent of Arabs living in "Greater Israel" have Jewish roots.

In addition to these crypto-Jewish customs, there are crypto-Jewish symbols to be found in traditional Palestinian embroidery. The seven-branched candelabra (menorah) is an unmistakable Jewish symbol, as represented in the Arch of Titus in Rome (see figure 4.7). The arch dates from around 82 CE and was built to commemorate the siege of Jerusalem. The Roman soldiers depicted in the arch have plundered the Second Temple and are carrying the spoils on their shoulders, including the menorah, which was used in the Temple service (and which forms the basis for the official emblem of the state of Israel).

Today, the menorah motif (complete with the correct number of candelabra branches and base) can be easily discerned in certain examples of traditional Palestinian embroidery (see figure 4.8). Similarly, the square motif, which is even more commonly represented in Palestinian embroidery, recalls the horned altar (*mizbeach*; as seen from above) upon which the temple sacrifices were placed (see figure 4.9). These Jewish symbols—the menorah and the mizbeach—have been hiding in plain view in Palestinian embroidery for centuries.

FIGURE 4.7 THE SPOILS OF JERUSALEM, ARCH OF TITUS, CA. 82 CE

SOURCE: Public domain; modified by Michael Dan.

FIGURE 4.8 PALESTINIAN EMBROIDERY SHOWING A REPEATING PATTERN OF THE SEVEN-BRANCHED MENORAH

SOURCE: Personal collection of Michael Dan.

FIGURE 4.9 RECONSTRUCTION OF AN ANCIENT ISRAELITE MIZBEACH (ALTAR), BEERSHEVA

SOURCE: Modified from Gugganji/Wikimedia Creative Commons BY-SA 3.0. Public domain.

INEFFICIENT BEHAVIOURS CAN BE VERY EVOLUTIONARILY STABLE

Why do conflicts persist? Not why do they begin, but why do they persist? This is perhaps the most difficult question in all of human history. In this chapter I've attempted to show that Jews and Palestinians are not that different from each other, even at the molecular level. The two groups have so much in common that an anthropologist from Mars would have a hard time telling them apart. And yet the conflict persists, much to the collective detriment of all players.

Shortly before Dawkins published *The Selfish Gene*, John Maynard Smith and George Price, in 1973, proposed the concept of an Evolutionarily Stable Strategy (ESS). In game theory, an ESS is a strategy that, if adopted by a given population in a given environment, cannot be bettered by any alternative strategy. In short, it survives even when a better (more efficient) alternative exists.

Smith and Price used a simple game of Hawk and Dove to illustrate the concept of an ESS. The game of Hawk and Dove is a variation of the game of Chicken, played over many rounds (i.e., an iterated game of Chicken). In Chicken, there are two players with an identical strategy. In Hawk and Dove, however, there is a hawk strategy and a dove strategy.

The hawk and the dove may be two members of the same species who are in conflict over the same resource. The hawk exhibits aggressive behaviour, and the dove is very passive. If a hawk wins the resource, the odds increase that the gene coding for hawkish behaviour will be passed on to the next generation. Likewise, if a dove wins the resource, the odds increase that the gene coding for dovish behaviour will be passed on to the next generation. Hawk and dove are simple placeholder terms; they just as easily could be pigeon and sparrow, your dog and your cat, or the neighbours Bill and Susan. The terms only refer to hawkish or dovish *behaviour* (as well as the genes coding for that behaviour).

Now, let's assume that a hawk will fight viciously for the resource and that a dove will merely engage in symbolic conflict, posturing and threatening but not actually fighting. If a hawk fights another hawk, the winner earns the resource and the loser may never recover. If a hawk fights a dove, the hawk will always win. If a dove fights another dove, the two will waste a lot of time until one dove finally gives up the resource. For excessive dallying, then, each dove will lose a few points but not nearly as many as the loser of a hawk vs. hawk encounter.

What Smith and Price were able to show is that if we begin with a population of 100 per cent doves and introduce a single hawk (due perhaps to a spontaneous mutation in a gene coding for aggressive behaviour), gradually over successive generations, the number of hawks in the population will increase. A population consisting uniquely of doves, therefore, is not evolutionarily stable: it's susceptible to invasion by hawks. The converse is also true: a population consisting purely of hawks is not evolutionarily stable because it is susceptible to invasion by doves (eventually, the doves would get together and share the resource among themselves).

Intuitively, we can grasp that there should be some ideal mix of hawks and doves such that the two will balance each other out over many generations. Such a population mix constitutes an ESS because it's resistant to invasion by additional hawks or doves. Remember, hawkish or dovish behaviour is not what's evolutionarily stable—it's the *mix* of hawks and doves that's stable over the long run.

And now comes the kicker. If we calculate the collective payoff of the ESS by adding up all the points lost by wounded hawks and exhausted doves, we come up with a number that is lower than if the population consisted only of doves—the so-called conspiracy of doves scenario.

To use the same language that we used in describing the Prisoner's Dilemma, an ESS is a Nash equilibrium that is evolutionarily stable. Evolution is notorious for producing stable, albeit Pareto-inferior, outcomes. In other words, "An ESS is stable," as Dawkins points out, "not because it is particularly good for the individuals participating in it, but simply because it is immune from treachery from within."[14]

The concept of an ESS has direct bearing on the Israeli-Palestinian conflict, but we have to be careful with our interpretation. For one thing, it would be a mistake to regard the Jews as the hawks and the Palestinians as the doves (or vice versa). Both sides have engaged in aggressive behaviour while demonstrating very little desire for rational co-operation. And prolonged fighting consumes lives and resources—resources that could otherwise be spent on more productive activities, such as raising the standard of living of Jews and Palestinians alike.

Additionally, it should be clear that "Jewishness" and "Palestinianness" are not genetically predetermined behaviours (as in real hawks and doves), but two different *cultural* behaviours that arose within the same genetic population (after all, Jews and Palestinians are virtually identical at the DNA level). And culture is something that can be consciously changed—sometimes profoundly so (ask any Frenchman about the impact of the French Revolution on the previously well-entrenched culture of monarchy and aristocracy).

So, what game theory and evolutionary biology are essentially telling us about the Israeli-Palestinian conflict is that neither side will ever succeed in crowding the other out. Both sides, therefore, need to move past their respective fantasies of throwing the other into the sea. There will always be a mix of Jews and Palestinians that will be stable over the long run, which means that Jews and Palestinians are forever destined to share the Land.

WE ARE MORE THAN OUR BIOLOGY

I find the concept of an ESS to be tantamount to an ancient curse, although I'm not necessarily disagreeing with it. What it adds up to is simply this: regardless of whether we're dealing with two species of birds fighting over the same nesting ground, or two ancient peoples fighting over the same piece of land in the Middle East, lives and resources will end up being wasted because of the natural persistence of highly inefficient patterns of behaviour. If the two birds (or the two peoples) could simply stop and think about what they were fighting over, then maybe they would arrive at a mutually satisfactory solution to the conflict (thus sparing much future bloodshed).

But that's not how the real world works. As every student of history knows, there's no such thing as a population made up exclusively of doves. Granted, if we all *behaved* like doves then our collective benefit would be maximized (and such thinking forms the basis for the teachings of Jesus, the political vision of Gandhi, and even the social contract of the modern welfare state). But for most of our history, humans have been trapped in vicious cycles of Pareto-inferior thinking, unable to mentally move into the co-operate/co-operate box of the Prisoner's Dilemma.

Even worse, if we believe that some higher power has commanded us to disregard any form of rational co-operation with the Other, then the task of maximizing collective utility becomes nearly impossible.

But unlike real hawks and doves, neither Jews nor Palestinians—nor any two groups of human beings—are merely the sum of their genetically predetermined behaviours. We are all much more than our biology. And so perhaps, one day, Jews and Palestinians will choose to play a different game, instead of always wounding and killing each other.

Chapter 5

NOT QUITE NORMAL

The secular Ashkenazi founders of political Zionism were well acquainted with the Westphalian system of governance, and they dreamed of the day when the Jewish nation would become "normalized" like every other nation of Europe—with a land base to call their own. The birth of the state of Israel, however, was anything but normal.

WHAT IS A STATE, ANYWAY?

The constitutive theory of statehood has no equivalent in either Jewish or Islamic law, which were formalized many centuries before the Peace of Westphalia (1648). According to the constitutive theory, a state is considered a person in international law if it is recognized as sovereign by other sovereign states (which typically includes a Great Power).

At the conclusion of the Second World War, there were five Great Powers (the United States, the USSR, the Republic of China, the United Kingdom, and France), all of whom were assigned permanent seats on the UN Security Council. Israel's de facto recognition by the United States and de jure recognition by the USSR on May 15, 1948, were enough to establish her legitimacy in international law. This was not a normal birthing process—it was more like an emergency C-section on a premature baby in acute distress: the newborn state was in the midst of an existential war with all her Arab neighbours, her population was in flux, and she lacked any permanent borders. But to Israelis this was, and would remain, their version of 'normal' for decades to come.

During the 1948 Arab-Israeli conflict, the UN made the usual attempts at reconciling both sides. But on September 17, 1948, the Zionist terrorist group Lehi assassinated Count Folke Bernadotte—a Swedish diplomat and the specially appointed United Nations Security Council Mediator. Two months later (on December 11, 1948), the UN General Assembly passed Resolution 194. These two events—the assassination of Bernadotte and the adoption of Resolution 194—were directly linked, since the wording of Resolution 194 begins with an expression of deep appreciation for the efforts of the late United Nations mediator.

Article 11 of Resolution 194 states that "the refugees wishing to return to their homes and live at peace with their neighbours should be permitted to do so at the earliest practicable date, and that compensation should be paid for the property of those choosing not to return and for loss of or damage to property." Israel objected to Resolution 194, but since Israel wasn't yet a member of the UN General Assembly, she was unable to voice any of her objections in an international public forum. The Soviet Bloc voted against Resolution 194; however, there were insufficient votes to prevent the resolution from being adopted by the General Assembly.

UN Resolution 194 enshrines the Palestinian "right of return," however, since it was never approved by the UN Security Council, it isn't legally binding. To this day, the state of Israel continues to resist all efforts by Palestinian refugees to return to historic Palestine.

ARMISTICE LINES INSTEAD OF BORDERS

Two months after the UN General Assembly passed Resolution 194 (on February 24, 1949), Israel signed an armistice agreement with Egypt. Although the fighting had ceased, the agreement did not provide for permanent borders. The latter took another three decades to establish. Then on March 4, 1949, the UN Security Council admitted Israel to the United Nations. On May 11, 1949, almost a full year after she declared her independence, Israel was finally admitted to the UN General Assembly.

Between March 23 and July 20, 1949, Israel signed armistice agreements with her remaining Arab neighbours—Lebanon, Transjordan, and Syria—thereby bringing to a close the Arab-Israeli conflict of 1948. The 1949 Armistice Line (also called the Green Line because it was depicted in green on UN maps) became Israel's de facto border. An analogy today would be the border between North and South Korea. The Korean War ended in 1953 with an armistice agreement but no peace treaty. The two countries are technically still at war with each other, but the armistice line is regarded by the international community as the de facto border.

After the fighting had ceased, the Arab state that was anticipated per UN Resolution 181 never materialized, and there were now 710,000 Palestinian refugees who either fled or were expelled from their homes and villages by Israeli military and paramilitary forces into the West Bank, Gaza Strip, Jordan, Lebanon, and Syria. For Israel's Arab neighbours, to have declared an Arab state in Palestine in 1948 would have meant the acceptance of a Jewish state in Palestine—something that they were not prepared to do at the time. In the language of game theory, the Arab world insisted on playing a zero-sum game: still numerically superior to the Jewish population, the Palestinians insisted on having all of Palestine to themselves.

A greater number of Jews (approximately 850,000) than Palestinians eventually fled from countries in the Middle East, and later settled in Israel, where they continued to be treated as second-class citizens, only this time by European Jews instead of by Muslims. The Arab refugees of the 1948 Arab-Israeli conflict now refer to themselves as Palestinians, which is a very confusing term, because the same term was also sometimes used by the Jews of Palestine when referring to themselves prior to May 14, 1948.

The Nakba, or catastrophic collapse of Palestinian Arab society in 1948, remains a gaping wound to this day. The official Israeli narrative asserts that the Palestinians fled of their own volition, presumably heeding their leaders' reassurances that the conflict would be over in a few days' time and that they would soon be able to return to their homes. In recent years, however, a darker, more credible account has emerged—that Israel engaged in acts of terror and ethnic cleansing, taking advantage of the fluidity of the situation to enlarge her territory to the maximum extent possible under the circumstances.

Two decades later (in 1969), Moshe Dayan, who was minister of defense at the time, publicly addressed the students of the Technion, in Haifa. His words confirm the Palestinian narrative.

> We came to this country which was already populated by Arabs, and we are establishing a Hebrew, that is a Jewish state here. In considerable areas of the country we bought lands from the Arabs. Jewish villages were built in the place of Arab villages. You do not even know the names of these Arab villages, and I do not blame you, because these geography books no longer exist; not only do the books not exist, the Arab villages are not there either. Nahalal arose in the place of Mahalul, Gevat—in the place of Jibta, Sarid—in the place of Haneifs and Kefar Yehoshua—in the place of Tell Shaman. There is no one place built in this country that did not have a former Arab population.[1]

GAME THEORY AND THE SOCIAL DILEMMAS

Anyone who visits Israel for any length of time and opens a newspaper or switches on a TV is immediately bombarded by a tidal wave of social discord. What's all the fighting about? Well, to begin with, the state of Israel has an almost paradoxical nature. The Israeli Declaration of Independence describes the state as a "Jewish state in Eretz-Israel." It's also understood that Israel is a democracy. (It wasn't until 1985 that Israel's democratic character was legally enshrined by means of an amendment to the Basic Law: The Knesset. In Israel, a series of Basic Laws takes the place of a constitution and cannot be overruled by subsequent laws.) Striking a balance between the Jewish and democratic character of the state has always been a challenge. The result has been a number of important social dilemmas.

The term "social dilemma" refers to a situation in which one individual benefits from selfish behaviour at the expense of another individual, or group of individuals. Identifying and resolving social dilemmas has been the preoccupation of human governance systems since prehistoric times. Every major religion in the world has evolved a version of the Golden

Rule. And even an atheist must credit organized religions for their ability to elicit social cohesion in the name of the greater good (even though the methods employed are often primitive and include the use of fear, threats, intimidation, and manipulation).

There are four main types of social dilemma, each of which may be represented as a symmetrical 2×2 matrix game. Exploring each will help us to decode all the discord that characterizes Israeli society.

In addition to the Prisoner's Dilemma (which is the classic example), there are also the games of Chicken, Deadlock, and Stag Hunt. The names of these games are not intuitive, and they need to be explained and illustrated with specific examples. Finally, there is the N-person Prisoner's Dilemma, which is a variant of the simpler 2×2 matrix game, and which also goes by the name Free-Rider Dilemma. Social dilemmas are common to every human society and to every human conflict, including the Israeli-Palestinian conflict.

Chicken

The game of Chicken is quite well known, and a favourite among game theorists. It came to prominence during the Cuban Missile Crisis of 1962, when the United States and the Soviet Union were headed for a potentially catastrophic nuclear showdown.

For a few years following the Second World War, the United States was the sole nuclear power in the world. During this time, Washington gave serious thought to launching a pre-emptive nuclear strike against Moscow on the basis that the window of advantage was fast closing and that there was no guarantee that a nuclear second strike would carry the same tactical advantage as a first strike. Public figures such as the philosopher Bertrand Russell and the mathematician John von Neumann voiced strong support for these efforts.

On August 29, 1949, the Soviets conducted their first nuclear weapons test and the arms race officially got underway. An arms race is a form of PD, but a nuclear war is more like a game of Chicken. In an arms race, both sides have to weigh the odds that the other will co-operate and *not* develop nuclear weapons. The Nash equilibrium, unfortunately, is for both sides to develop the weapons.

In the classic version of Chicken (as played by adolescent boys with cars), two drivers will head at full speed towards each other. Swerving at the last second is viewed as a form of social co-operation, whereas continuing to drive straight ahead is regarded as an antisocial behaviour bordering on psychopathy. If neither driver swerves (i.e., if both betray social norms), the outcome is a double suicide. If one driver swerves and the other continues to drive straight ahead, then the one who continues straight ahead wins. If both drivers co-operate and swerve at exactly the same instant (in opposite directions, obviously), then the game is a tie.

The outcome matrix for the game of Chicken is depicted in figure 5.1.

		car B	
		swerve	straight
car A	swerve	cars A and B swerve simultaneously	car A swerves, car B drives straight
	straight	car A drives straight, car B swerves	cars A and B drive straight ahead

FIGURE 5.1

With 4 representing the most desirable outcome, and 1 the least desirable outcome in all of these games, figure 5.2 summarizes the payout matrix for Chicken.

		B	
		C	D
A	C	3, 3	*2, 4*
	D	*4, 2*	1, 1

C = co-operate, D = defect/betray; Nash equilibria in bold italics text

FIGURE 5.2

This is a slightly different numbering system than for a PD, because a double betrayal amounts to what is referred to in 1960's cold war language as MAD, or Mutually Assured Destruction. Unlike a PD, there are

110   MICHAEL DAN

two Nash equilibria in a game of Chicken, and that is for one player to swerve and the other to drive straight ahead (it doesn't matter which one, as both are equally likely). The Cuban Missile Crisis of 1962 concluded with both the United States and the Soviet Union swerving—a payoff of 3 each. This was not the Nash equilibrium (thankfully).

Around 1966, Israel developed her own nuclear weapons program, but chose to neither admit nor deny that she had done so. The rationale for such a policy of 'nuclear ambiguity' was to avoid, for as long as possible, a nuclear arms race with other regional players. Recall that in a non-zero-sum game, such as PD or Chicken, both sides know the other player's choices and order of preference. Uncertainty over your opponent's nuclear capabilities adds an extra dimension of doubt to the game since a nuclear weapons program is very expensive to embark upon on and to maintain. So, if you're not certain that your opponent even possesses nuclear weapons, why go to the trouble and expense of developing them yourself?

Israel conducted a surprise air strike against a nuclear reactor facility in Osirak, Iraq, in June 1981. Codenamed Operation Opera, the attack itself did not involve nuclear weapons, although it did prevent Iraq from developing them. Although widely condemned in the media, Operation Opera was cautiously applauded for diminishing the risk that nuclear weapons might fall into the hands of a terrorist group. It was an example of a pre-emptive strike against a nuclear facility.

A variation on the game of Chicken is known as the Volunteer's Dilemma, which is simply Chicken with more than two players. Suppose that there's a power failure in your neighbourhood and all the lights on your street go out. Somebody has to call the power company, but that takes effort. In a Volunteer's Dilemma, one person must take on a chore that will benefit the entire group. To use the Chicken analogy, the entire group may be driving straight ahead (defecting), but the volunteer swerves (co-operates). The Volunteer's Dilemma is an important aspect of secular-religious relations in Israel, which we will come to later.

Deadlock

Anyone who's ever held a staring contest with a sibling or classmate is familiar with the game of Deadlock. The Nash equilibrium for this game is for both players to keep staring at each other until their eyeballs hurt, because whoever blinks first loses (see figure 5.3). Figure 5.4 describes the game.

FIGURE 5.3   PTE. PATRICK CLOUTIER OF THE ROYAL 22E RÉGIMENT (THE VAN DOOS), CANADIAN FORCES, face to face with First Nations (Anishinaabe) warrior and University of Saskatchewan economics student Brad Larocque during the 1990 Oka Crisis, Oka, Quebec.

SOURCE: Shaney Komulainen. Used with permission of the Canadian Press.

		your sibling	
		blink	stare
you	blink	both lose	you lose
	stare	you win	both keep staring

FIGURE 5.4

MICHAEL DAN

The game of Deadlock is represented by the payout matrix in figure 5.5.

B

		C	D
A	C	2, 2	1, 4
	D	4, 1	*3, 3*

C = co-operate, D = defect/betray; Nash equilibrium in bold italics text

FIGURE 5.5

A more serious example of the game of Deadlock is the current stand-off between Israel and Hezbollah along the Lebanese border. Both sides have their weapons pointed at each other, and whoever lets down their guard first will be the loser.

Stag Hunt

Stag Hunt owes its name to a passage in a book by Jean-Jacques Rousseau in which the philosopher and writer describes a group of individuals who must work co-operatively to hunt a stag. The problem with this arrangement is that in the process of hunting a stag, an occasional hare may pass by, in which case a hunter will be tempted to abandon the group and go after the hare.

Figure 5.6 shows the outcome matrix for a two-person Stag Hunt.

hunter B

		stag	hare
hunter A	stag	A and B hunt a stag together	A is abandoned while B goes off chasing a hare
	hare	B is abandoned while A goes off chasing a hare	A and B go off chasing after hares

FIGURE 5.6

And figure 5.7 shows the payout matrix for a Stag Hunt.

For each hunter, the first choice is to co-operate with the other hunter to catch the stag. Failing this, each hunter would be satisfied with catching a hare while the other hunter doesn't catch anything. The next-to-last

$$\begin{array}{c}
\text{B}
\end{array}$$

		C	D
A	C	*4, 4*	1, 3
	D	3, 1	*2, 2*

C = co-operate, D = defect/betray; Nash equilibria in bold italics text;
Pareto-inferior in shaded text

FIGURE 5.7

choice would be for both hunters to catch a hare. And the final choice would be for the other hunter to catch a hare while you're the one left empty-handed. There are two Nash equilibria in a Stag Hunt: either both hunters catch a stag, or both hunters catch a hare. But two hares won't feed as many people as one stag, which is why a Stag Hunt is a social dilemma.

The secular-religious status quo in Israel is an example of a Stag Hunt. On June 19, 1947, David Ben-Gurion sent a letter to the Agudat Yisrael (a Haredi political party originally formed in Poland) that guaranteed that kashrut, the Sabbath day, family law, Jewish burial, etc., in the future state of Israel (which hadn't yet been declared) would fall under the control of the Orthodox Chief Rabbinate. This established an atmosphere of mutual co-operation, in which Haredi and secular Jews agreed to work together to build the Jewish state. In reality, the secular community in Israel has always cared little for the Haredi community, and vice versa. Both would be pleased to go their own separate ways if they had the chance to do so (i.e., to hunt a hare). But for the sake of Jewish unity, both Haredi and secular communities manage to present a united front (which is also very helpful from a public relations perspective). Since both mutual co-operation and mutual betrayal are equally stable from the point of view of the Nash equilibrium, there is the possibility that one day the secular and Haredi communities in Israel will split irreparably over issues such as conversion or mixed prayer space at the Western Wall. Such an outcome would be Pareto-inferior, of course.

MICHAEL DAN

N-person Prisoner's Dilemma

In 1833, the British economist William Forster Lloyd published an essay that introduced the term "tragedy of the commons" to explain the effect of unregulated grazing of cattle on communal land (known as "commons" in the early nineteenth century). Since each farmer wants his cattle to produce the maximum amount of milk, he encourages them to overgraze. Eventually, this leads to a vicious cycle in which more and more farmers are overgrazing their cattle. The commons becomes depleted of grass, and all the farmers suffer collectively.

The tragedy of the commons was popularized in 1968 by the American ecologist Garrett Hardin, and later by Al Gore in his 2006 film *An Inconvenient Truth*. It's an example of an N-person Prisoner's Dilemma: each individual in a group has the choice of either co-operating with all the other individuals or betraying them. If only one individual betrays, then that individual receives the temptation payoff and the entire group must bear the burden of the sucker payoff. It's a perfect description of how wealthy nations enjoy all the benefits of burning fossil fuels while the rest of the world must live with the consequences of climate change.

Another term for the N-person Prisoner's Dilemma is the Free-Rider Dilemma. This is probably the most common PD in everyday life. The Free-Rider Dilemma is the opposite of the Volunteer's Dilemma. In the latter, the volunteer incurs a personal cost for the benefit of the group. In the Free-Rider Dilemma, the free-rider incurs a personal benefit at the expense of the group. Society will tolerate only so many free-riders before a conflict erupts, and the Haredim are notorious for being regarded as Free-Riders by the rest of Israeli society.

REJECTING MODERNITY, ACCEPTING THE WELFARE STATE

The Haggadah, which Jews around the world recite every Passover, describes the Jewish people as a "nation within a nation" (in reference to their alleged enslavement by the Egyptian nation). But the term "nation" is not used in the modern sense of the word because the concept of a modern sovereign state only arose with the Peace of Westphalia (in 1648), and the Haggadah is at least three centuries older (e.g., the oldest Sephardic Haggadah in the world is from Sarajevo, and dates from 1350).

The modern state of Israel must therefore find a way to accommodate the right of her Jewish (and non-Jewish) citizens to *reject* modernity, including modern concepts of nationhood, human rights, civics, and international law. This is analogous to a society accommodating the right of a parent to refuse to vaccinate their child against common childhood infectious illnesses.

Life-threatening reactions to vaccination are exceedingly rare, so if only one or two among tens of thousands of children develop a serious reaction to a vaccine, then the risk of a vaccination program is still justified compared to the alternative, which would be the unchecked spread of a potentially lethal infectious illness throughout a population. But the only way to ensure that an individual child never develops a serious or life-threatening reaction to a vaccine is to never vaccinate them. And if too many children go unvaccinated, then the entire population will suffer due to the failure to achieve what epidemiologists refer to as "herd immunity," which can be thought of as a "public good" in the same way that breathable air, potable water, and arable land are all public goods.

In a population with adequate herd immunity, a single unvaccinated child is unlikely to develop an infection. But the unvaccinated child is also a free-rider in a Free-Rider Dilemma because they are benefitting from a pubic good without giving anything back in return.

Modern concepts of civics, human rights, and international law may also be regarded as public goods: if enough of the world's nations respect them, then the outcome is to the mutual benefit of all nations. Alternatively, if a citizen of the state of Israel receives social welfare payments and protection by the Israeli Defense Forces (IDF) but refuses to give anything back to the state or to accept modern concepts of civics and international law, then they are eroding the public good of the state. Such practices are common not just to Israel, but throughout the Middle East, where a significant proportion of the population continues to reject concepts of modernity, yet derives much individual and collective benefit from modernity (e.g., public health, public education, and the Internet).

THE NATURE OF ISRAELI DEMOCRACY

Israel is not a democracy in the Anglo-American tradition, with regional representation based on current census data. Most North Americans are astonished to learn that none of the 120 Members of the Knesset (MKs) are directly chosen by the voters of Israel, nor are they even indirectly accountable to them.

The Israeli system of democracy is called a closed party list system. There are dozens of political parties in Israel, each one vying for a slice of the national vote. If a particular party succeeds in surpassing a certain threshold, it's allotted a seat in the Knesset. The more votes as a percentage of the national total, the more seats allotted. Each party generates its own list of potential MKs in a process that happens behind closed doors. If the party gets enough votes, its entire list will sit in the Knesset. Typically, this never happens.

In other words, when the voters in Israel go to the polls, they essentially vote for a political platform and not for an individual who campaigned in their riding on behalf of a party. There's little political transparency or accountability.

In addition, there's no formal mechanism for the voters of Israel to alter the course of party policy once the Knesset is in session. In the Anglo-American democratic tradition, a registered voter can always invite their local representative over for a cup of tea and express their opinion about a particular policy or proposed piece of legislation, thereby influencing the democratic process in real time. No such mechanism exists in the Israeli system, at least not in a formal sense.

There is also no such thing as a majority government in Israel. Since inception, every Israeli government has been a coalition government led by an Ashkenazi Jew—except in times of national crisis, when a unity government (also dominated by Ashkenazi Jews) is formed. Israeli coalition governments often create strange bedfellows, and coalitions typically hang by a thread at the best of times. What's more, there's an unofficial policy of prohibiting Arab parties (and also communists) from being included in any coalition government, presumably for reasons of national security.

Arab MKs are notoriously under-represented in the Israeli political system, although on more than one occasion, an Arab has acted as deputy speaker of the Knesset—and even exceptionally, a cabinet member. But in its present form, Israeli democracy doesn't allow for anything close to proportional representation of Palestinian citizens of Israel in real positions of power. Imagine if America had a policy of barring blacks from Congress, or Canada were to prohibit French Canadians from sitting in Parliament, or New Zealand refused to allow Maoris a representative political voice.

Every major decision in Israel regarding peace treaties or national security is made at the cabinet level, and in the case of the Israeli-Palestinian conflict, a very complicated multi-step process would have to be collapsed into as few steps as possible in order to win cabinet approval. If a coalition is too weak, then even a minor point risks getting tossed out and re-negotiated.

Although Israel describes herself as a democracy, she reluctantly embraces non-Orthodox Jewish traditions. Liberal Jews who wish to pray at the Western Wall in an egalitarian manner, according to their own religious traditions, typically require police protection, not because of threats from Muslims praying directly above them on the Haram al-Sharif, but because of threats from Haredi Jews praying right beside them, in the Western Wall plaza. Israel is probably the only country in the world where certain groups of Jews are denied the right to pray publicly according to their preferred religious tradition.

THE SIX-DAY WAR

In June 1967, Israel fought a six-day-long defensive war against her immediate Arab neighbours after Egypt blockaded the Straits of Tiran. Although it's clear that the latter constituted a *casus belli* (an act of war), it's equally clear that the Israeli battle plan had been prepared years in advance.

In less than a week, Israel succeeded in extending her borders to include not only the whole of historic Palestine but also the vast Sinai desert and a little piece of the former French Mandate for Syria and Lebanon, in the Golan Heights. The Palestinian Arab refugees who had fled the IDF in 1967, and who had settled in refugee camps in the West Bank and Gaza, once again found themselves under Israeli control.

The conflict ended with the famous UN Security Council Resolution 242, the preamble of which refers to the "inadmissibility of the acquisition of territory by war and the need to work for a just and lasting peace in the Middle East in which every State in the area can live in security." The main operative paragraph of Resolution 242 affirms the following two principles:

> (i) Withdrawal of Israeli armed forces from territories occupied in the recent conflict;
>
> (ii) Termination of all claims or states of belligerency and respect for and acknowledgment of the sovereignty, territorial integrity and political independence of every State in the area and their right to live in peace within secure and recognized boundaries free from threats or acts of force.

There is some controversy over the French translation of the text (both texts being considered legally binding). The French text reads, "Retrait des forces armées israéliennes des territoires occupés lors du récent conflit," which translates back into English as, "Withdrawal of Israeli armed forces from *the* territories occupied in the recent conflict" (emphasis added). The original English text, however, implies withdrawal from a portion of the territories; the French text implies withdrawal from *all* the territories (yet another dilemma to add to the growing list of dilemmas). It's a repetition of the same sort of ambiguity that's found in the Balfour Declaration concerning the extent of Palestine that the Jews would be allowed to settle: all, or only a portion of it. As a result of the ambiguity inherent in Resolution 242,

Israel decided to keep the Golan Heights in fulfillment of the internationally guaranteed right to live within secure boundaries.

Israel continues to rely on the concept of "secure boundaries" (as embodied in Resolution 242) to justify the annexation of the Golan Heights (which were never part of Mandatory Palestine in the first place). But the logic is essentially circular, since Israel may now define her territory as that which she believes to be secure.

COLONIZATION, NOT OCCUPATION

Settler colonialism involves the displacement of a native population by a population of colonizers who eventually become the dominant population. Jabotinsky was well aware that in 1922 the Arabs of Palestine outnumbered the Jews by a ratio of 9:1, and he was never shy with his colonial metaphors. In *The Iron Wall* he reminds us that

> it made no difference whatever whether the colonists behaved decently or not. The companions of Cortez and Pizzaro or (as some people will remind us) our own ancestors under Joshua Ben Nun, behaved like brigands; but the Pilgrim Fathers, the first real pioneers of North America, were people of the highest morality, who did not want to do harm to anyone, least of all to the Red Indians, and they honestly believed that there was room enough in the prairies both for the Paleface and the Redskin. Yet the native population fought with the same ferocity against the good colonists as against the bad.
>
> Every native population, civilised or not, regards its lands as its national home, of which it is the sole master, and it wants to retain that mastery always; it will refuse to admit not only new masters but, even new partners or collaborators … Every native population in the world resists colonists as long as it has the slightest hope of being able to rid itself of the danger of being colonised.

The Zionist colonization project did not cease with the creation of the state of Israel in 1948, nor did it cease with the Six-Day War in 1967. It continues to this day with the construction of new settlements in East

Jerusalem, the West Bank, and the Golan Heights. And every Israeli government since 1967, whether Labor or Likud, has encouraged the construction of settlements because the dream of a Zionist state in the whole of Palestine is yet unfulfilled. The persistence of organizations such as the Jewish National Fund (established in 1901) and the Jewish Agency for Israel (established in 1929), both of which predate the creation of the state of Israel, reflect the unfinished business of colonizing historic Palestine with Jewish settlers.

The Palestinians who live under direct and indirect Israeli military rule are clearly a colonized population. But what about the Palestinian Territories themselves? Are they occupied, colonized, or neither occupied nor colonized? This is probably one of the most controversial and polarizing questions in Israel today, but the answer is really quite simple.

Let's begin by reviewing the sequence of events leading up to Israel's capture of the West Bank (including East Jerusalem).

As the War of Independence drew to a close in mid-1949, Israel signed a series of armistice agreements with her Arab neighbours but remained technically at war with them. On May 22, 1967, Egyptian president Gamal Abdel Nasser closed the Straights of Tiran to Israeli maritime traffic, an act regarded as a *casus belli* by Israel. Two weeks later, on June 5, 1967, Israel wiped out almost the entire Egyptian air force in a surprise attack. It was only after Jordan fired a shot across the 1949 Armistice Line that Israel crossed into Jordan and seized control of the West Bank, including East Jerusalem.

There is no doubt that the Six-Day War was a defensive conflict from the Israeli perspective, but that still doesn't justify the expansion of Israeli territory by means of war. If it were permissible under international law for a country to expand their territory in a defensive war, then what would stop one country from provoking their neighbour, only to overrun their neighbour's territory in 'self-defence'? What's to stop the all-powerful US Army from taunting the much smaller Canadian Army into firing a single bullet south across the forty-ninth parallel, thereby providing the former with an excuse to march on Ottawa?

The Palestinian territories (the West Bank and the Gaza Strip) and the Golan Heights were illegally occupied by Israel in 1967 because Israel acquired them by means of war. In the alternative, if the West Bank and the Gaza Strip are legally disputed territories, then nobody is the clear owner and nobody should have the right to colonize them until the question of legal ownership is resolved.

Since 1967, however, some Israelis have claimed the right to colonize the West Bank and the Gaza Strip based on Article 6 of the 1922 Palestine Mandate, which permits "close settlement by Jews on the land, including State lands and waste lands not required for public purposes." But there is a problem with this argument because the mandate system, which was established under Article 22 of the Covenant of the League of Nations, was only meant to be a temporary measure, applicable to former Ottoman territories "inhabited by peoples not yet able to stand by themselves under the strenuous conditions of the modern world." Article 28 of the 1922 Palestine Mandate specifically addresses the issue of termination of the Mandate, and expressly guarantees that only Articles 13 and 14 (but not Article 6) will survive said termination. Given that Israel's independence was recognized by the international community in 1948, it would be difficult to argue that the Jews of historic Palestine remain as a people "not yet able to stand by themselves under the strenuous conditions of the modern world," and that they continue to require the legal protection of the 1922 Palestine Mandate.

Initially, the Zionist movement had the highest regard for international law. Herzl and Weizmann dreamed of establishing a national home for the Jewish people in Palestine, secured by international law. The game changed right after the founding of the state of Israel—which continues as a settler colonial project to this day. And settler colonialism is always a zero-sum game.

During one particularly heated cabinet debate in 1955, then prime minister Moshe Sharett declared that if it wasn't for UN General Assembly Resolution 181 of 1947, the state of Israel would never have been founded. Ben-Gurion, who was defense minister at the time, shouted back: "Not at all! Only the daring of the Jews founded this country and not some Oom-Shmoom resolution!" The meaning of Ben-Gurion's words requires a bit of deconstruction. *Oom* is a contraction of the Hebrew *umot m'ukhadot*, which translates as United Peoples, or United Nations. The suffix *Shmoom* represents a negation or diminution, as in Joe Shmoe. It's an expression straight from the shtetl of Płońsk, where David Ben-Gurion was born and raised. Who says that Jews aren't natural comedians?

THE LAW OF RETURN

As a sovereign state, Israel is free to make her own laws and to set her own immigration policies. As a multi-ethnic society of many faiths, however, Israel has always favoured one particular ethnonational group: the Jews. The Law of Return was enacted by the Knesset in 1950, granting the exclusive right of Jews to automatically obtain Israeli citizenship. Initially, Jews were legally defined as anyone who was born to a Jewish mother or who underwent a Jewish conversion (if a Conservative or Reform conversion, then it had to have been performed outside of Israel). In 1970, the Law of Return was amended to extend the right of automatic citizenship to the child and grandchild of a Jew, the spouse of a Jew, the spouse of a child of a Jew, and the spouse of a grandchild of a Jew. Under the amended Law of Return, anyone who would have been considered to be a Jew under the 1935 Nuremberg Laws would now be protected by the state of Israel. Israel has now effectively prepared herself, both legally and militarily, for the next Holocaust should it ever unfold exactly as it did in Nazi Germany in the 1930s.

The Israeli Law of Return is of course considered to be racist by all Palestinians (including Palestinian citizens of Israel), many of whom can trace their family roots back to the days of the Islamic conquest and whose relatives are currently dying in Syrian refugee camps (and elsewhere). But the Law of Return also protects the *non*-Jewish spouses, children, and grandchildren of Jews (including converts to Judaism), so it's not an entirely racist law. It would best be described as a Jewish nationalist law, one that protects the individual and collective rights of Jewish Israelis at the expense of minorities in Israel.

THE RIGHT TO SELF-DEFENCE

The defence industry is an important sector of the Israeli economy, thanks in part to a stream of significant subsidies from the United States. Every sovereign nation has the right to self-defence, and even though there are a few sovereign nations without armed forces (such as Liechtenstein, Costa Rica, and a number of small island-nations in the Caribbean and South Pacific), it would be difficult to imagine Israel, or any other country in the Middle East, aspiring one day to reduce the size of their army. The entire region seems to be locked into a permanent arms race. According to an article published in the *Guardian* in 2015, it was estimated that "arms sales to the top five purchasers in the region"—Saudi Arabia, the United Arab Emirates, Algeria, Egypt, and Iraq—would surge to more than $18 billion" from $12 billion the year before. "Among the systems being purchased are fighter jets, missiles, armoured vehicles, drones and helicopters."[2]

According to the Stockholm International Peace Research Institute (SIPRI), Israel was number ten among the top-twenty arms exporters in 2010–14.[3] Between 2004 and 2011, Israel signed arms transfer agreements worth $12.9 billion, putting it in eighth place among the world's biggest arms suppliers.[4] During this same time frame, Israel's arms transfer agreements with developing nations totalled some $8.7 billion. Israel is a world leader in unmanned aerial vehicle (UAV), or drone, technology; and three Israeli defence companies—Elbit Systems, Israel Aerospace Industries (IAI), and Rafael Advanced Defense Systems—are among the top one hundred arms-producing and military service companies in the world. Elbit is publicly traded on the Tel Aviv Stock Exchange, and IAI and Rafael are state-owned. IAI was founded in 1953 by Al Schwimmer and Shimon Peres—the same Shimon Peres who received a Nobel Peace Prize in 1994.

Defence exports are not the same as arms transfer agreements, and in 2012, Israel's defence equipment exports are believed to have reached $7 billion.[5] Israel exports most of her weapons to the United States and Europe, followed by Southeast Asia and South America. Exports to

African countries are minimal. The Ministry of Defense approves all weapons export deals and does not permit the export of weapons to states that violate human rights.

On a per capita basis, Israel's defence industry is probably the largest in the world, and it's a testament to Israel's free speech and to her free press that some of the fiercest critics of that defence industry come from within Israel herelf.[6]

Politicians and public figures from France, the United Kingdom, or the United States who condemn Israel's domestic policy must also acknowledge that their own countries are bigger arms exporters than Israel. And countries such as Australia, Canada, the Netherlands, Norway, Sweden, and Switzerland—which are often held up as models of healthy, peace-loving democracies—must also acknowledge that they are among the top twenty arms-exporting nations in the world. Canada, in particular, was at one time the second biggest arms exporter to the Middle East.[7]

Today, Israel has become the country that it wishes it could have been on the eve of the Second World War: militarized and fully prepared for the next Holocaust. For many Israelis, it's impossible to dislodge the cultural notion that the Jewish people are eternally persecuted and have nobody but themselves to rely on, and that Israel is the only place on earth where they may live in safety. This kind of closed thinking may have been appropriate for early-twentieth-century Europe but it no longer makes sense. In most of the Western world today, there are no more quotas on Jewish university students. Jewish businesses don't get boycotted or torched, and Jews can aspire to reach the highest levels of public and professional life without having to face the devil of institutionalized antisemitism. (The same isn't always true for the 50 per cent of humanity who are often discriminated against, sometimes abused, and on occasion even murdered simply because they are women.)

Some would argue that Israel, by her very existence, has made all this possible. But one can just as easily argue that Israel, by her continued military rule over the Palestinians, is in fact fanning the flames of global antisemitism rather than helping to extinguish them.

THE JEWISH NATIONAL FUND

The Jewish National Fund (JNF, or *Keren Kayemet LeYisrael*) was created at the Fifth Zionist Congress in Basel in 1901, and it has remained one of the main instruments of the Zionist project ever since. From the outset, the JNF has dedicated itself to planting trees in Eretz Yisrael and for over a century now, the ubiquitous blue-and-white JNF *pushke* (collection box) has been an iconic item in Jewish homes and institutions all over the world.

The JNF website states that the organization was created as "the sole agency for the development and infrastructure of land in Israel."[8] It also describes itself as "the caretaker of Israel on behalf of its owners—Jewish people everywhere." The term "Jewish peole" is interpreted in a nationalist sense, implying that the 14.7 million members of the worldwide Jewish community are the legal owners of JNF land, which constitutes some 13 per cent of the total land base in Israel (over 600,000 acres).

Over the years, the JNF has planted forests for security reasons (over 250 million trees, including non-native pines), and also to demarcate Jewish national spaces. It owns land in the West Bank and, rather disturbingly, has deliberately planted trees on the sites of former Arab villages abandoned in the 1948 Arab-Israeli conflict—all but erasing them from memory.

Until very recently, the JNF has not been a particularly financially transparent organization, refusing for over a century to disclose its financial statements to the public.[9] Prospective donors, therefore, have had a hard time trying to understand exactly where their money was going. It took enormous public pressure to get the JNF to finally release details of its financial records in 2015.[10] These records showed that the JNF holds lands worth $2 billion, and that it generated annual revenues of some $567 million (a return on assets of over 28 per cent). Donations accounted for only 6.2 per cent of total revenues, or $35.2 million, of which 57 per cent ($20.2 million) came from North America. Expenses included a payment of about $332 million to the Israel Land Authority (ILA) to manage JNF lands (roughly 59 per cent of revenues), and $146 million in salaries and pensions to the JNF's 950 employees (roughly 26 per cent of revenues). In 2015, the JNF also reported donations of some $15.1 million to the World Zionist Organization,[11] and $4.3 million to Nefesh B'Nefesh,[12] an organization devoted to helping families, retirees, students, and young professionals from the US, Canada, and the UK make Aliyah to Israel. A donation to the JNF, therefore, includes an involuntary contribution to other Jewish charities, some of which have nothing to do with trees.

Despite all of its financial secrecy, the JNF enjoys consistently widespread support from the North American Jewish community. In June 2013, the JNF hosted a Negev Dinner in Toronto in honour of then–prime minister Stephen Harper.[13] Most of the 4,600 guests were unaware that their carefully fundraised dollars were going towards a financially secretive and racist organization.

By law, only Jewish nationals can buy, mortgage, or lease JNF land. Arab nationals—even Palestinian citizens of Israel, who supposedly enjoy equal rights under Israeli law—may not make use of JNF land except for recreational purposes. Imagine if 13 per cent of the land area of the United States (an area greater than California and Texas combined) were owned by a non-profit organization that refused to sell or even rent land to blacks—or perhaps to Jews. Such racist behaviour would hardly be regarded as befitting a democratic state.

The JNF responds to the charge of racism as follows:

> The JNF is not the trustee of the general public in Israel. Its loyalty is given to the Jewish people in the Diaspora and in the state of Israel … The JNF, in relation to being an owner of land, is not a public body that works for the benefit of all citizens of the state. The loyalty of the JNF is given to the Jewish people and only to them is the JNF obligated. The JNF, as the owner of the JNF land, does not have a duty to practice equality towards all citizens of the state.[14]

This kind of zero-sum thinking directly contradicts the principles of Zionism as embodied in Israel's Declaration of Independence, which promises "complete equality of social and political rights to all …

inhabitants irrespective of religion, race or sex." The Jewish National Fund is not a Zionist organization; it's a nationalist organization. It should be re-named the Jewish Nationalist Fund.

PALESTINIANS AND PALESTINIAN ISRAELIS

The Palestinian people were officially recognized by Israel in 1993, when Israeli prime minister Yitzhak Rabin exchanged Letters of Recognition with Palestine Liberation Organization chairman Yasser Arafat (as the representative of the Palestinian people). This was supposed to mark a change from a zero-sum game to a game of rational co-operation. The signing of the Oslo I Accord established the Palestinian nation as a reality in international law, and today many countries maintain diplomatic relations with the Palestinian nation (which also goes by the name State of Palestine, or simply Palestine).

The term "Palestinian nation" includes those Palestinians living in the West Bank and Gaza, as well as all Palestinian refugees of the 1948 Arab-Israeli conflict (basically all six million members of the Palestinian diaspora, and not only those Palestinians living in refugee camps served by the United Nations Relief and Works Agency for Palestine Refugees in the Near East [UNRWA]). Palestinians who live in Israel, and who are Israeli citizens, belong to both the Palestinian nation and the Israeli nation. In Israel, such individuals are called Arab-Israelis, or Israeli Arabs, or sometimes Palestinian Israelis. The terms "Arab-Israeli" or "Israeli Arab" did not exist before 1948, and they are politically charged terms because they essentially negate the existence of a separate Palestinian nation. They promote the view that the Palestinian people do not exist per se, and that they are but a sliver of the greater Arab people.

Palestinian Israelis (who make up 21 per cent of Israel's population) are represented in the Knesset by the Joint List, which consists of four Arab parties (Hadash, United Arab List, Balad, and Ta'al) who collectively hold only 10.8 per cent of the seats. Israel would be a stronger democracy if 21 per cent of the seats in the Knesset were held by Palestinian Israelis, just as the United States would be a stronger democracy if 50 per cent of the seats in Congress were held by women.

As things currently stand, there's a strong desire—particularly among Jewish ultranationalists—to transfer (i.e., expel) all Palestinians from Israel. As part of an extensive survey conducted by the Pew Research Center between October 2014 and May 2015,[15] a cross-section of Israeli Jews was asked if they agreed with the statement "Arabs should be expelled or transferred from Israel." Among the national religious, 71 per cent agreed or strongly agreed with this statement, whereas among secular Jews, the proportion was only 36 per cent. Overall, almost half of Jewish Israelis want to expel Arabs, and among right-wing Jewish Israelis, the proportion is more like 72 per cent. This is both astonishing and representative of what social scientists refer to as a lacuna in Israeli democracy: "transfer" is merely a euphemism for ethnic cleansing. How could any democracy even abide the idea of ethnically cleansing its own citizens? The question is analogous to asking Americans if they think that blacks or Jews should be deported from the United States and sent back to Africa or the Middle East.

The same survey also found that roughly eight in ten Arab Israelis (79 per cent) say there is a lot of discrimination against Muslims in Israel today, while just 21 per cent of Israeli Jews share this view.

The Jewish 'nation' includes all the Jews in the world, but it is not a nation in international law. The Israeli nation, on the other hand, is a nation in international law but not in Israeli domestic law. If we count Palestinian citizens of Israel as Palestinians, then the Palestinian nation includes all the Palestinians in the world. Sound confusing? That's because it is.

A sovereign nation is one that exercises control over its own destiny. Palestinian national sovereignty has been recognized at the UN General Assembly level, but not yet at the Security Council level. In 1995, as part of the Oslo II Accord, Israel recognized full Palestinian sovereignty over Area A of the West Bank and also the Gaza Strip, and partial sovereignty over Area B of the West Bank. The United States has yet to fully recognize

Palestinian sovereignty, which is curious given that Israel already does to a limited degree. Palestinian national sovereignty is now a de facto reality at the UN, even though a few UN member states don't recognize the state of Palestine (non-member observer status was granted to Palestine on November 29, 2012—exactly sixty-five years to the day after UN Resolution 181 was passed).

Inside the Green Line, Palestinian citizens of Israel enjoy many of the same *individual* rights and freedoms as Jewish Israelis. But physical separation on the basis of nationality and 'soft' disenfranchisement has been getting worse in recent years. When the prime minister of Israel issues tweets about "Arab voters heading to the polling stations in droves" (as Benjamin Netanyahu did during the 2015 national election), it doesn't exactly encourage the full participation of minorities in the democratic process.

According to Israel's Nation-State Law (which was passed in July 2018), only Jewish citizens of Israel have the *collective* right to national self-determination in Israel. National projects that seek to Judaize spaces, encourage Jewish settlement, and create demographic imbalances are now legally justified. This is analogous to saying that Canada is an English state, English Canadians are a nation, and only English Canadians possess collective rights in Canada. I wonder how long Quebecers would tolerate such political nonsense before voting overwhelmingly in favour of separation.

Beyond the Green Line (in East Jerusalem and Area C of the West Bank), Palestinians live under the direct control of the IDF. Although Jews make up just over half the population of historic Palestine, in the Palestinian Territories there's a clear case of a minority controlling a majority, which is the hallmark of a nondemocratic state.

Other recent examples of the breakdown of Israeli civil society are as follows: In 2010, two rabbis from the Od Joseph Chai yeshiva in Yitzhar, rabbis Yitzhak Shapira and Yosef Elitzur, published a book, *The King's Torah*, which opined that the prohibition against murder only applies to "a Jew who kills a Jew," and that "babies and children of our enemies may be killed because it is clear that they will grow up to harm us."[16] These same views were echoed by Israeli justice minister Ayelet Shaked in 2014 when she referred to Palestinian children as "little snakes" in a Facebook post (which was subsequently and speedily deleted).[17] An investigation into rabbis Shapira and Elitzur over the contents of their book was closed in 2012 due to a lack of evidence.[18] *The King's Torah* may still be purchased in Israeli bookstores.

In a second example, in 2015, twenty years after the assassination of Prime Minister Yitzhak Rabin, 25 per cent of Israelis supported commuting the sentence of his assassin, Yigal Amir (a Jewish Israeli citizen). While in prison, Amir managed to marry a Russian immigrant, Larissa Trimbobler, who divorced her previous husband for the express purpose of marrying Rabin's assassin. The couple's wedding was originally forbidden by prison authorities, so Trimbobler devised a wedding-by-proxy ceremony in which the murderer's father stood in for his son. After rabbis deemed the wedding to be valid according to Jewish law, the High Court of Justice ordered Israeli authorities to register the couple as married. They were subsequently allowed conjugal visits, although not before Amir managed to pass a bag of his semen to his wife during a regular prison visit.[19] The two now have a son, Yinon, whose name is one of the biblical terms for the Messiah.

And in 2016, an eighteen-year-old Israeli army medic, Elor Azaria, fatally shot a Palestinian terrorist who only minutes earlier had been 'neutralized' after stabbing another Israeli soldier at a military checkpoint in Hebron. The Palestinian terrorist, Abdel Fattah al-Sharif, was unarmed following his 'neutralization' and had been lying prone on the ground for about ten minutes when Azaria approached and shot him in the head at point-blank range, killing him instantly. After a trial that grabbed the entire country's attention and pitted the IDF against politicians, Azaria was sentenced to only eighteen months in prison (which was subsequently reduced to fourteen months). Prime Minister Benjamin Netanyahu, and 75 per cent of the Israeli public, openly supported pardoning Azaria altogether.[20] An appeal was made to President Reuven Rivlin, who refused to grant a pardon. For his decision, Rivlin was widely accused of treason by the Israeli press, and a fake image of him wearing a *kaffiyeh* (the traditional Arab headdress) was circulated on social media.[21]

ISRAEL AND THE JEWISH DIASPORA

Although not strictly a social dilemma, the game Battle of the Sexes (now called Bach or Stravinsky out of respect for the women's movement, or simply Low Battle according to the Bruns classification[22]) is very helpful in understanding the relationship between Israel and the Jewish Diaspora. In Low Battle, two players must choose between going to a Bach or a Stravinsky concert. Player one prefers Bach, and player two prefers Stravinsky. The payout matrix is summarized in figure 5.8.

		Player two	
		Bach	Stravinsky
Player one	Bach	*4, 3*	1, 1
	Stravinsky	1, 1	*3, 4*

Nash equilibria in bold italics text

FIGURE 5.8

There are two Nash equilibria in this game, both of which involve one player getting their wish and the other one caving in.

Low Battle is a simplified version of the game of Battle, which ranks the undesirability of both players going not only to different concerts but also to the *wrong* different concerts. Figure 5.9 illustrates the payout matrix for Battle.

		Player two	
		Bach	Stravinsky
Player one	Bach	*4, 3*	2, 2
	Stravinsky	1, 1	*3, 4*

Nash equilibria in bold italics text

FIGURE 5.9

In this particular game, the combination "player one goes to the Stravinsky concert while player two goes to the Bach concert" is considered less desirable than the combination "player one goes to the Bach concert and player two goes to the Stravinsky concert."

Why is Battle helpful in understanding the tension between Israel and the Jewish Diaspora? In 1885, the American Reform Judaism movement produced the Pittsburgh Platform, which had the following to say about Jewish nationalism:

> We recognize, in the modern era of universal culture of heart and intellect, the approaching of the realization of Israel's great Messianic hope for the establishment of the kingdom of truth, justice, and peace among all men. *We consider ourselves no longer a nation, but a religious community*, and therefore expect neither a return to Palestine, nor a sacrificial worship under the sons of Aaron, nor the restoration of any of the laws concerning the Jewish state. [emphasis added].

Such a position is the exact opposite of political Zionism, which regards the Jewish people, first and foremost, as a nation and not as a religious community (most early Zionists, in fact, were atheists).

Today, the epicentre of the Jewish Diaspora is located in the United States, and most American Jews are affiliated with the Reform movement (the same one that produced the 1885 Pittsburgh Platform). Most Israeli Jews, on the other hand, identify strongly with Jewish nationalism. The tension between the two is a game of Battle that is represented by the matrix in figure 5.10.

		Israel	
		Universalism	Nationalism
Jewish diaspora	Universalism	*4, 3*	2, 2
	Nationalism	1, 1	*3, 4*

Nash equilibria in bold italics text

FIGURE 5.10

With the loss of the Gaza Strip to Hamas in 2007, and very soon the loss of the Jewish majority in historic Palestine, the government of Israel has now passed a law that places the collective rights of Jews above the collective rights of non-Jews. Most Jewish Israelis have accepted this new law, but most Diaspora Jews have not, insisting instead that Zionism must uphold the Jewish principles of dignity and universal justice as enshrined in Israel's Declaration of Independence.

THE IMPACT OF ANNEXATION ON THE FUTURE OF THE JEWISH STATE

The game of Battle can also help us understand the impact of annexation on the future of the Jewish state. Recall that Israel is by definition both a Jewish and a democratic state. To many individuals this represents a paradox, but if we can accept the notion that 'Jewish' in the Israeli context is not just an ethnicity or a religion but also a national identity (as in *l'om yehudi*), then the paradox of Jewish and democratic may be resolved by re-framing it as a game of Chicken between Israel's identity and her politics. That is represented by the 2×2 matrix in figure 5.11.

		Identity	
		Jewish	not Jewish
Politics	democratic	a Zionist state (3, 3)	*a secular state (2, 4)*
	not democratic	*a theocratic state (4, 2)*	a fascist state (1, 1)

Nash equilibria in bold italics text

FIGURE 5.11

As in any game of Chicken, there are two Nash equilibria. One sacrifices democracy in the name of preserving the state's Jewish identity, and the other sacrifices the state's Jewish identity in the name of preserving democracy. The former would lead to a theocratic state, and the latter to a secular one. Neither of these options is acceptable within a Zionist framework, even though the *utility* of all three options (theocratic, secular, or Zionist) is the same (4 + 2 = 2 + 4 = 3 + 3). The task of the Israeli Supreme Court is to ensure that the state's Jewish identity and democratic principles are always in balance, and that anti-democratic and anti-Jewish forces never collide. But such a task is only achievable in the context of a Jewish national majority.

If we now envision a scenario in which Israel annexes the remainder of the West Bank and the Gaza Strip (with the resulting loss of a Jewish national majority), then the game of Chicken is reduced to a game of Battle (see figure 5.12).

		Identity	
		Jewish	not Jewish
Politics	democratic	a Zionist state (2, 2)	*a state for all citizens (3, 4)*
	not democratic	*a Jewish ultranationalist state (4, 3)*	a Palestinian state (1, 1)

Nash equilibria in bold italics text

FIGURE 5.12

There are two Nash equilibria in this game: one represents an undemocratic, apartheid-like state dominated by Jewish ultranationalists, and the other, a state for all citizens. Both options have equal utility (4 + 3 = 3 + 4), but an apartheid-like state is obviously morally repugnant and possibly even illegal under international law. The Zionist option (i.e., a democratic state with a Jewish character) would now fall off the table because Jewish nationals would be in the minority. And the last option would be an undemocratic, non-Jewish state (which many on the Israeli right would call a Palestinian state, although there's no reason why a state with a Palestinian majority can't also be a democratic state).

Zionism, therefore, is only possible if there's a Jewish national majority in the Jewish state. One could even argue that any proposed annexation of the remainder of the West Bank and the Gaza Strip would be illegal under Israeli domestic law because it would preclude the possibility of Israel continuing as a Zionist state.

Chapter 6

AN ITERATED GAME OF CHICKEN

The Gaza Strip is a human catastrophe. We don't need game theory to tell us that. There aren't enough negative superlatives to describe it: the most densely populated *poor* place on earth; an open-air prison; a death spiral. To visit for even a single day is to incur a mental trauma; humanity, forgotten by humanity, on the brink of collapse like those mouse over-crowding experiments from the 1960s. How did the world ever allow this to happen?

With a population in 2018 of some 1.87 million individuals,[1] the Gaza Strip is the third most densely populated polity in the world (among polities with a population above one million), surpassed only by Singapore and Hong Kong. But whereas Singapore and Hong Kong boast a per capita GDP (PPP) of $85,700,[2] and $57,000,[3] respectively, the Gaza Strip has a per capita GDP (PPP) of about $4,300,[4] which makes it the most densely populated *poor* place on earth, exceeding Bangladesh, Rwanda, or Haiti by a long shot.[5]

Among all the poor places on earth, the Gaza Strip is still wealthier than the poorest nations of Africa (e.g., the Democratic Republic of the Congo, Burundi, or the Central African Republic). But it is small—very small—and very much lacking in agricultural land. At only 360 square kilometres, the Gaza Strip has just 179 square kilometres of agricultural land (by one very generous estimate[6]). This makes its population to agricultural land ratio fifteen times greater than Rwanda's. In other words, there is fifteen times less agricultural land per person living in the Gaza Strip than in Rwanda, where "population and land pressure, coupled with

137

unsustainable agricultural practices" have been recognized as important factors leading up to the [Rwandan] genocide.[7]

Over the centuries, the area of Gaza has been conquered and ruled by the Canaanites, Ancient Egyptians, Philistines, Ancient Israelites, Assyrians, Greeks, Bedouins, Seleucids, Ptolemies, Hasmoneans, Romans, Byzantines, Umayyads, Abbasids, Tulunids, Fatimids, Crusaders, Ayyubids, Mamluks, Ottomans, the British, Egyptians, Israelis, and, most recently, Hamas. But for purposes of understanding the current situation, it isn't necessary to look back any further than 1948.

PALESTINE REFUGEES, PALESTINIAN REFUGEES, AND UNRWA

Prior to the 1948 Arab-Israeli conflict, the population of Gaza City was around 34,000. Afterwards, it swelled considerably due to an influx of Palestinian Arab refugees, but we don't have the exact figures from that era. In 1949, in an effort to deal with the refugee crisis, the United Nations created the United Nations Relief and Works Agency for Palestine Refugees in the Near East (UNRWA). For the most part, refugees were housed in camps, many of which continue to exist to this day. The Palestine refugees of the 1948 Arab-Israeli conflict and their descendants now constitute the largest and oldest unsettled refugee population in the world.

According to UNRWA, "Palestine refugees" are "persons whose normal place of residence was Palestine during the period June 1, 1946, to May 15, 1948, and who lost both home and means of livelihood as a result of the 1948 conflict."[8] In addition, the descendants of Palestine refugee males, including legally adopted children, are also considered to be Palestine refugees for purposes of UNRWA.

The term "Palestine refugee" is frequently confused with the term "Palestinian refugee" and today the two are practically synonymous. As originally defined, however, a Palestine refugee was either a Jewish refugee *or* a Palestinian Arab refugee of the 1948 Arab-Israeli conflict (i.e., any person whose normal place of residence was Palestine during the period June 1, 1946, to May 15, 1948, and so on). In 1952, the Israeli government took over the responsibility of settling all the Jewish refugees of the 1948

Arab-Israeli conflict. But more than seventy years after the end of the conflict, no Arab state has assumed responsibility for the Palestinian Arab refugees of the 1948 Arab-Israeli conflict and their descendants, whose numbers now exceed 6 million (of which an estimated 1.5 million still live in UNRWA camps).[9]

UNRWA continues to have its mandate extended (and funded) by the UN General Assembly year after year. And it's no stretch to say that the entire international community continues to pay the financial cost of the failure to completely resolve the Palestine refugee issue. At present, there are approximately 1.1 million Palestine refugees living in the Gaza Strip alone (roughly 59 per cent of the total population), concentrated in eight camps: Nuseirat, Beach (Al-Shati), Bureij, Deir el-Balah, Jabalia, Khan Younis, Maghazi, and Rafah. The largest is Jabalia Camp, with 110,000 registered refugees living in a 1.4-square-kilometre area.

UNRWA is unique among refugee NGOs because it has no mandate to settle any refugees. Its only mandate is to provide services to the refugees of a single conflict: the 1948 Arab-Israeli conflict.

THE GAZA STRIP UNDER EGYPTIAN RULE (1949–67)

On January 6, 1949, Israel and Egypt entered into discussions on the island of Rhodes with the goal of reaching an armistice agreement. The talks floundered following the February 12, 1949, assassination in Cairo of Hassan al-Banna, the Muslim cleric who founded the Muslim Brotherhood (his killers were never apprehended, but King Farouk of Egypt and his Iron Guard remain the prime suspects). By the end of February 1949, talks had resumed, and Israel and Egypt signed an armistice agreement concluding the 1948 Arab-Israeli conflict. The agreement set out an Armistice Line, which was not to be construed in any way as an international border (there was no peace treaty between Israel and Egypt until 1979). The Armistice Line was drawn along the previous 1922 border between Egypt and Mandatory Palestine, with the exception of a strip of land around Gaza City. The strip of land later became known as the Gaza Strip.

About six months prior to the armistice, the Arab League (having rejected the 1947 UN partition plan for Palestine) established an All-Palestine Government, which aspired to be a Palestinian government in exile. In practice, the All-Palestine Government (whose president was Hajj Amin al-Husseini, the former chairman of the Arab Higher Committee) only exercised symbolic authority over the newly created Gaza Strip, and even then, only until 1959. As per the 1949 Israel-Egypt armistice agreement, executive power over the Strip resided at all times with Cairo.

On July 26, 1956, Egyptian president Gamal Abdel Nasser nationalized the Suez Canal, hoping to charge tolls that would pay for construction of the Aswan High Dam. The canal, together with the Straits of Tiran, were subsequently closed to Israeli shipping. On October 29, the Israeli army crossed the 1949 Armistice Line into Egypt and, in an effort that was entirely planned and coordinated with the British and the French, attempted to retake control of the canal and to depose Nasser. The Egyptian forces were defeated, but not before they had blocked the canal to all shipping. The United States, the USSR, and the United Nations subsequently threatened Britain and France with economic sanctions, and by December 1956, Britain and France had withdrawn their troops from the Suez Canal. Israel, however, occupied the Sinai (including the Gaza Strip) until March 1957, making it very clear that any future closure of the Straits of Tiran would be regarded as a *casus belli*.

THE GAZA STRIP UNDER ISRAELI RULE (1967–94)

Nasser once again closed the Straits of Tiran to Israeli shipping in May 1967, while mobilizing the Egyptian army along the border with Israel. On June 5, 1967, Israel launched a series of pre-emptive strikes against Egyptian airfields, destroying nearly the entire Egyptian air force in a few hours. In subsequent fighting, Israeli forces avoided entering the Gaza Strip (Israeli defense minister Moshe Dayan had expressly forbidden it). But after Egyptian positions in the Gaza Strip opened fire on the Israeli settlements of Nirim and Kissufim (located about seven kilometres east of Khan Yunis), the IDF chief of staff, Yitzhak Rabin, overrode Dayan's instructions and gave orders to enter the Strip. After two days of fierce fighting, Gaza City and the entire Gaza Strip fell into Israeli hands. This caused a second exodus of Palestinian refugees (the first being in 1948), with some fleeing from the Gaza Strip into Jordan, and about eleven thousand fleeing from the Gaza Strip into Egypt.[10]

Following eighteen years of Egyptian military rule, the Gaza Strip had suddenly fallen into Israeli hands. The Palestinians, not surprisingly, were anxious about Israel's intentions, but Israel maintained a nominally hands-off policy of "government but not administration." This allowed Palestinian civil servants to continue with their work with minimal interference from Israel. In game theory, we would call this 'live and let live.'

But increasingly, the IDF began to interfere directly in the Gaza Strip—especially in 1971, when Ariel Sharon ordered the demolition of over two thousand shelters in the Beach Camp, for the purpose of widening the roads (allegedly for security reasons). When Israel and Egypt reached a final peace agreement in 1979, six years after the Yom Kippur War, the Gaza Strip remained under Israeli control instead of reverting to Egyptian control (as was the case before 1967). So, in exchange for giving up the Sinai Desert and for peace with the Egyptians, Israel acquired the Gaza Strip and the Palestinians.

THE ORIGIN OF HAMAS

In 1984, the IDF arrested a forty-seven-year-old nearly blind wheelchair-bound imam, Sheikh Ahmed Yassin, who had been a quadriplegic since a childhood wrestling accident. Yassin, a Palestinian refugee of the 1948 Arab-Israeli conflict and resident of the Beach Camp, was charged with weapons possession and sentenced to a twelve-year jail term (he was released after serving only one year as part of a prisoner exchange deal). Previously, Yassin had been involved in the Muslim Brotherhood, the organization founded by the Egyptian cleric Hassan Al-Banna (it was Al-Banna's assassination in Cairo in 1949 that had interrupted the Egyptian-Israeli armistice talks). The Muslim Brotherhood had maintained a presence in the Gaza Strip since the 1950s, working quietly to establish various charitable and social organizations in addition to a net-work of mosques.

During the First Intifada (which lasted from 1987 to 1993), Yassin and Abdel Azziz al-Rantisi co-founded the organization known as Hamas, the paramilitary wing of the Muslim Brotherhood in Palestine. Al-Rantisi was Hamas's political leader and spokesman in the Gaza Strip for many years, and Yassin's role was that of spiritual guide for the organization. From the outset, Hamas opposed the Oslo peace process, advocating instead for armed struggle and acts of terrorism against Israel. Its 1988 charter, for example, calls for the replacement of Israel and the Palestinian Territories with an Islamic state.

The relationship between Israel and Hamas is a complicated one, as one historian has noted. "Israel for years tolerated and, in some cases, encour-aged them [Hamas] as a counterweight to the secular nationalists of the Palestine Liberation Organization and its dominant faction, Yasser Arafat's Fatah. Israel cooperated with [Sheikh Ahmed Yassin] even as he was laying the foundations for what would become Hamas."[11] Simply put, by tacitly supporting Hamas, Israel was hoping to divide and conquer the Palestinians.

Yassin was again arrested by the Israelis in 1989; this time he was sen-tenced to life in prison. In 1997, however, he was released as part of an arrangement with the Jordanian government following the failed assas-sination attempt by the Mossad of Khaled Mashal, the head of the Kuwait branch of Hamas.

In mid-1991, in response to the Oslo peace process, Hamas created a military wing: the Izz al-Din al-Qassam Brigade (or simply, Qassam Brigade), named after the Syrian-born imam and Palestinian nationalist whose death sparked the 1936 Palestine riots and general strike. Since its inception, the Qassam Brigade has operated separately from the rest of Hamas, which continued to focus primarily on providing religious and social services.

In April 1993, Hamas conducted its first suicide car bomb attack. A twenty-seven-year-old electrical engineer named Yahya Ayyash (cre-atively nicknamed "The Engineer") rigged three large propane tanks to a Volkswagen minibus, which was exploded at Mehola Junction, in the West Bank, killing one individual.

Meanwhile, in February 1994, on the Jewish holiday of Purim, a thirty-seven-year-old American-born Jewish physician, Baruch Goldstein, entered the Cave of the Patriarchs/Ibrahimi Mosque in Hebron and massacred twenty-nine Muslim worshippers and wounded at least 125 others, before being beaten to death by anyone he managed not to gun down.

THE GAZA STRIP UNDER PALESTINIAN RULE (1994–PRESENT)

In spite of the increasing violence, and as part of the Oslo I peace accord, Yasser Arafat and Israeli prime minister Yitzhak Rabin signed the Gaza-Jericho Agreement in May 1994. The latter provided for the creation of the Palestinian Authority and limited Palestinian self-rule in the Gaza Strip and around the area of Jericho. The Hebron massacre, still fresh in people's minds, led to an escalation in Palestinian suicide bombings, and over the next two years Ayyash played a role in at least nine separate suicide bombings for Hamas and Palestinian Islamic Jihad. These killed a total of seventy-seven individuals.

In January 1996, Ayyash himself was killed by the Shin Bet (Israel's domestic security agency, analogous to the FBI) using a cell phone packed with fifteen grams of RDX explosive, which was remotely detonated. It was a very neat and 'surgical' operation, in counterpoint to the indiscriminate human carnage caused by Ayyash during his career as a master bomb maker. Following Ayyash's targeted assassination, four separate suicide bombings were carried out by members of the Qassam Brigade, which killed fifty-nine Israelis in February and March 1996.

By the time the Second Intifada got underway (in 2000), Hamas had developed the Qassam rocket, whose initial range of four kilometres was gradually improved to fourteen kilometres. Between 2001 and 2006, a total of 702 rockets and 2,935 mortar shells were launched from the Gaza Strip into southern Israel,[12] most of them not landing even close to their intended targets. Meanwhile, the Israelis were making vast improvements to their capacity for targeted assassinations.

ISRAEL PUSHES BACK AGAINST HAMAS

On July 22, 2002, the IDF dropped a one-ton bomb on the Gaza City home of Salah Shehade, leader of the Qassam Brigade during the Second Intifada, killing not only Shehade but also his wife, his daughter, and seven members of the Matar family, who lived next door. Eight houses in the vicinity were destroyed, and nine were partially destroyed. Between fifty and one hundred and fifty people were injured in the targeted assassination of Shehade, who was suspected of masterminding a campaign of suicide attacks against hundreds of Israeli citizens.

In January 2004, Hamas offered the Israelis a ten-year truce (*hudna* in Arabic) in return for the creation of a Palestinian state and the complete withdrawal by Israel to the 1967 borders. The offer was rejected on the basis that it was clear that Hamas intended to resume military activity against Israel once the truce was over.

In fact, shortly thereafter both of Hamas's founders—Yassin followed within a month by al-Rantisi—were assassinated by the Israeli Air Force. Apache attack helicopters and Hellfire missiles were used in both targeted assassinations, and numerous bystanders were killed.

In May 2004, following the deaths of five Israeli soldiers in a Palestinian attack, the IDF conducted a military operation (Operation Rainbow) in the southern Gaza Strip. Fifty-nine Palestinians were killed, and three hundred homes razed along the Gaza-Egypt border. A zoo and seventy hectares of agricultural land were also destroyed.

Israel stepped up her campaign against Hamas that September. Izz El-Deen Sheikh Khalil, a senior level Hamas member who was believed to be in charge of the group's military wing outside of the Palestinian territories, was killed in a car bombing in Damascus. As usual, the Israelis never confirmed their involvement, but this did not deter Hamas from threatening to target Israelis who lived abroad, in retaliation for what was presumed to be another Israeli targeted assassination.

On November 11, 2004, Yasser Arafat died in a French military hospital of a hemorrhagic stroke secondary to a blood condition known as disseminated intravascular coagulopathy. At the time of his death, he had amassed a personal fortune in excess of $1 billion from the VAT tax receipts on goods purchased by the Palestinian people. The tax receipts had been deposited directly into Arafat's personal bank account at Bank Leumi in Tel Aviv, per the 1993 Oslo I Accord.

In retrospect, it's hard to believe that Israel ever agreed to such provisions. Perhaps they thought that if Arafat ever acted egregiously against Israel's interests, they could always freeze his assets. But either way—peace or no peace—Arafat was going to get rich off the Oslo Accords.

The following January, Mahmoud Abbas (Abu Mazen) was elected to succeed Arafat as president of Palestine. Not surprisingly, Hamas and Islamic Jihad—both opponents of the peace process that Abbas and his Fatah Party supported— boycotted the election. For instance, in the Gaza Strip, a Hamas stronghold, only about half of the eligible voters cast ballots.

In fact, in municipal elections in Palestine that ended in May, Hamas had proclaimed a *tahdiyah* (period of calm) and it ended up polling relatively well—an ominous portent for the stability of the peace process.

ISRAEL'S UNILATERAL DISENGAGEMENT FROM THE GAZA STRIP (2005)

Israel began a process of unilateral disengagement from the Gaza Strip in August 2005. All twenty-one Israeli settlements, together with about eight thousand settlers, were evacuated by August 22. Those settlers who refused to leave were evicted (many literally clinging to their homes while TV crews filmed) by Israeli police units under direction from the IDF. The evacuated settlers then received a government compensation package, and their former homes were razed to the ground by demolition crews. In all, 2,800 formerly Jewish homes and community buildings (that could have been used by Palestinians), were intentionally destroyed by Israel.

The idea of a unilateral disengagement from the Gaza Strip had been publicly proposed for the first time by Prime Minister Ariel Sharon back in December 2003. Senior Israeli cabinet ministers had been lukewarm to the plan; it was feared that any disengagement would mean losing sovereignty over a portion of Eretz Yisrael (i.e., the partition dilemma, see chapter 1). On May 2, 2004, the Likud party (headed by Sharon) held a referendum on the plan and it was rejected by 65 per cent of the party membership. The plan was amended, two cabinet ministers were dismissed, and finally it was accepted by the remainder of the cabinet on June 6, 2004. Two religious party ministers quit in protest, however, leaving Likud without a majority in the Knesset. On October 11, 2004, the Knesset voted 53 to 44 against Sharon's address at the opening of the winter session, but on October 26, the Knesset gave preliminary approval for the plan by a margin of 67 to 45. Benjamin Netanyahu and three other cabinet ministers from Sharon's own party threatened to resign unless Sharon agreed to a national referendum on the plan within two weeks.

As we know, Yasser Arafat died in November 2004, which turned out to be fortuitous for Sharon. First, Netanyahu withdrew his threat to resign from cabinet. Second, on December 30, 2004, Sharon closed a deal with Shimon Peres and the Labor Party, thus forming a national unity government and regaining a majority in the Knesset. From that point onward, it was possible for Sharon to achieve sufficient votes in cabinet and in the Knesset to approve the unilateral disengagement from the Gaza Strip. Imagine now, how complicated things would have been if Israel had to consider a bone fide peace offer from the Palestinians!

On November 15, 2005, Israel signed the Agreement on Movement and Access (AMA) with the Palestinian Authority—a treaty that aimed to improve the freedom of movement and economic activity within the Palestinian territories, including the Gaza Strip, and to open an international crossing between Egypt and Gaza at Rafah. The AMA promised the construction of a seaport in Gaza, and to continue to explore the possibility of an airport. Things were finally starting to look promising for the residents of the Strip.

Following her unilateral disengagement from the Gaza Strip, Israel continued to control borders (except for the Rafah crossing into Egypt), as well as a security zone within the border, which encroached on valuable agricultural land. The world hailed Sharon as a peacemaker. Then on December 18, 2005, he suffered a minor stroke, followed by a major stroke a month later, which left him in a permanent coma (he eventually died in 2014).

HAMAS DOES REMARKABLY WELL IN DEMOCRATIC ELECTIONS

Meanwhile, legislative elections were held in the Palestinian Territories the following January and Hamas did remarkably well, taking 74 of 132 seats. The elections were monitored by international observers and were regarded as fair and democratic. Hamas subsequently called for a unity government with its rival, Fatah, but refused to recognize Israel's right to exist, renounce violence, or accept previous agreements and obligations including the Roadmap for peace.

The United States and the European Union subsequently cut all funds to the Palestinian Authority, and on February 19, 2006 (the day after the new parliament was sworn in), Israel refused to hand over $55 million in monthly tax and custom revenues collected on behalf of the Palestinians. Israel also increased controls on checkpoints but did not otherwise impose a blockade on the flow of people or goods.

Nine months earlier (in May 2005), the Australian-born American Jewish president of the World Bank, and the Quartet's Special Envoy for Gaza Disengagement, James Wolfensohn, arrived in the Middle East "in order to monitor," according to an historian, "the Israeli disengagement from Gaza and to help heal the badly ailing Palestinian economy."[13] At first, Wolfensohn was "full of hope" and managed to raise $9 billion ($3 billion a year for three years) "to bolster the Palestinian economy." Three months following the disengagement—in November 2005—Wolfensohn served as the mediator between Israel and the Palestinian Authority in negotiations on transit routes and on access to and from the Gaza Strip. He also donated his own personal money to help the Palestinians buy Israeli-owned greenhouses in the Gaza Strip, in an effort to foster Palestinian economic activity.

It was around this time that Wolfensohn's optimism all but dried up. The flow of people and goods through the Gaza border was poorly coordinated, and the greenhouse initiative—symbolic of the future Palestinian economy—failed.

"What really doomed the greenhouse initiative … were Israeli restrictions on Gazan exports." In early December 2005, he writes,

> the much awaited first harvest of quality cash crops—strawberries, cherry tomatoes, cucumbers, sweet peppers and flowers—began. These crops were intended for export via Israel to Europe. But their success relied upon the Karni crossing [between Gaza and Israel], which, beginning in mid-January 2006, was closed more than not. The Palestine Economic Development Corporation, which was managing the greenhouses taken over from the settlers, said that it was experiencing losses in excess of $120,000 per day … It was excruciating. This lost harvest was the most recognizable sign of Gaza's declining fortunes and the biggest personal disappointment during my mandate.[14]

In February 2006, Wolfensohn warned that the Palestinian Authority was on the verge of collapse, but the international community took no heed of his warning. In April, Wolfensohn resigned as the Quartet's Special Envoy for Gaza Disengagement and headed back to the United States. The greenhouses were eventually burned to the ground by (justifiably) frustrated Gazans.

ROCKETS, TUNNELS, AND SCHELLING'S DILEMMA

The June-to-August period marked the peak of the 2006 rocket attacks on Israel. On June 8, 2006, the Israeli Air Force interrupted the relative calm that had prevailed for the past five months with the targeted assassination of Jamal Abu Samhadana using missiles fired from Apache attack helicopters. At the time, Samhadana was director general of the police forces in Gaza and founder of the Popular Resistance Committees. He was suspected of plotting rocket attacks against Israel.

The next day, Islamic Jihad fired rockets into Israel, and the IDF retaliated with a devastating bombardment of the launch site on a beach near Beit Lahia. Eight members of the Ghaliya family were killed and at least thirty other civilian individuals were injured. The incident became known as the Gaza beach explosion. A video of eleven-year-old Huda Ghaliya, reacting to the death of family members, was widely broadcast.

These incidents are a perfect example of Schelling's Dilemma. In an atmosphere of intense mutual distrust, fear leads to an arms race, which leads to more fear. And it doesn't take much to trigger a pre-emptive strike.

In the early morning of June 24, 2006, for the first time since the disengagement of August 2005, members of the IDF entered the Gaza Strip. The IDF broke into a house near Rafah and detained two members of the Muamar family on suspicions of belonging to Hamas and plotting to carry out imminent attacks on Israel. The incident became known as the Muamar family detention incident, and it triggered another round of escalating violence, even though it was largely ignored in the major English media.

The following day, members of the Qassam Brigade, the Popular Resistance Committees, and the Army of Islam crossed from Gaza into Israel through an underground tunnel near the Kerem Shalom crossing and captured Corporal Gilad Shalit. After being held in isolation and captivity for more than five years, Shalit was released on October 18, 2011, in exchange for 1,027 Palestinian prisoners who were collectively responsible for 569 Israeli deaths.

Three days after the capture of Gilad Shalit, on June 28, 2006, Israel initiated Operation Summer Rains, the first major ground operation in the Gaza Strip since Israel's unilateral disengagement in August 2005. The goals of the operation were to suppress rocket fire from Gaza and to secure the release of Corporal Shalit. On the first day of the operation, Israel bombed the only electrical power plant in the Gaza Strip.

Operation Autumn Clouds began on November 1, 2006, and ended on November 26 with a ceasefire between the IDF and Hamas but no release of Shalit. A total of 1,247 rockets and 28 mortar shells were fired into Israel from the Gaza Strip in 2006.[15]

In November 2006, US president George W. Bush instructed Secretary of State Condoleeza Rice and Deputy National Security Advisor Elliott

Abrams to push Egypt, Jordan, Saudi Arabia, and the United Arab Emirates into a quixotic American-backed plan for a coup against Hamas. The plan involved the three Arab countries purchasing American-manufactured weapons for delivery to Mohammed Dahlan, a former national security adviser to Mahmoud Abbas; with the co-operation of the Israelis, the plan was designed so that Dahlan could enter the Gaza Strip and overthrow democratically elected Hamas.[16]

At the time, the Palestinian Legislative Council (PLC; the legislative body of the Palestinian Authority) had power over civil matters and internal security in Area A of the West Bank and in the Gaza Strip. In March 2007, the PLC (with the blessings of the Saudis) established a national unity government: Abbas remained as president, and Hamas colleague Ismail Haniyeh was installed as prime minister. This was regarded by Israel and the West as a form of betrayal because any Palestinian government that includes Hamas—basically a terrorist organization—would be automatically regarded as illegitimate.

THE BATTLE OF GAZA AND SUBSEQUENT BLOCKADE

In the second week of June 2007, Fatah fighters, led by Mohammed Dahlan and backed by the Bush administration, attempted to overthrow Hamas in the Gaza Strip. Unfortunately, the United States had miscalculated badly, and Fatah was brutally defeated by the better-equipped Hamas forces. Following Hamas's victory, Israel and Egypt sealed their borders with the Gaza Strip, allegedly because the Palestinian Authority could no longer provide security on the Palestinian side of the border. A complete land, sea, and air blockade of the Gaza Strip (home then to some 1.5 million individuals) was imposed (in possible violation of Article 33 of the Fourth Geneva Convention, which prohibits collective punishment of a civilian population). A total of 938 rockets and 663 mortar shells were fired into Israel from the Gaza Strip in 2007.[17]

From February 28 to March 3, 2008, the IDF conducted Operation Hot Winter in response to continued rocket fire into Israel from the Gaza Strip (mostly Qassam, but for the first time, also Grad missiles). At least

112 Palestinian militants and civilians were killed, along with three Israelis. Almost half the Palestinian casualties were civilians, including children. Both the UN and the EU criticized Israel for her "disproportionate use of force."

On November 3, 2008, just over sixteen months into the land, sea, and air blockade of the Gaza Strip, the Israelis informed the United States in a diplomatic cable that they were intentionally maintaining the Gaza economy "on the brink of collapse ... without pushing it over the edge."[18] This was the embodiment of collective punishment and zero-sum thinking.

A total of 1,270 rockets and 912 mortar shells were fired into Israel from the Gaza Strip in 2008.[19] The total number of casualties from rocket attacks from the Gaza Strip following the 2005 disengagement was two in 2006, two in 2007, and five in 2008. Clearly, the rockets were more successful as weapons of terror than as weapons of mass destruction (the average casualty rate was 2.6 deaths per thousand rockets fired at Israel between 2006 and 2008).

In June 2008, with the help of Egyptian mediation, a *tahdiyah* (period of calm) of six months was agreed upon. It could have lasted longer, but on December 27, 2008, the IDF commenced Operation Cast Lead, its largest military operation in the Gaza Strip since the Six-Day War. There is no doubt that the Israelis were the ones to break the ceasefire.

OPERATION CAST LEAD

The goals of Operation Cast Lead were to stop rocket fire into Israel and weapons smuggling into the Gaza Strip. The Israeli offensive began with a week-long air attack. The Israeli Air Force targeted all suspected rocket launching sites and weapons caches; some civilian sites such as police stations; and political and administrative institutions in densely populated areas, including Gaza City, Khan Yunis, and Rafah. A ground invasion, with air support, began on January 3, 2009, and within two days the IDF was operating in densely populated urban areas of the Gaza Strip. The IDF chief rabbi, Avichai Rontzki, issued a publication that was distributed to soldiers in front-line units, describing the appropriate code of conduct in the field: "When you show mercy to a cruel enemy, you are being cruel to pure and honest soldiers. This is terribly immoral. These are not games at the amusement park where sportsmanship teaches one to make concessions. This is a war on murderers. À la guerre comme à la guerre."[20]

Hamas responded with rockets that hit the cities of Beersheba and Ashdod for the first time. Israel declared a unilateral ceasefire on January 18, 2009. Between 1,387 and 1,417 Palestinian combatants and civilians lost their lives in Operation Cast Lead. Non-governmental sources confirmed a high percentage of civilian deaths. The number of Israeli casualties was 13, including 4 from friendly fire.

The president of the UN Human Rights Council established a fact-finding mission on the Gaza conflict in April 2009, headed by South African Justice Richard Goldstone, a distinguished prosecutor with the International Criminal Tribunal for the former Yugoslavia and the International Criminal Tribunal for Rwanda. Goldstone and his colleagues issued a report in 2010 accusing both the IDF and Palestinian militants of war crimes and possibly crimes against humanity, in addition to "extensive destruction of property, not justified by military necessity and carried out unlawfully and wantonly."[21]

The report went on to state that the

mission finds that the conduct of the Israeli armed forces constitute grave breaches of the Fourth Geneva Convention in respect of wilful killings and wilfully causing great suffering to protected persons and as such give rise to individual criminal responsibility … It also finds that the direct targeting and arbitrary killing of Palestinian civilians is a violation of the right to life.[22]

The Goldstone Report was criticized by the Israeli government, and its findings disputed. Later that year, South African Zionists attempted to ban Goldstone from attending his own grandson's bar mitzvah.[23] In 2011, Goldstone published an op-ed piece in *The Washington Post*, expressing doubt over his own findings. The other three authors of the Goldstone Report did not publicly change their views.

THE GAZA FREEDOM FLOTILLA

On May 31, 2010, a humanitarian-aid flotilla consisting of three passenger ships and three cargo ships destined for the Gaza Strip was boarded in international waters by Israel's Shayetet 13 naval commandos (an ultra-elite Special Forces unit, equivalent to the US Navy SEALs). Known as the Gaza Freedom Flotilla, the humanitarian effort was organized by the Free Gaza Movement and the Foundation for Human Rights and Freedoms and Humanitarian Relief, an Islamic aid group based in Turkey.

The three cargo ships were carrying ten thousand tons of humanitarian aid worth an estimated $20 million, including books; building materials such as cement (which was prohibited under the blockade); electricity generators; food; footwear; medicines and medical equipment; mobility scooters; operating theatre equipment and wheelchairs; sofas; textiles; toys; and cash. No weapons were found on board except for clubs and slingshots. Nine activists (eight with Turkish citizenship and one American) were killed in the raid, and dozens injured. Seven Israeli soldiers were injured. The ships were eventually towed to the Israeli port of Ashdod, and the activists imprisoned and later deported to their home countries. Most of the cargo was eventually delivered to Gaza under UN supervision about a month later. Following the incident, Israeli-Turkish relations became severely strained as Israel refused to issue an apology.

By June 2012, the blockade of the Gaza Strip had entered its sixth year. Despite a partial lifting of the blockade in 2010 by both Israel and Egypt, 34 per cent of the Gaza Strip's workforce (including half its youth) remained unemployed, 44 per cent of Gazans were food insecure, and 80 per cent were aid recipients. In 2011, less than one truckload of goods per day exited Gaza, which was less than 3 per cent of the average amount of exports during the first half of 2007. Fuel and electricity shortages resulted in outages of up to twelve hours per day, and over 90 per cent of the water from the Gaza aquifer was unsafe to drink without treatment.

There was a deficit of some 71,000 housing units in the Gaza Strip.[24] The economy remained stagnant, and according to the UN, "the quality of infrastructure and vital services, including in the areas of health, education and water and sanitation, have significantly declined as a result of the import restrictions and the rapid population growth." There was no way that Gaza would ever become economically self-sufficient under the circumstances. Both sides continued to stubbornly violate international humanitarian law.

OPERATION PILLAR OF DEFENSE

On November 14, 2013, the IDF commenced Operation Pillar of Defense, an eight-day operation in response to a barrage of more than one hundred rockets launched at Israel in a twenty-four-hour period, the firing of an anti-tank missile at an IDF jeep within Israeli territory, and an explosion caused by IEDs near the Israeli end of a tunnel originating in the Gaza Strip.[25]

On the first day of the operation, Ahmed Jabari, the Hamas second-in-command, was killed in a targeted assassinated by the Israeli Air Force. Jabari had played a key role in the Hamas takeover of the Gaza Strip in June 2007, the capture of Corporal Gilad Shalit, and the acquisition of longer-range rockets by Hamas. In just over a week, the IDF struck over 1,500 sites in the Gaza Strip, and Hamas fired over 1,456 rockets into Israel, reaching Rishon LeZion, Beersheba, Ashdod, Ashkelon, and Tel Aviv, which was hit for the first time since the 1991 Gulf War. Rockets were also fired at Jerusalem by Hamas. According to the UNHCR, 174 Palestinians were killed and hundreds more wounded. Among the six Israelis killed, three were from a direct hit on a home in Kiryat Malachi.

More than 420 rockets were intercepted by the Iron Dome missile defence system, which was deployed for the first time in March 2011.[26] During Operation Pillar of Defense, the Iron Dome intercepted about 90 per cent of the rockets launched from the Gaza Strip that would have landed in populated areas of Israel. A truce between Israel and Hamas was reached on November 21, 2012, with both sides claiming victory. Rocket fire from the Gaza Strip into Israel was subsequently curtailed.

On June 12, 2014, three Israeli teenagers disappeared while hitchhiking near the West Bank settlement of Alon Shvut, in Gush Etzion. One of them, Gilad Shaer, was able to call the police and notify them that he and his two friends had been kidnapped. This resulted in the eleven-day-long Operation Brother's Keeper, during which the West Bank was placed in a state of lockdown, and Israel arrested around 350 Palestinians, including nearly all of Hamas's West Bank leadership. Five Palestinians died during the operation. Two weeks later, the bodies of the three teenagers were found near Hebron. It's not completely clear if senior Hamas officials knew about or sanctioned the kidnapping and murder of the teenagers until after it had occurred. Hamas in Gaza responded to the situation by firing rockets at Israeli settlements in the West Bank.

On July 2, 2014, sixteen-year-old Mohammed Abu Khdeir disappeared from East Jerusalem. Two weeks later, three Israelis admitted to kidnapping and burning him alive in response to the kidnapping and murder of the three Israeli teens.

OPERATION PROTECTIVE EDGE

Six days later, the IDF commenced Operation Protective Edge, its third military incursion into the Gaza Strip since Hamas came to power in June 2007. The aim of the campaign was to stop rocket fire from the Gaza Strip into Israel. Initially, the campaign involved only air strikes by the IDF.

Then, on July 16, 2014, Hamas issued ten conditions for a ceasefire with Israel in exchange for a ten-year hudna (truce). The conditions were:

(1) removing Israeli tanks from the Gaza border to a distance to allow Palestinian farmers to work their lands near the border freely; (2) releasing all the prisoners arrested following the killing of the three teenage settlers; (3) removing the siege from Gaza and opening the crossings for goods and people; (4) opening a sea port and an international airport under UN inspectors; (5) expanding a fishing zone

for ten kilometres from the shore; (6) turning the Rafah crossing into an international crossing under the inspection of the UN and ally Arab countries; (7) halting fire while the Palestinian factions commit to a ceasefire for ten years based on having international inspectors on the border with Gaza; (8) that Israel should ease the access to and give permits to worshippers from Gaza strip to Al-Aqsa mosque; (9) that Israel cannot become involved in the internal Palestinian political issues and the political reconciliation process and what follows of elections for presidency and parliament; and (10) re-establishing the industrial zones and improving the development in the Gaza Strip.[27]

At face value, Hamas's list of conditions seemed to make sense. But on the grounds that acceptance of the conditions would be tantamount to rewarding Hamas for the past eight days of violence, Israel not only flatly rejected them but also doubled down on her military efforts by authorizing a ground invasion the very next day.

On July 20, 2014, Israel dropped one hundred one-ton bombs on Shuja'iyya,[28] a densely populated neighbourhood of Gaza City, killing more than seventy Palestinians who were already packed into refugee shelters, and wounding hundreds more. Survivors of the massacre claim that Hamas had used them as human shields.

Ten days later, the IDF bombed an UNRWA school.[29]

All in all, after striking 5,263 targets in the Gaza Strip, at least thirty-four "terror tunnels" were discovered and destroyed by the IDF during Operation Protective Edge. Hamas, Islamic Jihad, and other militant groups fired 4,564 rockets and mortars into Israel. More than 735 were intercepted by Iron Dome, which had been operating with an interception rate of over 90 per cent since 2012.[30] Two-thirds of Hamas's ten-thousand-strong rocket arsenal was either used up or destroyed. According to the UN Human Rights Committee, a total of 2,251 Palestinians, including 551 children, were killed in Operation Protective Edge, versus 72 Israelis (including 6 civilians). Approximately 910 of the 1,700 adult Palestinians who were killed were civilians. The total number of wounded Palestinians was 11,231, including 3,436 children. More than 18,000 homes were destroyed or seriously damaged, and 1,500 children were orphaned; 73 hospitals or health care facilities in the Gaza Strip were either destroyed or seriously damaged.[31]

On August 15, 2014, the *New York Times* reported that the

> damage to Gaza's infrastructure from the current conflict is more severe than the destruction caused by either of the last two Gaza wars … The fighting has displaced about a fourth of Gaza's population. Nearly 60,000 people have lost their homes, and the number of people taking shelter in UNRWA schools is nearly five times as many as in 2009. The cost to Gaza's already fragile economy will be significant: the 2009 conflict caused losses estimated at $4 billion—almost three times the size of Gaza's annual gross domestic product.[32]

A ceasefire was finally reached between Israel and Hamas on August 26, with both sides again claiming victory.

ISRAEL AND HAMAS DO, IN FACT, CO-OPERATE

It's very difficult to grasp the full impact of the blockade plus three wars on the people and infrastructure of Gaza. Although the total number of Palestinian casualties (combatant plus civilian) in the three Gaza wars is relatively small (around 3,800; or roughly two per one thousand inhabitants), the number of civilian casualties, including women and children, is disturbingly high. The IDF claims that it took great care to avoid such casualties, and we know for a fact that Hamas used civilians as human shields.

As a physician I know first-hand that not all casualties involve physical injury. In the dirty, violent, and crowded camps of Gaza, there is now an entire generation of children who have spent every minute of their lives living under a land, sea, and air blockade. Almost every one of them has lived through at least one war, and some through two or three. They have witnessed first-hand acts of violence and terror against their families, committed by the IDF, or Hamas, or some militant Islamic faction—it doesn't really matter which. These highly traumatized children will grow up to become the terrorists of tomorrow. An equally disturbing thought is that there is now an entire generation of Israeli children who will grow up knowing that one day it will be their job to hunt down and kill these terrorists—these former children of Gaza. The obvious question any Israeli must ask him- or herself is: why? Why contribute so much to ensure a future generation of sworn enemies with whom one must contend in an existential battle of survival?

If Hamas were to formally renounce all violence and accept Israel's right to exist, then there would be a basis for rational co-operation at a high level, and the rebuilding of the Gaza Strip could begin. But the truth is that Israel and Hamas do, in fact, co-operate, but not at a high level and not in a way that many would like to see.

The game that Israel and Hamas have been playing since 2007 is an *iterated* game of Chicken of indefinite duration with the payout matrix in figure 6.1.

Hamas

		quiet	escalate
Israel	quiet	quiet for quiet (3, 3)	*missiles and tunnels* *(2, 4)*
	escalate	*continued blockade* *(4, 2)*	military operation (1, 1)

Nash equilibria in bold italics text

FIGURE 6.1

In this game of Chicken, both Israel and Hamas repeatedly drive straight ahead towards each other but swerve at the last minute in order to avoid a head-on collision. A head-on collision would be something like another war, which is the last choice either party wants (although sometimes Israel refers to war with Hamas as "mowing the lawn"— in other words, a routine chore). The first choice for Israel is to maintain the blockade of Gaza for as long as possible. If Israel succeeds in doing so without any retaliation from Hamas, then Israel scores a victory. The first choice for Hamas is to build tunnels and lob missiles at Israel for as long as possible. If Hamas succeeds in doing so without provoking another war, then Hamas scores a victory. Either scenario ("continued blockade" or "missiles and tunnels") represents a Nash equilibrium in this game, which is why they are such stable scenarios.

Another option is called "quiet for quiet," which is a form of low-level co-operation between Israel and Hamas. In the quiet-for-quiet scenario, both Israel and Hamas drive straight towards each other, but swerve at exactly the same time. The rockets stop briefly, and the blockade is loosened a bit. A small amount of humanitarian aid trickles through and that's about it. The "grass" grows back. It's the same game … over and over again.

The Gaza Strip is now lost to Jewish settlement for the foreseeable future. The most that its residents can ever hope for is a generous helping of quiet for quiet. The Land of Israel has now been partitioned, and the world has grown numb to the suffering in Gaza. This game of Chicken will likely continue for a very long time.

Chapter 7

A SMALL HOUSE

A small house can accommodate hundreds of friends,
but not two enemies.
— ARAB PROVERB

It's astonishing how many individuals—not to mention diehard Zionists and western democracies—continue to believe in the two-state solution for historic Palestine. Since 1937, there have been no less than three major attempts at a two-state solution, and all three have failed miserably. Why then, after more than eight decades of beating a political dead horse, would anyone expect the horse to get up and gallop on the fourth try?

The first to propose two-states for two peoples was the 1937 Palestine Royal Commission (Peel Commission); however, a year later the 1938 Woodhead Commission concluded that partition was simply not feasible. This led to the infamous 1939 White Paper and, on the very eve of the Holocaust, restrictions on Jewish immigration to Mandatory Palestine, which was a disaster for the Jewish people.

The second attempt occurred a decade later, when the United Nations Special Committee on Palestine (UNSCOP) proposed the partition of Mandatory Palestine and the creation of separate Jewish and Arab states. On November 29, 1947, the UN General Assembly adopted Resolution 181 (in favour of partition), and the following day a civil war broke out. Six months later, a Jewish state emerged—much larger than originally envisioned by either the 1947 UN partition plan or the 1937 Peel Commission plan—but no Arab state. Instead of an Arab state, 710,000 Palestinian Arabs ended up as refugees—a disaster, this time, for the

Palestinian people. The part that most people forget is that on the day that Israel declared her independence, she also declared that she was prepared to accept a two-state solution (with an economic union) for the whole of Eretz Yisrael. This is explicitly stated in Israel's Declaration of Independence.

Then, from 1993 to 2014, the Oslo peace process attempted for the third time to divide historic Palestine into two states. But Israel continued to build settlements beyond the 1967 border, insisting all the while that they were not an impediment to peace (imagine if it were the other way around, and the Palestinians were building new villages *inside* the 1967 border). After rejecting an offer of 93 per cent of the West Bank (excluding East Jerusalem) plus the Gaza Strip in 2000, the Palestinian counter-offer was the Second Intifada. The result today is a Palestine that's physically and politically fragmented and divided, with little hope of ever forming a contiguous and functionally sovereign state. In short, another disaster for the Palestinian people.

MUTUAL RECOGNITION NOT ENOUGH

The Palestinian people have always seen themselves as a colonized nation; the Jewish people, as an exiled nation with irredentist claims to Eretz Yisrael. These two incompatible worldviews can never be knitted together into a single society without meaningful efforts towards reconciliation and restitution.

Astonishingly, in 1988, the Palestinian National Council (PNC) recognized the state of Israel along the 1967 border. This represented a huge concession because it meant that the PLO had effectively relinquished claim to 78 per cent of the area of historic Palestine. It also meant that the maximum territory that Israel would ever have to surrender in any future peace deal with the Palestinians would be the West Bank (including East Jerusalem) and the Gaza Strip, but no more. At the time, few understood the significance of these developments because previously the PLO's explicit objective had always been to pursue the zero-sum game of "throwing the Jews into the sea" and liberating all of Palestine. But after the PNC agreed to accept only 22 per cent of historic Palestine as the basis for a future Palestinian state, there was no going back. Why didn't they start by asking for 45 per cent, which was the area of Mandatory Palestine allotted to an Arab state according to the 1947 UN Partition Plan for Palestine? Anyway, as Faisal Huseini famously said, 22 per cent means "there can be no compromise on the compromise."

In international law, a nation can only sign a peace treaty with another nation. So, in order for Israel to sign a peace treaty with the Palestinians, the Palestinians first had to become a nation in international law.

On June 15, 1969, Golda Meir bluntly stated in an interview with the *Sunday Times* that

> there were no such thing as Palestinians. When was there an independent Palestinian people with a Palestinian state? It was either southern Syria before the First World War, and then it was a Palestine including Jordan. It was not as though there was a Palestinian people in Palestine considering itself as a Palestinian people and we came and threw them out and took their country away from them. They did not exist.

The Oslo Accords changed all of this. In a letter dated September 9, 1993, Prime Minister Yitzhak Rabin informed Chairman Yasser Arafat that "the Government of Israel has decided to recognize the PLO as the representative of the Palestinian people." Likewise, Arafat sent a letter of recognition to Rabin, offering the PLO's recognition of Israel. This simple exchange of letters of recognition solidified the nation-to-nation relationship between Israel and the Palestinian people. But mutual recognition alone is not enough for successful binational relations.

There are many examples of binational and multinational states, such as Afghanistan, Belgium, Bosnia and Herzegovina, Brazil, Canada, China, Ethiopia, India, Indonesia, Iraq, Madagascar, Montenegro, Nigeria, Pakistan, Russia, Serbia, South Africa, Spain, Suriname, Turkey, and the United Kingdom. And what all these states have in common is a shared vision and a shared society. Israel and Palestine dream only of displacing each other from what's left of the West Bank (Israel has already relinquished all claims to the Gaza Strip). Colonization is a zero-sum game.

THE ISRAELI ANTI-PEACE CAMP

The fact that the Oslo I Accord was signed by a democratically elected government meant very little to Baruch Goldstein, a thirty-seven-year-old American-born physician, settler, and Jewish ultranationalist. In the Middle East, the method of choice for changing the course of history is often violence rather than democratic institutions. On February 25, 1994, a date that coincided with the Jewish holiday of Purim, Goldstein entered the Cave of the Patriarchs/Ibrahimi Mosque in Hebron and gunned down 154 Muslim worshippers (29 of whom died of their injuries) before being beaten to death by survivors of the massacre. This dealt a severe blow to the peace process—which, of course, was Goldstein's intention all along. But the loss of momentum was insufficient to prevent Israel and Jordan from signing a peace treaty some eight months later (on October 26, 1994).

Then on the evening of November 4, 1995, as Israeli prime minister Yitzhak Rabin walked towards his car following a peace rally in Tel Aviv, he was shot several times in the chest by Yigal Amir, a twenty-five-year-old Orthodox Jewish law student from Bar-Ilan University. After a frantic twenty-five-minute drive to a hospital that was only five minutes away by foot, Rabin died on the operating table from massive blood loss.

Yigal, together with his brother, Hagai, had spent the previous two years planning every detail of Rabin's assassination. In the months leading up to Rabin's murder, both brothers drew ideological support from a circle of right-wing rabbis and a chorus of religious nationalist voices (including Likud), all of whom objected vehemently to Israel withdrawing from "Jewish" land in the West Bank—land that Israel has colonized since 1967, despite widespread condemnation from the international community.

At trial, Yigal calmly explained that his motive for Rabin's murder derived from two Talmudic laws: *din rodef* (the law of the pursuer) and *din moser* (the law of the informer). The law of the pursuer allows for the extra-judicial killing of an individual who is pursuing another individual with the intent of murdering them. It's murder to prevent a murder. According to Amir's interpretation of the law of the pursuer, Rabin was a Jewish king who was about to murder the Jewish settlers of Judea and Samaria (the biblical names for the West Bank) by handing them over to the Palestinian Authority.[1] According to the law of the informer, Rabin could also be regarded as having betrayed his fellow Jews by informing on them in a non-Jewish court (the international community, presumably). Thus, for having violated these two important Talmudic laws, Rabin merited killing twice over—without trial and without warning.

Of course, Prime Minister Yitzhak Rabin was not a king, nor Israel a monarchy (it's a republican form of government). And under the Oslo I Accord, all settlers remained under Israeli rule, subject only to Israeli law. But that's not how the Amir brothers and their circle of rabbis saw things. They could only see the Oslo I Accord through a Talmudic lens. Their understanding of civics and international law was at least fifteen hundred years out of date. They lacked the modern vocabulary to comprehend what the Oslo I Accord was even attempting to accomplish. They only understood the struggle for historic Palestine as a zero-sum game. Over time, more and more on both sides of the conflict would come to embrace this view.

THE MINIMAX PRINCIPLE

Apart from recognizing the PLO (now re-branded as the Palestinian Authority) as the sole legitimate representative of the Palestinian people, Israel conceded basically nothing else of substance between 1993 and 2005. No territorial concessions, no permanent halt to settlement construction in the Seam Zone or Area C (see below), no refugee concessions, and certainly no concessions on Jerusalem (the Likud charter, which has never been revised, explicitly opposes the creation of a Palestinian state in the West Bank).

The 1994 peace treaty with Jordan (which was prompted by the signing of the Oslo I Accord the previous year) should be viewed as a welcome by-product of the peace process, enough to secure Israel against any external threats from one of her key Arab neighbours. Neither the Israeli-Egyptian peace treaty of 1979 nor the Israeli-Jordanian peace treaty of 1994 is conditional on Israel setting aside any territory for the Palestinians. Article 8 of the Israeli-Jordanian peace treaty only stipulates that Israel and Jordan will "seek to resolve" the issues of Palestinian refugees "in a quadripartite committee together with Egypt and the Palestinians." All three countries (Israel, Egypt, and Jordan) have therefore settled their main differences while bypassing the core issues of the Palestinians.

If the Palestinians can be accused of anything, it's that they misunderstood the progress that Israel was making with other Arab players. By 1994, Israel had a peace treaty with Egypt (1979), it had annexed the Golan Heights (1981), and it maintained a presence in south Lebanon (which lasted until 2000). Once a peace treaty with Jordan was signed, Israel had an effective buffer zone on all sides. There was simply no need to take the peace process with the Palestinians any further, and Israel could simply stall and stall, while at the same time placing increasingly difficult demands on the Palestinians. The latter included demilitarization of any future Palestinian state, maintenance of a permanent Israeli military presence in the Jordan Valley, permanent Israeli control over Palestinian airspace, and Israeli sovereignty over the Haram al-Sharif (the third holiest site in Islam). Such demands, of course, undermine the whole notion of Palestinian sovereignty.

In the realpolitik of peace agreements, "any agreement that by itself brings an end to an immediate crisis will be deemed sufficient by the people in charge of the deal-making."[2] Stated another way: once the Israelis had reached the point where they had minimized their maximum possible loss, they put on the brakes. It was a classic case of bait and switch: the Oslo peace process began as an exercise in rational co-operation (a two-person non-zero-sum game) and then deteriorated into a zero-sum game once the First Intifada was brought under control and Israel had a peace treaty with Jordan.

In 1995, as part of the Oslo II Accord, the West Bank was divided into three areas (Areas A, B, and C), with Area C encompassing some

61 per cent of the territory of the West Bank (excluding East Jerusalem, which was annexed by Israel in 1967). Area A is under full Palestinian administrative and security control; Area B is under joint Palestinian and Israeli security control; and Area C is under full Israeli administrative and security control. Area C includes the Jordan Valley, which Israel insists it must control for reasons of national security. Although Oslo II was intended to be a temporary measure, it has now become a permanent arrangement. This is yet another famous example of leaving business unfinished because an intermediate step is more favourable than the final arrangement.

In a two-person zero-sum game, the strategy that minimizes your loss in a worst-case scenario is called the minimax strategy. For Israel, the minimax strategy involved recognition of the Palestine Authority and a commitment *not* to build settlements in Areas A and B of the West Bank, but otherwise no substantial concessions when it came to the remaining core issues of the conflict (borders, security, refugees, and Jerusalem).

THE PEACE PROCESS AFTER 2000

Following the collapse of the 2000 Camp David Summit (in July), the Palestinians prepared for a Second Intifada. Two months later, Ariel Sharon (who was the official opposition leader at the time and not yet the prime minster of Israel) visited the Temple Mount, surrounded by a throng of Likud supporters and Israeli security forces. This was precisely the sort of direct provocation that the Palestinians had been looking for, and it sparked a campaign of suicide bombings against Jewish civilian targets.

There were five suicide bombings in 2000, forty in 2001, forty-seven in 2002, and twenty-three in 2003. Then in 2003, Israel completed the "first continuous segment" of a seven-hundred-kilometre-long separation barrier that runs along the Green Line and encircles the major West Bank settlements, annexing as much as 10 per cent of the West Bank. The number of suicide bombings dropped to seventeen in 2004. The separation barrier is the incarnation of Jabotinsky's iron wall.

In 2002, the Arab League proposed a peace initiative, known as the Arab Peace Initiative (or Saudi Initiative). That same year, the UN Security Council passed Resolution 1397, which affirms "the vision of a region where two States, Israel and Palestine, live side by side within secure and recognized borders" and welcomed "the contribution of Saudi Crown Prince Abdullah." It marked the first time that the two-state solution was mentioned at the Security Council level.

The following year, former Oslo negotiators prepared the Geneva Initiative, a draft Permanent Status Agreement to end the Israeli-Palestinian conflict based on "previous official negotiations, international resolutions, the Quartet Roadmap, the Clinton Parameters, and the Arab Peace Initiative."[3] The combined effect of these very serious peace proposals ultimately pressured the Sharon government into disengaging unilaterally from the Gaza Strip.

Writing in *Haaretz*, Peter Beinart explained the rationale as follows:

Sharon saw several advantages to withdrawing settlers from Gaza. First, it would save money, since in Gaza Israel was deploying a disproportionately high number of soldiers to protect a relatively small number of settlers. Second, by (supposedly) ridding Israel of its responsibility for millions of Palestinians, the withdrawal would leave Israel and the West Bank with a larger Jewish majority. Third, the withdrawal would prevent the administration of George W. Bush from embracing the Saudi or Geneva plans, and pushing hard—as Bill Clinton had done—for a Palestinian state. Sharon's chief of staff, Dov Weisglass, put it bluntly: "The significance of the disengagement plan is the freezing of the peace process. And when you freeze that process, you prevent the establishment of a Palestinian state, and you prevent a discussion on the refugees, the borders and Jerusalem. Effectively, this whole package called the Palestinian state, with all that it entails, has been removed indefinitely from our agenda. And all this with authority and permission. All with a presidential blessing and the ratification of both houses of Congress."[4]

In August 2005, Ariel Sharon ordered the withdrawal of the IDF and the dismantling of all Israeli settlements in the Gaza Strip. This represented the loss of a piece of Eretz Yisrael (albeit only 360 square kilometres) in exchange for essentially nothing. It also meant the loss of any hope for a Jewish state in the *whole* of Eretz Yisrael. Religious Zionist leaders organized the largest prayer rallies and mass protests since the Madrid Conference of 1991 (which they also opposed), completely flooding the Western Wall plaza and spilling outside of the Old City of Jerusalem. The eight thousand Jewish settlers who were forced to evacuate their homes had to be dragged away by the police instead of the IDF for fear of sparking a mutiny within the ranks of the armed forces. Some four months later, Sharon suffered a series of strokes, the last of which left him in a permanent coma. No doubt this was regarded as a form divine retribution by the Orthodox rabbis who placed an ancient curse on him and pleaded with the Almighty to send the Angel of Death to dispatch him to the next world.

Prime Minister Netanyahu delivered a seminal speech at Bar-Ilan University in 2009 in which he departed from the official platform of his own party and publicly endorsed for the first time the concept of a Palestinian state alongside Israel. He then proceeded to outline a series of conditions that would have eviscerated all prospects of Palestinian sovereignty. Palestine was to be a completely demilitarized state; Jerusalem would be the undivided capital of Israel; Palestine would have to recognize Israel as a Jewish state; and there would be no return of any Palestinian refugees to Israel. By this point it became clear that Netanyahu was playing a zero-sum game, pretending all the while to be interested in rational co-operation.

In January 2011, a collection of nearly seventeen hundred confidential documents (minutes, e-mails, reports, draft agreements, maps, etc.) regarding the Israeli-Palestinian peace process was leaked by a French lawyer of Palestinian descent, Ziyad Clot, to the Al Jazeera television network. Clot, who was a member of the Palestinian Negotiations Support Unit (NSU), sought to undermine his boss, Saeb Erekat, the Palestinian chief negotiator, for inadequately representing the case of Palestinian refugees.

The authenticity of the Palestine Papers (as they came to be known) has been confirmed by both *Al Jazeera* and *The Guardian*. According to one document—minutes of a trilateral meeting dated June 15, 2008—the Palestinian Authority was prepared to concede most of East Jerusalem including the Armenian Quarter, except for Har Homa. Erekat called it "the biggest Yerushalayim in Jewish history." His offer was rebuffed by Israel, and a few months later, Israel launched Operation Cast Lead.

As we know, the Obama administration attempted to jump-start the peace process in 2013 and 2014 and—as expected—the talks collapsed. With the passing of Shimon Peres in September 2016, the Oslo peace process finally and symbolically departed this earth. Today, any discussion of two states for two peoples is entirely out of the question. All of the main protagonists (Rabin, Peres, Arafat, Clinton, and Bush) are either dead or long into their political retirement. Historic Palestine is now partitioned, not by a political border, but by a seven-hundred-kilometre-long security barrier.

ISRAEL'S "PEACE DIVIDEND" IS SMALL

In 2015, the Costs-of-Conflict Study Team of the RAND Corporation published a monograph on the net costs and benefits that would ensue if the long-standing conflict between Israelis and Palestinians follows its current trajectory over the next ten years, versus other possible trajectories ranging from a two-state solution to another violent uprising. The authors concluded that a

> two-state solution provides by far the best economic outcomes for both Israelis and Palestinians. Israelis gain over two times more than the Palestinians in absolute terms—$123 billion versus $50 billion over ten years. But the Palestinians gain more proportionately, with average per capita income increasing by approximately 36 per cent over what it would have been in 2024, versus 5 percent for the average Israeli. A return to violence would have profoundly negative economic consequences for both Palestinians and Israelis ... the per capita gross

domestic product (GDP) would fall by 46 percent in the West Bank and Gaza (WBG) and by 10 percent in Israel by 2024.[5]

Splashing some cold water on the RAND Corporation study, David Rosenberg commented in *Haaretz* that

> for Israel the peace dividend, as RAND sees it, is pretty paltry. On a per capita basis, GDP would be just 5 per cent higher—or just $2,200 in the tenth year after peace—than if the status quo continues. In RAND's worst-case scenario of an intifada, like the kind in the early 2000s, Israel's GDP per capita would be a not-intolerable 10 per cent lower (the economy shrunk even more during the Second Intifada).[6]

Without peace Israel has been doing quite well, which RAND tacitly acknowledges by using as its baseline the country's economic performance in 1999–2014. Average annual growth was 4.1 per cent, despite an intifada and four short wars. Israel's high-tech economy draws billions of dollars annually in foreign investment. The global boycott, divestment, and sanctions (BDS) movement has had no discernible impact so far.

Thanks to a host of supporters and enablers, there isn't a strong economic case to be made for peace with the Palestinians. Israel's continued colonization and control of the West Bank, the Golan Heights, and East Jerusalem give it a sense of security that it would not otherwise have. Most Israelis would agree that a 10 per cent drop in GDP by 2024 is a small price to pay for that added sense of security.

Israel has always maintained that the 1967 borders are indefensible. At their narrowest point, there's only 13.8 kilometres between the Green Line and the Mediterranean coast. Any advancing army could easily cut Israel in half. The settlements of East Jerusalem and the West Bank are now connected to the rest of the country by an extensive network of road, water, electricity, and communications infrastructure. Withdrawing completely to the 1967 border would require perhaps decades of civil engineering work. Under the Oslo Accords, Israel wasn't obliged to evacuate even a single settlement.

AMERICAN ENABLEMENT OF ISRAELI INTRANSIGENCE

Since the start of Prime Minister Benjamin Netanyahu's second term (in 2009), Israel has pursued a zero-sum game with the Palestinians, playing for time and conceding nothing beyond a ten-month-long halt in settlement construction in 2009–10. To a great extent, Israel's intransigence is aided and abetted by the United States.

In 2006, the value of total direct United States aid to Israel since 1949 was conservatively estimated to be $108 billion (current, non-inflation-adjusted dollars).[7] Today, that figure would be in excess of $125 billion, making Israel the largest cumulative recipient of US foreign aid since the Second World War.[8] For a proper perspective on this figure, American grants and loans to the world from 1945 to 1953 (including the Marshall Plan) totalled $44.3 billion, just over a third of this figure.[9]

Of the $3.8 billion in aid that Israel receives in annual military aid from the United States (accounting for slightly more than 50 per cent of total US annual military financial aid worldwide), about three-quarters goes towards the purchase of US-manufactured military equipment, and about one-quarter goes towards the procurement in Israel of defence articles and services, including research and development. Stated another way, the United States subsidizes its own arms industry to the tune of some $2.25 billion per year via Israel's military efforts in the Middle East; on top of which, American taxpayers write an annual cheque for some $750 million per year, payable to the state of Israel, which goes directly to the Israeli arms industry. Total US military aid to the Palestinian Security Services was around $60 million per year, but in January 2019 it was cut off at the request of the Palestinian Authority because of concerns over lawsuits by US victims of terror under the recently passed Anti-Terrorism Clarification Act (ACTA).[10]

An important feature of US foreign aid to Israel is that it is deposited at the beginning of each fiscal year as a lump sum, directly into Israel's US bank accounts, where it immediately begins to collect interest. Aid to other countries is issued in quarterly instalments. In addition, there is no accountability for specific purchases. US funds are comingled with Israel's general funds, at which point the paper trail disappears. Other countries receive US aid for specific purposes and must give a detailed account of how every dollar is spent.

Some of the aid that Israel received from the United States may be in violation of US laws. The Arms Export Control Act stipulates that US-supplied weapons be used only for "legitimate self-defence," and the US Foreign Assistance Act prohibits military assistance to any country "which engages in a consistent pattern of gross violations of internationally recognized human rights." When Israel bulldozes the homes of relatives of Palestinian terrorists, whose only crime was that they are related by blood to actual Palestinian terrorists, Israel must be very careful not to use any American-built bulldozing equipment.

INTERNATIONAL ENABLEMENT OF PALESTINIAN INTRANSIGENCE

UN General Assembly Resolution 194 was discussed in chapter 5. This resolution, which is not legally binding (since it was never adopted by the UN Security Council), embodies what many refer to as the "Palestinian right of return."

Since it was first adopted in December 1948, Resolution 194 has been renewed by the UN on a regular basis, and today it forms part of the core identity of the Palestinian people. It should be noted, however, that the refugees referred to in Article 11 of Resolution 194 include both Palestinian Arab and Jewish refugees.

UN Resolution 194 is unique in several respects. Most notably, it establishes international support for the return of the instigators of a conflict to their former homes. As many right-wing Israelis like to point out, the Palestinians attacked the state of Israel in 1947, they lost and were either expelled or left of their own volition, and now they are rewarded with the right to return to their homes as if there had been no conflict in the first place. The situation is analogous to refugees of the Chinese Civil War (1945–50) who fled with the Kuomintang to the island of Taiwan being allowed to return to mainland China as if there had never been a civil war. The reality today is much different, of course. The Republic of China

(ROC) and the People's Republic of China (PRC) are technically still in a state of war. The ROC, which was a founding member of the United Nations, was expelled from the UN in 1971 and replaced by the PRC. Any nation that recognizes the ROC government is automatically precluded from doing business with the PRC.

In December 1949, a year after UN Resolution 194 was passed, the United Nations passed UN Resolution 302, which established the United Nations Relief and Works Agency for Palestine Refugees in the Near East (UNRWA). The initial purpose of UNRWA was to provide emergency relief to both Jewish and Arab refugees of the 1948 Arab-Israeli conflict. In 1952, however, Israel assumed full responsibility for all the Jewish refugees of the conflict, which left UNRWA to focus exclusively on the needs of the Palestinian refugees. Had there been a Palestinian state in 1952 to assume responsibility for Palestinian refugees, then UNRWA might have only lasted for a few years. But there wasn't, and so over the past seven decades UNRWA has evolved into a veritable pseudo-state that provides Palestinian refugees with "governmental and developmental services in areas such as education, health, welfare, microfinance, and urban planning,"[11] all of which go way beyond its initial mandate of emergency relief. UNRWA has created a state of entitlement and chronic dependency among Palestinians, for which there is currently no solution.

UNRWA is a very different organization from its younger sibling, the United Nations High Commissioner for Refugees (UNHCR), which was established in 1950 to safeguard the rights and well-being of all other refugees in the world. UNRWA is today the only agency in the world that is focused on a single ethnic group and a single conflict: the Palestinian Arab refugees of the 1948 Arab-Israeli conflict and their descendants (now totalling some 5.15 million individuals living in the West Bank, the Gaza Strip, Jordan, Lebanon, and Syria). But in the absence of any final resolution of the Israeli-Palestinian conflict, the UN General Assembly simply continues to renew UNRWA's mandate, thereby subsidizing the *non*-resolution of the conflict.

In 2015, UNRWA had an annual operating budget of some $1.247 billion,[12] of which around 30 per cent ($381 million) came from the United States, but in August 2018 the Trump administration cut all aid to UNRWA. The European Union contributed $137 million, and the United Kingdom, $100 million to UNRWA in 2015.[13] The largest contribution from a single Arab country was $96 million from Saudi Arabia, followed by $32 million from Kuwait. The total contribution of all Arab countries was $153 million (or 13.6 per cent of the annual budget). Israel does not contribute financially to UNRWA, but it helps in other ways, primarily by providing coordination and logistical support.

According to UNRWA, refugee status can be inherited via Palestinian refugee fathers, including by their adopted children.[14] This has resulted in a complicated category of individual, the oxymoronic "citizen refugee," who may be a full citizen of a neighbouring Arab country, such as Jordan, but is also able to claim Palestinian refugee status through UNRWA.

Unlike the UNHCR, UNRWA has no specific mandate to aid Palestinian refugees to integrate into their local country, resettle in a third country, or repatriate when possible. UNRWA is a needs-based, as opposed to a rights-based, organization that has never been tasked with finding a durable solution to the Palestinian refugee problem. This unique situation has enabled both Israeli and Palestinian peace negotiators to engage in all sorts of games of indecision and brinksmanship, knowing full well that the world will somehow find a way to house, clothe, feed, and educate some 5.15 million Palestinians living in the West Bank, the Gaza Strip, Jordan, Lebanon, and Syria.

If UNRWA were to have its mandate terminated and its mission taken over by the UNHCR, such that Palestinian refugees would be treated like every other refugee population in the world, this would create a conflict with UN General Assembly Resolution 194, which enshrines the Palestinian Right of Return. But if Resolution 194 were to be approved by the UN Security Council, this would create a conflict with UN General Assembly Resolution 181, which supports the creation of two states, one with a Jewish majority and one with an Arab majority. The dilemma posed by Resolution 194 is not a Zionist dilemma—it's an international community dilemma.

THE 1946 PARTITION OF INDIA IS NOT A MODEL FOR THE PARTITION OF HISTORIC PALESTINE

The British East India Company governed India from 1757 to 1858. Between 1858 and 1947, the British Crown was directly sovereign over the Indian subcontinent. Things did not go well for the British Empire following the Second World War, and around the same time that Great Britain began extricating herself from Mandatory Palestine, she was faced with even bigger challenges in India. The political exit strategy for India involved partition according to the Two-Nation Theory—a complicated arrangement that recognized Hindus and Muslims as two separate and distinct nations.

Sound familiar?

Gandhi rejected partition in favour of a binational, one-state solution. Such a solution would have required a very high degree of co-operation and coordination between Hindu and Muslim nationals, but it would have been the Pareto-superior solution. We would therefore place Gandhi's one-state solution in the double co-operation quadrant of a 2×2 game matrix. The two-state solution, which entailed Hindu and Muslim nationals each forming their own independent state, occupies the double autonomy quadrant of the game matrix. The other two quadrants represent situations of either Hindu or Muslim hegemony, which the other side wished to avoid at all costs.

The partition of India is a good example of a Prisoner's Dilemma. In the end, Gandhi's Pareto-superior, one-state solution was defeated and the Pareto-inferior, Nash equilibrium prevailed (see figure 7.1). Today, more than seventy years after the trauma of partition—in which fourteen million people were displaced and over one million perished—there are not two but three independent states in the Indian subcontinent (in 1971, the state of Pakistan underwent a further partition with the independence of Bangladesh).

		Muslim nation	
		co-operation	autonomy
Hindu nation	co-operation	Gandhi's vision (3, 3)	Muslim hegemony (1, 4)
	autonomy	Hindu hegemony (4, 1)	*India and Pakistan* *(2, 2)*

Nash equilibrium in bold italics text; Pareto-inferior in shaded text

FIGURE 7.1

The partition of the Indian subcontinent, however, is not a model for the partition of historic Palestine because tiny Palestine doesn't have room for two independent states. A 2018 study by the Tony Blair Institute for Global Change[15] reported that

> Israel has a central role as a trading partner for the PA, compared with other regional partners. The share of all Arab countries combined in Palestinian exports of goods in 2016 was 6 per cent, against an Israeli share of 92 per cent. All other world markets combined accounted for just 2 per cent.

In other words, if Palestine were to cease all export trade with Israel, the Palestinian economy would completely collapse. So, when we talk about the two-state solution for historic Palestine, what we really mean is the two-*interdependent*-state solution rather than the two-*independent*-state solution. This is something that the international community has known for over eighty years but has yet to fully come to terms with.

Recall that the 1937 Peel Commission recommended a "customs union" between the Jewish and Arab states, but that the 1938 Woodhead Commission concluded that the Peel Commission's recommendations would be impossible to implement. Also recall that one of the key features of the 1947 UN Partition Plan for Palestine was an 'economic union' between the proposed Arab and Jewish states. So, in this sense, the 1947 UN Partition Plan for Palestine is nothing like the 1946 partition of India: the latter was never contingent on the free movement of people and goods between the two states of the former Raj, whereas the proposed partition of Mandatory Palestine was completely dependent on free trade between Arab and Jewish states.

If the two-interdependent-state solution for historic Palestine necessitates a high level of economic co-operation and integration between Israel and Palestine, and if colonization and military rule over the Palestinians also requires the constant interaction between Jews and Arabs (albeit of a very different kind), then there's no way for Israel to ever separate completely from Palestine (and vice versa).

KING SOLOMON SPLITS THE BABY

If the two-state solution is now dead, then what is the current relationship between Israel and Palestine? The partition of historic Palestine has its parallels in the biblical story of King Solomon ruling between two women, both claiming to be the mother of the same newborn child (1 Kings 3:16–28). Calling for a sword, King Solomon decreed that the baby would be divided in two and each woman given half. Upon hearing the judgment, one woman begged the king to give the baby to the other woman rather than see it be killed. The other woman, however, preferred to see the baby die rather than let either of them have it. King Solomon gave the baby to the real mother, the woman who was willing to relinquish her claim to the child rather than see it die.

From a game theory perspective, both women were playing a non-zero-sum game in which they could either give in to the other woman or stand firm. If one woman gave in while the other stood firm, the one who stood firm would get the baby. If both women gave in (i.e., mutual co-operation), King Solomon would probably get the baby (this option isn't even discussed in the biblical story). If both women stood firm (i.e., mutual defection), the baby would die.

The real mother's preferences resembled a game of Chicken because she viewed mutual defection as a catastrophic outcome. The imposter mother's preferences resembled a game of Deadlock because she viewed mutual defection as her next-best choice, second only to getting the baby for herself. Since both mothers had different preferences, the game is asymmetrical. The payout matrix is shown in figure 7.2.

		real mother (Chicken)	
		give in	stand firm
imposter mother (Deadlock)	give in	King Solomon gets the baby (2, 3)	baby is given to real mother (1, 4)
	stand firm	*baby is given to impos-ter mother (4, 2)*	baby is cut in two (3, 1)

Nash equilibrium in bold italics text

FIGURE 7.2

There is a Nash equilibrium in this game, and that is for the imposter mother to stand firm while the real mother gives in. King Solomon, who was a wise king, understood the nature of the game and gave the baby to the real mother. Game theorists have a name for this game that is a cross between Deadlock and Chicken: it's called Bully. In the classic example of dividing the baby, the imposter mother bullied the real mother into giving up her child, but King Solomon called out the bully.

Today, dividing historic Palestine into two contiguous states is no longer an option, so in this sense the 'splitting the baby' analogy breaks down somewhat. The territory over which the Palestinian people have any degree of semi-autonomy (Areas A and B of the West Bank) is completely fragmented. The partition dilemma has now been effectively resolved. The only choice that Israel is willing to offer the Palestinians is more coloniza-tion or less colonization. And the only choice available to the Palestinians is to either accept or reject more colonization or less colonization. These choices form the basis for a 2×2 non-zero-sum game with the same pay-out matrix as King Solomon splitting the baby (see figure 7.3).

In this asymmetrical game, the most that the Palestinians can hope to achieve is some form of semi-autonomy in the context of Israeli coloniza-tion. Should Israel decide to offer the Palestinians less autonomy, then this would mean the full colonization of historic Palestine (minus the Gaza

Palestine (Chicken)

		accept colonization	resist colonization
Israel (Deadlock)	offer more autonomy	Palestinian semi-autonomy (2, 3)	mild criticism of Israel (1, 4)
	offer less autonomy	*full colonization of historic Palestine minus the Gaza Strip (4, 2)*	BDS, take Israel to the ICC, another intifada, etc. (3, 1)

Nash equilibrium in bold italics text

FIGURE 7.3

Strip). Full colonization may take the form of the so-called "Israeli solution," which would involve annexation of the remainder of the West Bank and an offer of residency (but not full citizenship) to all Palestinians (see below). Palestinian acceptance of full colonization by Israel is the Nash equilibrium in this game. Politically, it represents the next stage in the relationship between Israel and Palestine. Should the Palestinian people choose to resist full colonization, then their options would include BDS, lodging a complaint against Israel with the International Criminal Court; another intifada; and so on.

There is one other possibility, however, and that is for Israel to offer more autonomy to the Palestinians and for the Palestinians to accept the offer but to also resist colonization. Obviously if resistance involved anything of a violent or subversive nature, then Israel would not offer more autonomy. In such a case, only mild criticism of Israel would be tolerated. But the most effective form of peaceful protest that the Palestinians can engage in is to simply have more babies.

THE "ISRAELI SOLUTION"

One possible solution to the Israeli-Palestinian conflict, as suggested by American-Israeli journalist Caroline Glick, involves the unilateral imposition of Israeli law on the entire West Bank (but not the Gaza Strip), similar to the imposition of Israeli law in East Jerusalem in 1967 and the Golan Heights in 1981.

There are numerous issues with Glick's so-called "Israeli solution." To begin with, it completely ignores the national rights of the Palestinian people. At a minimum, they should be allowed to decide via a referendum whether they wish to disband the Palestinian Authority and live under Israeli law. The Israeli solution also relies heavily on the theory that the number of Palestinians living in the West Bank has been grossly over-estimated since 1997, when the Palestinian Central Bureau of Statistics (PCBS) assumed responsibility for the collection of demographic data for the state of Palestine. This seems like a bit of wishful thinking. If I were a Palestinian demographer, I would be tempted to systematically *under-represent* the number of Palestinians living in the West Bank so that in the event that an Israeli solution or some other form of one-state formula were ever to be unilaterally imposed in the future, there would be a nice demographic surprise waiting for Israel.

From the database of the Israeli Central Bureau of Statistics (CBS) and the United States Census Bureau, International Programs (USCB), it's possible to reconstruct the Jewish population percentage of an Israeli solution. From a high of 69.52 per cent in 1968, the percentage of Jews in the territory of Israel plus the West Bank (but not including the Gaza Strip) is projected to decline to 53.87 per cent by the year 2050 (see figure 7.4 and Appendix for details; historical data represented by the solid line, projected data by the dashed line).

The situation with the Palestinian Authority is particularly tenuous. The PA is the only legitimate representative of the Palestinian people; once the PA is gone, there will truly be nobody left for Israel to talk to.

In February 2016, the Israeli minister of immigrant absorption and of Jerusalem affairs, Ze'ev Elkin (Likud), gave a speech at Bar-Ilan University warning that the "question is not if the PA collapses but when it is going to collapse. The PA has no mechanism in place to choose a successor once [President] Abbas relinquishes power, which would likely mean that the most probable scenario is a violent succession struggle in the PA."[16] Elkin

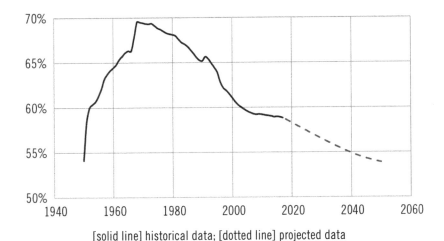

[solid line] historical data; [dotted line] projected data

FIGURE 7.4 PERCENTAGE OF JEWS IN ISRAEL PLUS THE WEST BANK
For calculation details, see Appendix.

SOURCE: Data from the Israeli Central Bureau of Statistics, and the United States Census Bureau (International Programs).

rejected the possibility of a democratic election in the PA, saying that if elections were to take place, that Hamas would likely win. "Most of the Fatah candidates will never win an election against Hamas. The only one who will is in Israeli jail—Marwan Barghouti."

In September 2018, Commanders for Israel's Security (a group of retired generals from Israel's various security agencies), reinforced by leading private sector and academic experts as well as senior veterans of other government institutions, published the results of a year-long study—unprecedented in scope—of the entire spectrum of ramifications of Israeli annexation of the West Bank.[17] The report was highly critical of the Israeli government's lack of any clear policy regarding the future of the area, as well as its lack of any comprehensive, in-depth analysis of the security, diplomatic, economic, legal, and social implications of annexation.

Briefly, the report concluded that creeping and legislated annexation of Area C could set in motion a cascade of events that would end with widespread violence, collapse of the Palestinian Authority, collapse of coordination and co-operation between Israeli and Palestinian security services, reoccupation of Areas A and B by the IDF, institution of military administration in Areas A and B, pressure to dissolve the military administration and demand for equal rights, full annexation and the reluctant granting of permanent residency to some 2.6 million West Bank Palestinians, an economic cost to Israel of some $14.5 billion annually (due to the cessation of international support for the Palestinians—Israel would now have to bear the full cost of all basic services including health, education, and infrastructure), the transformation of Israel into 'an apartheid state,' civil war, and finally the granting of Israeli citizenship to 2.9 million Palestinians in the West Bank and East Jerusalem. This last stage would mark the undisputed end of political Zionism.

Post-Zionism doesn't begin suddenly (the steep erosion of minority rights in Israel, and the creeping and legislated annexation of Area C are already underway). Post-Zionism is a gradual process that will eventually reach a tipping point. The tipping point could be anything from an accidental collision between an IDF truck and a Palestinian car (as in the case of the First Intifada), the poorly timed visit of an Israeli government official to an Islamic holy site (as in the case of the Second Intifada), or the spontaneous collapse of the Palestinian Authority.

Chapter 8

THE DEMOGRAPHIC DEADLOCK

In the mythology of the Zionist movement, Eretz Yisrael has the capacity to absorb millions of Jews—returning after two thousand years of exile—only to make the desert bloom and bring about the return of even more Jews to Eretz Yisrael. In the Jewish text *Pirkei Avot* (Ethics of the Fathers), we read that one of the ten miracles of the Holy Temple was that "they stood crowded but had ample space in which to prostrate themselves."

Today, the Land is full; there are now over thirteen million people living in historic Palestine, and it's doubtful that many more can be accommodated without everyone suffering a collective drop in their standard of living—Jews and non-Jews alike. Such a dystopian future—a future in which the addition of *more* Jews to Eretz Yisrael would *subtract* from the well-being of the Jewish collective (never mind the Palestinian collective)—was never imagined by the founders of the Zionist movement. But such a day is already upon us.

A CENTURY OF GEOMETRIC GROWTH IN HISTORIC PALESTINE

How did the Zionist project—from the perspective of the late 1930s—envision the demographics of the future Jewish state? Testifying before the Palestine Royal Commission in 1937, David Ben-Gurion astonished commission members when under questioning he opined that Palestine would one day be home to some six million people. The transcript of his testimony is as follows:

> Ben-Gurion: I have met Aouni Bey Abdul Hadi [a Palestinian political figure] ... He was a man who cannot be bought; he has no office,

and he is an important Arab Nationalist. I thought that if I could come to terms with him, it would be worthwhile to get a man who was not biased, and who could not be bought, and who really cared for the future of the Arab people. It is only if such people come to terms that it is lasting. I said to him: "We are here; we will come here whether you like it or not. You do not like it, and I can understand why you do not like it, but here we are; it is a fact; you will not prevent us from coming; why should we fight each other, perhaps we can help each other." ... I said to him: "As I am being frank with you about our aim, I am telling you that we do not mean to have a spiritual centre in Palestine [in reference to Cultural Zionism]; we want to have millions in Palestine; we do not want to be here at your mercy; we want to be a free people." He asked me, "How many do you think you can have here?" I said: "In this part of the world, at least four million."

Sir Horace Rumbold: Four million in Palestine?

Ben Gurion: Yes.

Sir Laurie Hammond: Total population is that?

Ben Gurion: No, I mean Jews. I am telling you what I said to him. This is my conviction, that in this part of the country, Palestine, we can bring in at least four million.

The prediction was astounding, and the committee seemed momentarily hard of hearing. "Four million Jews?" the chairman repeated.

"Yes," Ben-Gurion assured him, but "not in one year, or even in ten years, but perhaps in thirty or forty years." Next, he was asked how many Arabs.

Ben-Gurion: At that time there will be about two million Arabs.

Question: A total population of six million?

Ben-Gurion: Yes. I believe in time, with modern methods of industry, Haifa will be a town of one million Jews. It may sound ridiculous to you; perhaps it is ridiculous, but we are an optimistic people. I remember that when I came to Palestine what is now Tel-Aviv was sand. Probably an economic expert would have said, "To build a city here, it is mad." But we were mad, and we were ridiculed, but we had to do it and we did it; we have to do it.

Ben-Gurion's confident optimism was echoed by his political rival, Ze'ev Jabotinsky, who also testified before the Peel Commission:

> Mr. Jabotinsky: The term "Palestine," when I employ it, will mean the area on both sides of the Jordan, the area mentioned in the original Palestine Mandate. That area is about three times the size of, say, Belgium. We maintain that the absorptive capacity of a country depends, first of all, on the human factor: it depends on the quality of its people or of its colonizers, and it depends on a second human factor, the political regime under which that colonization is either encouraged or discouraged to go on … An area of Palestine's size populated at the rather moderate density of, say, Wales can hold eight million inhabitants; populated at the density of Sicily can hold twelve million inhabitants; populated at the density of England proper, or of Belgium, which is, of course, a very exceptional case, it could hold eighteen million inhabitants … Palestine is good for holding the one million present Arab population, plus one million economic places reserved for their progeny, plus many millions of Jewish immigrants—and plus peace.

In 1937, the population of the original Palestine Mandate was roughly 1.5 million (800,000 Arabs[1] and 400,000 Jews[2] in Mandatory Palestine, plus 300,000 Arabs in Trans-Jordan). Today, it hovers around twenty-three million people, which exceeds Jabotinsky's "very exceptional case" scenario by over 25 per cent.

MEETING AND EXCEEDING ALL DEMOGRAPHIC PROJECTIONS

Both Ben-Gurion and Jabotinsky were confident that historic Palestine could accommodate four million Jews. The four million number was eventually reached in the early 1990s. They also seemed to agree on the idea of two million Arabs living in historic Palestine. That number was reached a decade earlier, in 1980.

With four million Jews and two million Arabs living in historic Palestine, under a Zionist ideal case scenario, the percentage of Jews would be 67 per cent. This seems to be a number that both Ben-Gurion and Jabotinsky were comfortable with. But over the past eight decades, just as historic Palestine's Jewish population has grown, so too has its non-Jewish population—and at a faster rate. By 2005, the two populations were roughly equal in number,[3,4] which is a scenario that both Ben-Gurion and Jabotinsky had hoped to avoid because a Jewish state without a Jewish majority isn't really a Jewish state.

Figure 8.1 depicts the Jewish and non-Jewish mid-year populations of historic Palestine from 1920 to 2017. (Details of how these numbers were derived are given in the Appendix section.)

We can see that in 1951 the Jewish population of historic Palestine surpassed the non-Jewish population, but that in recent years the Jewish and non-Jewish population curves have almost converged.

Figure 8.2 depicts the percentage of Jewish nationals living in historic Palestine from 1920 to 2017. This is merely a different way of presenting the same data as in figure 8.1.

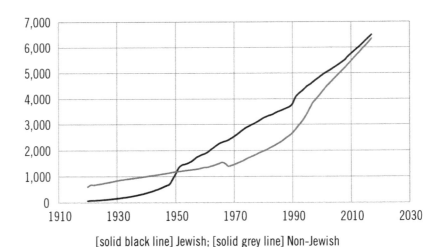

[solid black line] Jewish; [solid grey line] Non-Jewish

FIGURE 8.1 POPULATION OF HISTORIC PALESTINE (THOUSANDS), 1920–2017
For calculation details, see Appendix.

SOURCE: Data from the British Census of Palestine (1922 and 1931), the Israeli Central Bureau of Statistics, and the United States Census Bureau (International Programs).

In 1951, the percentage of Jewish nationals living in historic Palestine exceeded 50 per cent for the first time in nearly two thousand years. The percentage peaked in 1973 at 63.53 per cent and has been steadily dropping since (save for a little bump in the early 1990s due to an influx of Russian Jews). It's currently hovering just above 50 per cent, right back where it was in the early 1950s.

What is the cause of the relative decline of the Jewish population? The question really needs to be asked the other way around: what is the cause of the relative strength of the non-Jewish population?

The answer is quite simple, and it has to do with income. According to the World Bank, the Gross National Income (GNI) per capita of Palestine is less than *one-tenth* of the GNI per capita of Israel ($3,100 vs $37,270), and poverty is universally associated with a high fertility rate. As things currently stand, the fertility rate in the Palestinian Territories (the West Bank and the Gaza Strip) is 4.1 children per woman in her child-bearing years, compared to an average Israeli fertility rate of 3.1, which is the highest of any OECD country, and well above the replacement rate of 2.1 (see figure 8.3).[5] These are the most recent fertility rates; the historical fertility rates have been even higher, in particular for the West Bank and the Gaza Strip.

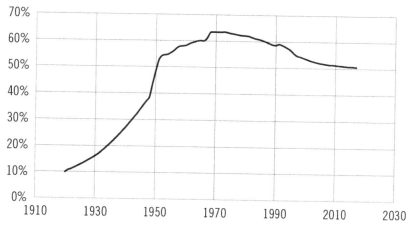

FIGURE 8.2 PERCENTAGE OF JEWS IN HISTORIC PALESTINE, 1920–2017

SOURCE: Data from the British Census of Palestine (1922 and 1931), the Israeli Central Bureau of Statistics, and the United States Census Bureau (International Programs).

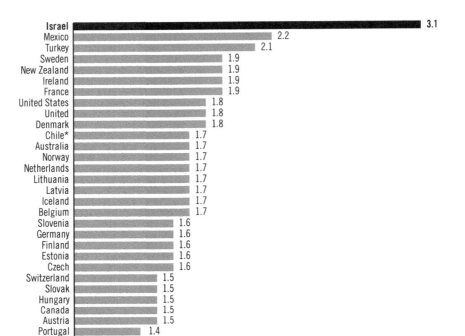

FIGURE 8.3 FERTILITY RATES IN OECD COUNTRIES, 2016

SOURCE: Dan Ben-David, Shoresh Institution and Tel Aviv University. Data: OECD.

Used with permission of the Shoresh Institution.

If Jewish Israelis would like to see a reduction in the fertility rate of the non-Jewish population of historic Palestine (including Palestinian citizens of Israel), then the simplest intervention would be to implement policies that raise the standard of living of the non-Jewish population (i.e., steady jobs, good housing, good public health, and modern education). But instead of helping to create a prosperous Palestinian middle class (on both sides of the Green Line), Israel has chosen to offer financial incentives and free fertility treatments to the Haredi population, who are mostly content with living in poverty and having an average of 7.1 children per woman of child-bearing age (which is on par with the fertility rate of Niger—which has the highest fertility rate in the world).

In 1798, just as the Industrial Revolution was getting underway, Thomas Robert Malthus published *An Essay on the Principle of Population*, in which he observed that throughout history population growth tends to follow a geometric pattern, whereas food production follows an arithmetic pattern. This leads to recurrent periods where population outstrips food supply, otherwise known as periodic famines. During the famine, the population is reduced and once again there is sufficient food for everyone. These so-called Malthusian traps have been greatly reduced by modern farming practices, but they continue to occur at the margins of society. Today, both the Haredi and the Palestinian populations of historic Palestine are living in the same sort of Malthusian trap as their ancestors did.

SEVENTY YEARS OF GEOMETRIC GROWTH IN ISRAEL PROPER

Figure 8.4 depicts the Jewish and non-Jewish populations of Israel proper from 1948 through 2017.[6]

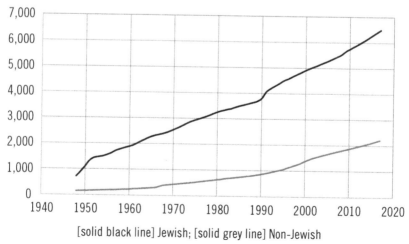

[solid black line] Jewish; [solid grey line] Non-Jewish

FIGURE 8.4 POPULATIONS OF ISRAEL (THOUSANDS), 1948–2017

SOURCE: Data from the Israeli Central Bureau of Statistics.

The percentage of Jews in Israel proper over the same time period is presented in figure 8.5.[7] Note, in particular, that since 1967 this number has included all settlers living in East Jerusalem plus the West Bank plus the Golan Heights, as well as Palestinian residents of East Jerusalem who have Israeli residency or citizenship.

In 2017, for instance, 1.818 million Arabs were living in Israel proper at the midpoint of the year. Let's put that number into critical perspective: that's about as many Arabs as there were Jews living in Israel in 1959, when Israel was 89 per cent Jewish.

The number of Arabs living in Israel proper has never been as high as it is today, and it's not about to decrease anytime soon because the Arab birth rate continues to be higher than the Jewish birth rate. At present, one in five Israelis is Palestinian, and one in four is non-Jewish—and this despite a fertility rate of more than seven children per woman of child-bearing age among the million-strong Haredi community.[8] (See figure 8.6.)

Taken together, these graphs illustrate the failure of the Zionist project to establish a stable Jewish majority in Eretz Yisrael after more than a century of continuous effort. At no point between 1937 and 2017 was there

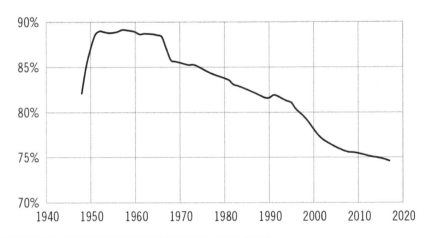

FIGURE 8.5 PERCENTAGE OF JEWS IN ISRAEL, 1948–2017

SOURCE: Data from the Israeli Central Bureau of Statistics.

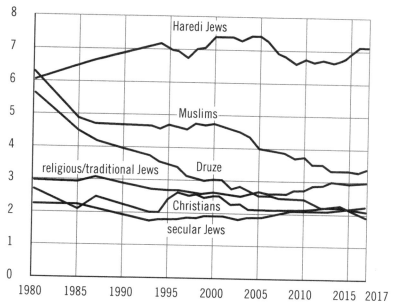

FIGURE 8.6 FERTILITY RATES IN ISRAEL, 1980–2017

SOURCE: Dan Ben-David, Shoresh Institution, and Tel Aviv University. Data: Central Bureau of Statistics and Hleihl (2017). Used with permission of the Shoresh Institution.

ever a two-thirds Jewish majority in the whole of Palestine, which was Ben-Gurion and Jabotinsky's comfort zone.

At some point in the future, however, the Jewish majority in Israel proper may dip below the 67 per cent mark (it's less than ten points away from there already).

THE SPECTACULAR GROWTH OF THE HAREDI COMMUNITY

Speaking at the Herzliya Conference in 2015 (widely regarded as Israel's centre stage for articulating national policy, and hosted every year by the Interdisciplinary Center in Herzliya), Israeli president Reuven Rivlin described his country as a

reality in which there is no longer a clear majority, nor clear minority groups. A reality in which Israeli society is comprised of four population sectors, or, if you will, four principal "tribes," essentially different from each other, and growing closer in size. Whether we like it or not, the make-up of the "stakeholders" of Israeli society, and of the State of Israel, is changing before our eyes.[9]

A typical Israeli cohort of first graders in 1990 was comprised of 52 per cent secular Jews (*Mamlachti*), 16 per cent national religious Jews (*Mamlachti dati*), 9 per cent Haredi Jews, and 23 per cent Arabs—each with their own separate education system and curriculum. Fast-forward twenty-five years to 2015, and the typical Israeli cohort of first graders is now comprised of 38 per cent secular Jews, 15 per cent national religious Jews, 22 per cent Haredi Jews, and 25 per cent Arabs. This represents a *huge* shift in Israeli demographics over a very short time frame. The potential impact on the future of the country is profound. The secular, national religious, and Arab tracks produce citizens who are more or less equipped to deal with modernity. The Haredi track, which continues to receive generous subsidies from the state, does not. By age fourteen, most Haredi boys have all but ceased their secular studies.

Haredi schools exist in other jurisdictions throughout the world, most notably in the United States, the United Kingdom, and Canada, but they receive no public funding, and must always teach a curriculum that meets the minimum state, local, or provincial standards. In Israel, Haredi schools receive state funding and teach a core curriculum that hasn't changed much since the late seventeenth century. To many people's embarrassment, the modern Jewish state has become a supporter and enabler of an anti-modern education track that could one day threaten the state's very existence.

Why is Israel—an OECD country and so-called modern state—using public funds to deliberately exclude a portion of her population from the twenty-first century? This trend, by the way, is now irreversible. The Haredim currently hold enough political power to keep their children ignorant of modernity for generations to come (in August 2016, the

Knesset passed legislation to exempt Haredi schools from teaching core curriculum subjects such as Hebrew and English language skills, science, and mathematics).[10]

The Israeli educational system has yielded to religious political pressure since at least the late 1970s, when laws were enacted that resulted in a large increase in the number of Yeshiva students. Since then, the country has completely failed to enforce a modern, national curriculum that is incumbent on all her students. As a result of the more than doubling of the Haredi population between 1990 and 2015, more and more Israeli students lack any foundational knowledge in mathematics, science, world history, world literature, English, or civics. Some critics regard this deliberate withholding of a well-rounded education in Haredi schools to be a form of child abuse.[11] This is not some wild argument.

In order to pursue higher education in Israel, students must first pass the *Bagrut* matriculation examination, but this is not the same as obtaining a high school diploma from the state. The Bagrut is analogous to the New York State Regents Examination, or the British A-levels. In 2014, an average of 52.7 per cent of Israeli high school graduates were eligible to receive a Bagrut certificate,[12] but in the Haredi community of Modi'in Ilit in 2012, the Bagrut pass rate was only 9 per cent.[13] That same year, there were only six thousand Haredim pursuing higher education in all of Israel,[14] and only a handful were enrolled in research universities.

In Israel, most students who wish to attend university must first complete compulsory military service, which is three years for men and two years for women. Haredim and Palestinian Israelis, who will soon make up half of Israel's population, don't usually serve in the army. A freshman class in a mixed Israeli university, such as the University of Haifa, typically consists of Arab men and women who are three years and two years younger, respectively, than their Jewish counterparts; and very exceptionally, one or two Haredim. This has profound impacts on mixing and socialization across President Rivlin's four "tribes."

HOW DID ISRAEL LET THIS HAPPEN?

The present situation with the Haredi community is essentially a creation of the state of Israel and her system of democracy. For instance, according to an article in *The Economist* in June 2015 about Haredi Jews and unemployment,

> at the state's foundation in 1948, Israel's first prime minister, David Ben-Gurion, accepted the rabbis' request to be allowed to rebuild the yeshivas which had been destroyed in the Holocaust in Europe. A first quota of 400 yeshiva students was exempted from military service. In 1977 the first Likud government, in which Haredi parties were coalition partners, removed that cap. Successive governments have expanded funding for yeshiva stipends as well as benefits for large families.[15]

After graduating from Yeshiva, Haredi married men typically join a *kollel*, where they continue to study Torah for up to eighteen hours a day, living off a meager stipend augmented by state subsidies and whatever income their wives can bring in. If a yeshiva or kollel student tries to legally enter the labour market or to learn other skills, he risks losing what little financial support he may receive from his community. It's a formula for multi-generational poverty.

The employment participation rate for Haredi men between ages 25 and 64 in 2014 was only 45.2 per cent, compared to a participation rate of 86 per cent among non-Haredi male Jews of a similar age (and lower than for any other group except for Arab women).[16] Poverty rates among the Haredi have been increasing since 2000. In 2013, 66.1 per cent of Haredi families lived below the poverty line.[17] It's not unusual to find entire Haredi families in Israel living in rented storage lockers in underground parking garages.

"From an economic viewpoint," commented President Rivlin in his Herezilya Conference speech of 2015, "the current reality is not viable." Furthermore,

[the] mathematics is simple, any child can see it. If we do not reduce the current gaps in the rate of participation in the work force and in the salary levels of the Arab and Haredi populations—who are soon to become one half of the work force—Israel will not be able to continue to be a developed economy. The severe and painful epidemic of poverty that is already having a major effect in Israel, will only expand and worsen. From a political viewpoint, Israeli politics to a great extent is built as an inter-tribal *zero-sum game*. [emphasis added]

THE QUIET GROWTH OF THE PALESTINIAN ISRAELI SECTOR

The Palestinian Israeli sector, as a result of many years of neglect and fear, has evolved a sort of cultural autonomy within Israeli society. Writing in *Haaretz* in 2016, David Rosenberg commented that Palestinian Israelis

are educated in their own schools in their own language, they are subject to Muslim (or Christian) religious law on personal status issues and they live for the most part in their own self-governing towns. There are no bans on minarets as there are in Switzerland or the veil as in the case in France, Belgium and the Netherlands. Arabic is an official language and appears on road signs and product labels. Muslim Arabs aren't drafted into the army.

Arabs are less likely than Jews to hold a job, and Arab women are the least likely of all. The poverty rate for Arabs is nearly four times as high as it is for Jews. Arabs perform worse than Jews on standardized school exams, and far fewer finish high school ready to go on to higher education. Arab towns get much less money for infrastructure and services, they have less land available for expanding and are not served well by public transportation.

In addition to not serving in the Israeli army, the Haredi and Palestinian Israeli sectors don't define themselves as Zionist. Palestinian Israelis justifiably won't sing Israel's national anthem, "Hatikvah," the first two lines of which read, "As long as in the heart, within / A Jewish soul still yearns." ("Hatikvah" was adopted at the First Zionist Congress in 1897 and its melody bears a strong resemblance to "The Moldau" by Czech composer Bedřich Smetana.)

The Start-up Nation that we keep hearing about is more like "a closed ecosystem where people know each other from the army, hire their friends and help them get funding."[18] According to the CIA World Factbook, "Israel's progressive, globally competitive, knowledge-based technology sector employs only about 8 percent of the workforce, with the rest mostly employed in manufacturing and services—sectors which face downward wage pressures from global competition. Expenditures on educational institutions remain low compared to most other OECD countries with similar GDP per capita."[19]

Israel's dependency ratio (ratio of the population aged 0–14 and 65+ to the population aged 15–64) is the highest of any OECD country (see figure 8.7). This problem is compounded by (1) the high proportion of working-age population that's not participating in the labour force (i.e., the Haredi and Palestinian Israeli communities), and (2) Israel's overall low literacy and numeracy scores compared to other OECD countries (see figure 8.8). "Israel's Arabic-speaking children account for a quarter of its first graders. Their average scores in math, science and reading in international exams are below those of many Third World countries. In fact, their scores are below those of most predominantly Muslim countries."[20]

In 2018, Prof. Dan Ben-David of the Shoresh Institution for Socioeconomic Research and the Department of Public Policy at Tel Aviv University issued a report entitled "Overpopulation and demography in Israel." The report noted that the

> majority of Haredi children—who account for almost one-fifth of Israel's first graders—do not even participate in the international exams (and thus, do not lower even further the already low national average to a level that would more accurately reflect the true state of education in Israel). Nearly all of the boys do not study any core curriculum subjects beyond eighth grade, and even what they do study until that juncture is quite partial (no English, no science and only rudimentary

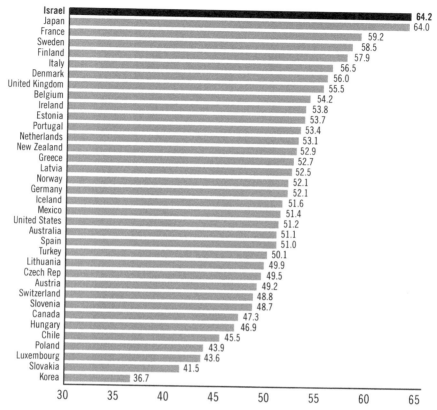

FIGURE 8.7 OECD COUNTRIES RANKED BY DEPENDENCY RATIO, 2015: RATIO OF POPULATION AGED 0–14 AND 65+ PER 100 POPULATION AGED 15–64

SOURCE: Dan Ben-David, Shoresh Institution and Tel Aviv University. Used with permission of the Shoresh Institution.

math) … the population groups with the highest fertility rates in Israel are receiving an education that will not enable them to support a developed economy in the future—with all of the national security implications that this will have on Israel's future ability to exist in the most violent region on the planet.

On the one hand, the country has adopted developed country norms stipulating that a child's basic right to an education requires mandatory school attendance. On the other hand, Israel is the only

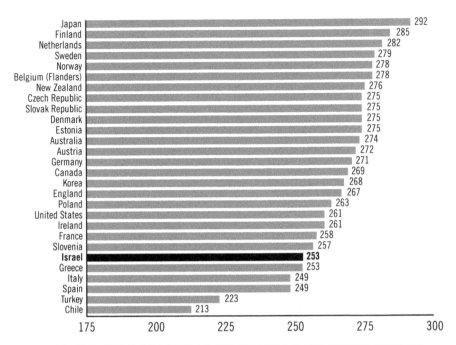

FIGURE 8.8 OECD COUNTRIES RANKED BY AVERAGE SCORE IN LITERACY AND NUMERACY PROFICIENCY, 2011–2014: P1AAC EXAM, 16–64 YEAR OLDS

SOURCE: Dan Ben-David, Shoresh Institution and Tel Aviv University. Data: OECD.

Used with permission of the Shoresh Institution.

developed country that allows parents to systematically deprive their children of a core curriculum that will provide them with tools and employment options in the future. As if this were not enough, Israel also provides varying degrees of funding for schools that do not teach a core curriculum.[21]

TWO TECTONIC DIVIDES: ZIONISM AND RELIGIOUS OBSERVANCE

Two tectonic divides now run orthogonally through Israeli society, fracturing it into four quadrants. One divide is between Zionists and those indifferent to Zionism[22] (the Haredi and the Palestinian Israeli sectors), and the other divide is along religious and secular lines within the

Jewish community itself. According to President Rivlin's numbers, the religiously educated sector (National Religious plus Haredi) now constitutes 37 per cent of the young population, compared to 38 per cent for the secular Jewish sector. This represents an equal split between these two groups—and a huge shift from just a couple of decades ago, not to mention the political Zionism of Theodor Herzl.

Another important study, published in 2018 by Shmuel Rosner and Camil Fuchs, looks not at the divisions that will characterize future generations of Israelis, but at the present generation.[23] Rosner and Fuchs describe a sector that they refer to as *Jewsraelis*: Jewish Israelis who identify with both Jewish tradition and nationalist identity, and who now make up 55 per cent of adult Jewish Israeli society. The other categories of the Rosner/Fuchs classification include 17 per cent Jews (religious but not nationalist, i.e., Haredim), 15 per cent Israelis (nationalist but who do not observe religious tradition), and 13 per cent Universalists (neither religious nor nationalist, i.e., the Tel Aviv crowd).

Historically, Israel has always regarded herself as a predominantly secular society. But as of 2018, this was no longer the case, which represents a huge paradigm shift. Today, the average Israeli adult is more politically right-wing and more likely to observe some degree of religious tradition than even a generation ago (even if they are also more religiously tolerant).

VOLUNTEERS OR FREE-RIDERS?

Haredi demographics long ago exceeded anything that Herzl or Ben-Gurion could have ever imagined. From a game theory perspective, Haredi Jews see themselves as volunteers in a Volunteer's Dilemma, having assumed the burden of studying Torah for the benefit of all Jews.

Secular Jews, on the other hand, see the Haredim as free-riders, draining the resources of the Israeli welfare state without contributing to either the economy or the state's defence. But the truth is that the Haredim are both at the same time; and their numbers continue to grow because their rabbis, in collusion with the state, encourage them to follow a high fertility strategy.

This is a serious matter. Demographic trends now threaten to erode the 'public good' of Israeli civil society even further. In 1947, when Ben-Gurion negotiated the status quo agreement with the Haredi community, there were only about 3,500 Torah scholars who qualified for exemption from the IDF. Today, there are over a million Haredim in Israel, and the country has four distinct educational streams that produce four very different civic and cultural experiences. The failure to create a single, unified educational system is yet one more indication that Israel remains an unfinished country even to this day.

THE IMPACT OF UNRESTRAINED POPULATION GROWTH ON THE ENVIRONMENT

The Middle East has always been an environmentally sensitive area. The Fertile Crescent witnessed the birth of agriculture some ten thousand years ago, and today, much like in the past, it must deal with issues of overcrowding, resource depletion, and environmental degradation.

Israel's self-recognized territory is 22,072 square kilometres (if you include East Jerusalem and the Golan Heights, which were annexed in 1967 and 1981, respectively), and her population, according to the 2018 edition of CIA World Factbook[24] is 8.816 million (this includes the Jewish Israeli population of 391,000 living in the West Bank and 201,000 living in East Jerusalem). The West Bank and the Gaza Strip cover an area of some 6,020 square kilometres and are home to 4.244 million Palestinians. This means that within the territory of historic Palestine plus the Golan Heights, there was a population of some 13.06 million in 2018.

The population density of historic Palestine, around 465 persons per square kilometre in 2018, is higher than in India. Belgium, by comparison, which was mentioned by Jabotinsky in his testimony before the Peel Commission, had a population density of 374 persons per square kilometre in 2018. If historic Palestine were to become a single state (the one-state solution), then it would be the fourth most-densely populated country in the world among countries with a population over ten million. But in the Gaza Strip, where the population density is already *more than five thousand persons per square kilometre*, the situation is nothing short of a human catastrophe.

Figure 8.9 shows the total population of historic Palestine from 1920 to 2017.[25]

We can see from this graph that the population has grown geometrically over the past century. From 673,200 in 1920 to over 13 million in 2017, the implied growth rate is 3.1 per cent per year. If this trend were to continue much longer, the population of historic Palestine would exceed the carrying capacity of the Land in very short order. If we factor in the threat of climate change, which is very real in the Mediterranean Basin,[26] then it's probably there already.

A report issued by Israel's Ministry of Environmental Protection in 2013 warned that more than five million Israelis (more than half the country) are at risk of "severe flooding events" due to climate change.[27] Other risks associated with flooding include outbreaks of transmissible diseases, including mosquito-borne diseases, and contamination of aquifers.

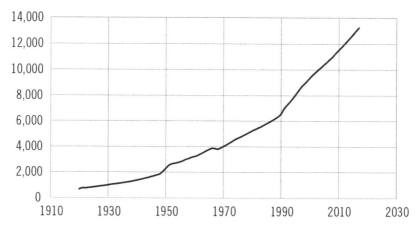

FIGURE 8.9 TOTAL POPULATION OF HISTORIC PALESTINE (THOUSANDS), 1920–2017

SOURCE: Data from the British Census of Palestine (1922 and 1931), the Israeli Central Bureau of Statistics, and the United States Census Bureau (International Programs).

As things currently stand, Israel experiences a high level of food security, but it is no longer self-sufficient when it comes to food production. Energy self-sufficiency has always been an issue (notwithstanding the recent discoveries of offshore natural gas), and Israel relies heavily on desalination technology for her agriculture and drinking water. A computer virus in a desalination plant could wreak havoc on the population and the economy. Israel's coastal aquifer is already threatened, as are many of the country's wildlife reserves. Her roads and transportation networks are notoriously congested; her schools and hospitals are demonstrably overcrowded.

Historic Palestine is also an "energy island," meaning that there are very limited interconnections with neighbouring countries. Israel is not electrically connected at the transmission level to any Middle Eastern country, but it's electrically connected to Greece via a submarine cable. Palestine is essentially totally dependent on Israel for electricity, either transmitted or as oil supply to the Gaza power plant (there is a small Egypt-Gaza interconnect). And the electrical supply situation in Gaza is particularly poor at 1,092 kWh/person/year compared to 5,437 kWh/person/year in the EU, or 6,058 kWh/person/year in Israel.

FOR HOW MUCH LONGER WILL ISRAEL BE A SAFE HAVEN FOR THE JEWISH PEOPLE?

For over a century now, one of the key assumptions of the Zionist movement was that the Jewish state would be available as a home, or safe haven, to all of the world's Jews should the need ever arise. This forms the basis for a social contract between Israel and the Jewish Diaspora (and the multi-billion-dollar American Jewish charity industry[28]). As things currently stand, however, Israel barely has the capacity to maintain the standard of living of her 8.816 million Jewish and non-Jewish citizens, let alone the 6.5 million Jews who live in the Diaspora (should they ever decide to move to Israel). And in order to maintain her current standard of living, Israel must literally steal land and water from the Palestinians. Add to this: (1) an average Israeli fertility rate of 3.1 per woman of child-bearing age (which is the highest of any OECD country, and a full child per family higher than the number two country, Mexico); (2) a per capita IVF rate that is the highest of any OECD country; and (3) the numerous difficulties and challenges that women age 19–40 face getting an abortion—and you have a formula for intractable overcrowding and ecological stress, not only in historic Palestine but also in Israel proper. In other words, a Malthusian trap.

Again, this is not some wild argument. In 2017, the Central Bureau of Statistics predicted that Israel's population would hit eighteen million by 2059.[29] That's more than double the 2017 population in just over four decades. Half the population in 2059 will be either Haredi or Arab, which means that unlike today, the Jewish state of the future will be just as poor as the shtetlech of nineteenth-century Eastern Europe.

My own projections are just as scary. Based on the United States Census Bureau's demographic projections for Israel, the West Bank, and the Gaza Strip, I was able to estimate the Jewish and non-Jewish populations of historic Palestine going out to 2050 (see Appendix for details of the calculations; historical data represented by the solid line, projected data by the dashed line). Figure 8.10 gives us a reasonable glimpse of what the future might look like.

From this chart, we can see two crossovers between Jewish and non-Jewish populations in historic Palestine. The first occurred in 1951, when the Jewish population surpassed the non-Jewish population, and the second is expected to occur some seventy years later, in 2021, when the number of non-Jews is projected to exceed the number of Jews once again. By 2050, the total population of historic Palestine could well reach 19.6 million, which is roughly 53 per cent higher than the 2017 level.

And the projections in figure 8.11 bode ill for Jewish sovereignty within Israel proper (once again, see the Appendix for details of the calculations; historical data represented by the solid line, projected data by the dashed line).

If current Jewish and non-Jewish demographic trends continue, the percentage of Jews in Israel proper may only be slightly above the

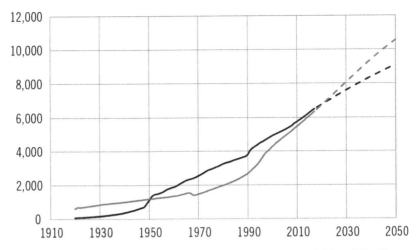

[solid black] Jewish historical; [solid grey] Non-Jewish historical; [dotted black] Jewish projected; [dotted grey] Non-Jewish projected

FIGURE 8.10 POPULATION OF HISTORIC PALESTINE (THOUSANDS), 1920–2050
For calculation details, see Appendix.

SOURCE: Data from the British Census of Palestine (1922 and 1931), the Israeli Central Bureau of Statistics, and the United States Census Bureau (International Programs).

two-thirds mark by 2050. By this time, the percentage of Jews living in historic Palestine will be well below 50 per cent. What will be the impact on Israeli democracy when Jews make up only two-thirds of all Israelis? Will 40 of the Knesset's 120 seats be set aside for non-Jews? (To even pose this question is to risk inducing a state of apoplexy in some individuals.) And what about the recently passed Nation-State Law? How long can Israel continue *not* to be a "state for all its citizens" when a third of them will be non-Jews?

WE ARE NOW LIVING IN THE POST-ZIONIST ERA

Political Zionism attempted to achieve four goals simultaneously: (1) the creation of a sovereign and democratic Jewish state (2) in the Land of Israel, with (3) a Jewish majority (that respects minority rights) and (4) the capacity to absorb all the Exiles (i.e., the Jewish Diaspora) should they ever wish to, or need to, return to Eretz Yisrael.

MICHAEL DAN

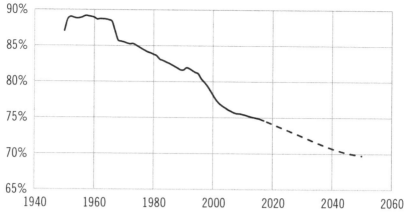

[solid line] historical data; [dotted line] projected data

FIGURE 8.11 PERCENTAGE OF JEWS IN ISRAEL, 1950–2050
For calculation details, see Appendix.

SOURCE: Data from the Israeli Central Bureau of Statistics.

By virtue of their interdependence, it's clear that if even one of these four goals is rendered unachievable then all of them are, and the Zionist project will never be fully realized.

Today, there is little doubt that Israel is a sovereign state, recognized in international law, and with normal relations with many other nations of the world including two Arab states. As a member of the OECD, Israel also has the most democratic institutions and the most diversified economy in the Middle East. Israel has much to be proud of, but some fifty years after asserting control over the whole of historic Palestine, Israel has already had to give up civil control over significant portions of that territory (including Areas A and B of the West Bank, and the entire Gaza Strip). This means that *the Zionist dream of a Jewish state, with a Jewish majority, in the whole of historic Palestine will likely never be fulfilled.*

Paradoxically, Israel is alive and thriving, but political Zionism is either failing or has already failed.

Two concepts that are easily conflated—but in the negative sense—are antisemitism and anti-Zionism. These are not the same concepts in the positive sense (i.e., philosemitism is not the same as Zionism), so why would their opposites be regarded as the same? There are plenty of Jews who are indifferent or even opposed to the settler movement, so does that make them bad Jews? Instead of conflating Judaism with Zionism, or Israel with Zionism, it makes more sense to decouple these terms and face the reality that political Zionism has achieved all it's ever going to achieve, and that we are now living in a post-Zionist era.

Perhaps this is for the better. If the over-arching objective of the Zionist movement is to ensure the long-term survival of the Jewish people, then does it even make sense to concentrate all of them in a hot, overcrowded, resource-poor country in the Middle East with hostile neighbours to the north, northeast, and southwest? Such thinking is both dangerous and messianic. If any of those hostile neighbours were ever to get their hands on nuclear weapons, their dreams of wiping out the entire Jewish people would be all the easier to realize. And if nuclear bombs don't wipe us all out, climate change or global pandemics might just do the trick.

Think of it this way: if there was an active gunman on the loose in your kid's school, would it make sense to assemble all the students in the gym? Herzl's vision was incomplete: the answer to state-sponsored anti-semitism isn't just a Jewish state—it's a *combination* of a Jewish state and a Jewish Diaspora that resides in religiously tolerant *non*-Jewish states.

In this book, I have argued that we came to the post-Zionist era by at least four different routes. Demographics helped to bring us here by creating a situation of near-equality between Jewish and non-Jewish populations in historic Palestine. Those who would dispute these numbers must still contend with a Palestinian population within Israel proper that continues to grow at a faster rate than the Jewish population.

Resolution of the dilemma of Palestinian national legitimacy helped to bring about the post-Zionist era because the Palestinian people are now a de facto reality in international law, recognized by both the state of Israel and the international community. This means that they, too, have a legitimate claim to historic Palestine. Prime Minister Golda Meir's pronouncement in 1969 that there is no such thing as the Palestinian people is, today, demonstrably false.

Partition helped to bring about the post-Zionist era because now that Israel has withdrawn from Areas A and B of the West Bank, as well as the Gaza Strip, there can be no Jewish state in the *whole* of historic Palestine. No amount of denial, delegitimization, or dehumanization of the Palestinian people will change that reality. Historic Palestine is now divided, as are the Palestinian people. Both Israelis and Palestinians alike must contend with the disappointments of a fragmented geography.

And finally, Jewish nationalism and ultranationalism helped to bring about the post-Zionist era by destroying values sacred to Zionism. As previously noted, the Israeli Declaration of Independence—one of the foundational documents of Zionism—favours a two-state solution with an economic union of the whole of Eretz Yisrael, as well as the complete equality of social and political rights of all inhabitants irrespective of religion, race, or sex. Jewish nationalism vehemently opposes these values.

A GAME OF DEADLOCK

The relationship between Jewish and Arab populations in historic Palestine can best be understood as a game of demographic Deadlock. Both sides have an interest in seeing the average fertility rate decline to below 2.1 children per woman of child-bearing age (which is the replacement rate). If this could be achieved, then population levels would stabilize and both Jews and Palestinians would be able to live in historic Palestine in a sustainable manner. Instead, Jewish and Palestinian populations are each competing for numerical superiority. The game may be represented by the payout matrix in figure 8.12.

	Palestinian fertility rate per woman of child-bearing age	
	<2.1	>2.1
Jewish fertility rate per woman of child-bearing age <2.1	both populations sustainable (2, 2)	Palestinian majority (1, 4)
>2.1	Jewish majority (4, 1)	*perpetual growth (3, 3)*

Nash equilibrium in bold italics text

FIGURE 8.12

In Deadlock, the goal is to keep staring at your opponent until they blink. In historic Palestine, this amounts to producing as many babies as possible, regardless of the consequences, in the hope of weakening the other side's resolve—analogous to the staring contest that took place between the Canadian Forces soldier and the First Nations warrior in Oka, Quebec, in 1990.

The Nash equilibrium in the game of perpetual growth is for both the Jewish people and the Palestinian people to engage in a high fertility strategy (i.e., mutual defection). This is precisely the wrong strategy from both a social and environmental perspective since the population density of historic Palestine is already high enough as it is (see figure 8.13).

Absent some monumental co-operation between Jews and Palestinians, the demographic Deadlock won't resolve itself spontaneously. The geometric growth is relentless. This is what President Rivlin meant when he warned that "the mathematics is simple; any child can see it." Israel and Palestine must work together to bring down the average fertility rate in historic Palestine to below 2.1, or a time will come (perhaps twenty years from now?) when every bright young Israeli who has the ability to do so, will simply hop on a plane and go live somewhere else. The ensuing "brain drain" will no doubt drive the demographics even further in the Palestinians' favour. (As things currently stand, there are already over 700,000 Israelis living outside of Israel, mostly in the United States. This amounts to roughly 10 per cent of the Jewish Israeli population.[30])

     MICHAEL DAN

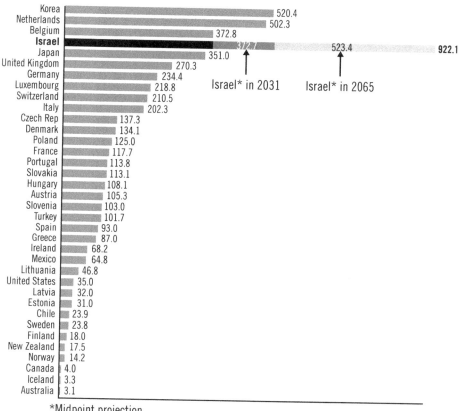

Country	Value
Korea	520.4
Netherlands	502.3
Belgium	372.8
Israel	
Japan	351.0
United Kingdom	270.3
Germany	234.4
Luxembourg	218.8
Switzerland	210.5
Italy	202.3
Czech Rep	137.3
Denmark	134.1
Poland	125.0
France	117.7
Portugal	113.8
Slovakia	113.1
Hungary	108.1
Austria	105.3
Slovenia	103.0
Turkey	101.7
Spain	93.0
Greece	87.0
Ireland	68.2
Mexico	64.8
Lithuania	46.8
United States	35.0
Latvia	32.0
Estonia	31.0
Chile	23.9
Sweden	23.8
Finland	18.0
New Zealand	17.5
Norway	14.2
Canada	4.0
Iceland	3.3
Australia	3.1

Israel* in 2031 → 523.4
Israel* in 2065 → 922.1

*Midpoint projection

FIGURE 8.13 POPULATION DENSITY IN OECD COUNTRIES, INCLUDING PROJECTED POPULATION DENSITY IN ISRAEL: PERSONS PER SQUARE KILOMETRE

SOURCE: Dan Ben-David, Shoresh Institution, and Tel Aviv University. Data: UN and Central Bureau of Statistics. Used with permission of the Shoresh Institution.

DISCOUNTING THE FUTURE

Robert Aumann, the Israeli-American economist who shared the 2005 Nobel Prize for Economics with Thomas Schelling "for having enhanced our understanding of conflict and co-operation through game-theory analysis," has written extensively about war and peace. In his Nobel Prize lecture, aptly entitled "War and Peace,"[31] Aumann discusses how war, far from being an irrational activity, is entirely rational to those who engage in it.

After citing Richard Dawkins, John Maynard Smith, and George Price (see chapter 4), Aumann discusses the relation of co-operative game theory to repeated games. He concludes that repetition acts as an enforcement mechanism: it makes co-operation achievable when it is not achievable in a one-shot game. A concrete example would be the game of Chicken between Israel and Hamas as played out in the Gaza Strip. The Nash equilibrium (in the one-shot game) is for one side to "swerve" while the other drives straight ahead. But in a repeated (iterated) game of Chicken, the equilibrium is for both sides to co-operate by simultaneously swerving. The result is "quiet for quiet," otherwise known as "peace."

Based partly on the results of his research, as well as his deep convictions as a religious Zionist, Aumann has advocated for a strong Israeli military response to any escalations by the Palestininans—which obviously didn't win him many friends among the Israeli left. He vehemently opposed Israel's unilateral withdrawal from the Gaza Strip in 2005 (which occurred just a few months before he was awarded the Nobel Prize), and he has publicly questioned the viability of a secular Zionist state.[32] He concluded his Nobel Prize lecture with the catchy phrase: "Nations must continue to *learn* war, in order *not* to fight."

But Aumann also issues a strong caveat: "In order for this to work, the discount rates of all agents must be low; they must not be too interested in the present as compared with the future." From the Palestinian perspective, the discount rate is not low, but high because Palestinians see a future in which the Jewish population of historic Palestine will soon be outnumbered by the non-Jewish population. Thus, the *economic* (i.e., rational) incentive for war persists, despite Israel's willingness to flex her military muscles in a repeated manner.

A high discount rate also helps to explain the seemingly irrational business of Hamas sending young Palestinians directly into the line of fire during the 2018 border protests. The rationale here is that there will always be more young Palestinians to take their place, and that eventually Israel will have to account for her actions in the international court of public opinion.

Chapter 9

AN ERSATZ PEACE

P eace is a recurring theme in the liturgy of Judaism. In the *Amidah* prayer, which observant Jews recite three times a day, peace is mentioned no less that six different times depending on the time of year the prayer is recited. But what exactly is peace?

Humans seem incapable of understanding the concept of peace except through metaphors. Isaiah 2:4 imagines a utopia in which nations "shall beat their swords into ploughshares and their spears into pruning hooks." The same biblical verse later describes how "nation will not lift up sword against nation and they will no longer study warfare." But peace is much more than just the absence of war; peace also demands that we actively seek *not* to engage in war.

In game theory, Peace may be represented by the 2×2 matrix in figure 9.1.

		Them	
		plough-shares	swords
Us	ploughshares	*4, 4*	3, 1
	swords	1, 3	2, 2

Nash equilibrium in bold italics text

FIGURE 9.1

This is a brilliant, albeit rather concise, representation of humanity's oldest desire: peace between nations. In the mathematics of game theory, Peace is a symmetrical game; both sides have the same preferences and neither side dominates the other. The first choice is to co-operate with a co-operative opponent (which is also the Nash equilibrium), and the last choice is to betray a co-operative opponent by taking up the sword against them. If a peace treaty must be broken, then it must be broken by mutual consent.

But what if peace is simply unattainable? Is there such a thing as "the next best thing to peace"—a form of *ersatz* peace? The answer is "yes," and it's a game called Coordination.

THE IMMOVABLE LADDER

First recorded in an engraving dating from 1728, the Immovable Ladder is a short wooden ladder located just above the entrance to the Church of the Holy Sepulchre in Jerusalem; it rests on an exterior ledge below the right main window (see figure 9.2). It was left there by a stone mason nearly three hundred years ago (nobody is certain of the exact date) and has only been moved twice since. Under the terms of the status quo agreement between the six Christian denominations that share the use of the church, no item may be moved, rearranged, or altered by any one group without the consent of the other five. Due to a long-standing disagreement between the Greek Orthodox Church and the Armenian Orthodox Church over who is responsible for care for the ledge on which the ladder rests, the ladder must not be moved until the question of responsibility is finally settled (the Armenians claim that they are the rightful caretakers of the ledge; the Greeks have asserted jurisdiction over the cornice below the ledge).

During his pilgrimage to the Holy Land in 1964, Pope Paul VI described the ladder as a visible symbol of Christian division. In 1981, an attempt was made to remove the ladder. The Israeli police were called in, but the culprit was never apprehended. In 1997, the ladder was pulled in through the window and hidden behind an altar by a Christian pilgrim who wanted "to make a point of the silliness of the argument over whose ledge it is." It was returned to the ledge a few weeks later, and a grate was installed in the window to prevent the ladder from being pulled in again.

FIGURE 9.2 THE IMMOVABLE LADDER, CHURCH OF THE HOLY SEPULCHRE, JERUSALEM

SOURCE: Michael Dan, 2018.

The Immovable Ladder is an example of a six-person game of Coordination. All six ecumenical Christian orders must reach unanimous consent over the fate of the ladder, or it doesn't get moved.

The simpler two-person game of Coordination has the payout matrix described in figure 9.3 (in this example, I use the Greek Orthodox and the Armenian Orthodox churches, but it could just as well be Israel and Palestine).

The numbering system for the game of Coordination differs only slightly from the game of Peace, but the implications are vast. Coordination, like Peace, is a symmetrical game; one side has no advantage over the

Armenian Orthodox Church

	move ladder	don't move
Greek Orthodox Church move ladder	***4, 4***	2, 1
don't move	1, 2	***3, 3***

Nash equilibria in bold italics text; Pareto-inferior in shaded text

FIGURE 9.3

other. And like the game of Peace, the first choice is to co-operate with a co-operative opponent, and the last choice is to betray the efforts of a co-operative opponent (in this case, by refusing to move the ladder if the other side wants to move it).

But unlike the game of Peace, the game of Coordination has two Nash equilibria: one is for both sides to co-operate (i.e., to move the ladder), and the other is for both sides to betray (i.e., to agree *not* to move the ladder). And this is what makes Coordination such an important game, because in this game it's perfectly acceptable to agree to disagree (which also happens to be a Pareto-inferior outcome). This is what His Holiness Pope Paul VI was alluding to when he stated that the ladder is a symbol of Christian disunity. From a Christian perspective, disunity is always Pareto-inferior to unity.

COORDINATION INSTEAD OF PEACE

Israel and Palestine may not know peace—either politically or in a game theory sense—for a very long time. But they can still coordinate their daily activities. In fact, they do it all the time.

COGAT is the primary unit of the Israeli Ministry of Defense that's responsible for coordinating civilian issues between the Government of Israel, the IDF, various NGOs, diplomats, and the Palestinian Authority. It's also responsible for implementing Israeli government policy in Area C of the West Bank. COGAT stands for Coordinator of Government

Activities in the Territories. The name "coordinator" reflects the important role that COGAT plays as an ersatz peacemaker.

The Shin Bet regularly coordinates its anti-terrorist efforts with the Palestinian Security Services, notably against Hamas. Both could work independently, but this would lead to a Pareto-inferior outcome, similar to the six Christian denominations who all agree to disagree over the issue of the Immovable Ladder. There are many other examples of Israeli and Palestinian coordination, and in the absence of a formal peace agreement, coordination is probably the best that both can do under the circumstances.

Of course, both could choose not to co-operate. And in the game of Coordination this would be an acceptable outcome. But they must not go so far as to undermine each other; that would mean they aren't playing by the rules of the game. In Coordination, it's okay to lead separate lives; it's just not okay to sabotage the other side.

MORE EMPATHY WILL NOT SOLVE THE PROBLEM

In January 2019, Simon Baron-Cohen, an autism researcher at Cambridge University (and cousin of comedian Sasha Baron Cohen), published an article in *The Guardian* entitled, "Only empathy can break the cycle of violence in Israel-Palestine."[1] It's a popular belief that if Israelis and Palestinians could only find enough commonalities, get to know each other a little better, and learn to see each other as fellow human beings, then they would eventually find a way to settle most of their differences. I don't buy the "empathy deficiency" argument, nor do I believe that "dialing up" the empathy from a 2 to a 10 will bring about peace in the Middle East.

From an historical perspective, the Middle East is probably the first place on earth where humans courageously proclaimed the importance of empathy and compassion, equity and justice, mercy and forgiveness. Anyone acquainted with the sacred texts of Judaism, Christianity, and Islam is no doubt familiar with these concepts. Modernity has very little to teach the Middle East about the importance of empathy that isn't already in the Torah, the New Testament, or the Qur'an.

In evolutionary terms, all of this makes perfect sense. The Middle East has always been a harsh and fragile environment. Agriculture developed in the Fertile Crescent ten thousand years ago in part *because* the hunter-gatherer lifestyle could no longer sustain the existing human population. Cultures in the Middle East that failed to evolve large-scale systems of co-operation and social cohesion eventually disappeared, along with the individuals who belonged to those cultures (who died out from either violence or starvation).

Co-operation is now part of the social DNA of every Abrahamic faith, which in part explains the enormous success of these faiths in spreading outside of the Middle East, beginning with Christianity in the first century CE. Why did Christianity spread to Scandinavia, or Islam take root in Indonesia? Game theory suggests that it was because of systems of co-operation and social cohesion that were stronger than the indigenous systems of those regions.

The main reason that there continues to be inequity and injustice, hatred and oppression, dispossession and poverty in the Middle East is not any lack of familiarity with the opposite of these concepts, but because of *systemic and structural factors* that facilitate the persistence of inequity, injustice, hatred, oppression, dispossession, and poverty.

Systemic injustice is common in many colonial and post-colonial societies, and the Middle East is a prime example of both. Israel, as already discussed, is a colonial society that practises systemic injustice towards Palestinians, including her own Palestinian citizens. And Canada is an example of a post-colonial society that, despite its reputation for fairness, continues to practise systemic injustice against Indigenous people.

CANADA'S SYSTEMIC INJUSTICE TOWARDS INDIGENOUS PEOPLE

Prior to the arrival of Europeans in Turtle Island (the Indigenous name for North America), there were approximately two million Indigenous people living in what would later become Canada. Initial encounters between Indigenous peoples and European peoples were mutually respectful. In 1613, the Hodinohso:ni (Iroquois) entered into a "peace and friendship" treaty with the Dutch in the Finger Lakes region of upstate New York. The treaty, which is still in effect today, is represented by a wampum belt with two parallel purple lines, running lengthwise against a white field. The two purple lines represent the Indigenous canoe and the European sailing ship, each travelling along the river of life together, neither touching nor interfering with the other. This was the Hodinohso:hi way of representing the concept of peaceful coexistence.

In 1759, the British defeated the French in a pivotal battle in the Seven Years' War, fought on the Plains of Abraham just outside Quebec City. The Seven Years' War was concluded with the 1763 Treaty of Paris, and France surrendered all her North American possessions to the British except for the tiny islands of St. Pierre and Miquelon, just south of Newfoundland. Chief Pontiac, an Odawa chief and former ally of the French, subsequently incited a rebellion against the British out of fear that they would attack him for having sided with the French during the Seven Years' War.

Pontiac's Rebellion was so successful, it prompted King George III of Great Britain to issue the Royal Proclamation of 1763, which included, as one of its most important features, the recognition of Aboriginal Title. In simple terms, Aboriginal Title is an acknowledgement that the Indigenous people of North America possessed title to the land on which they lived by virtue of having always lived there. One very important aspect of the Royal Proclamation of 1763 is that it prohibited the "sale" of Indigenous land to anyone other than the British Crown. Aboriginal Title could only be extinguished through the treaty process, which involved a nation-to-nation relationship. From 1763 to the present, the Indigenous people of Turtle Island have signed dozens of treaties with the British Crown (initially directly, and later as represented by Canada) based on this nation-to-nation relationship.

Canada passed the Indian Act in 1876 in order to regulate the lives of Indigenous people who, either directly or through their ancestors, had signed treaties with Canada. Although the Indian Act has undergone many revisions over time, it continues to be a racist piece of legislation aimed at controlling the lives of Indigenous people. From the outset, the

Indian Act created a category of individual known as a "Status Indian." At various points in the past, Status Indians were considered to be wards of the Crown and were prohibited from voting in federal elections. If they lived on Indian Reserves, they could not own the land or the homes in which they lived. They could not leave the reserve without the permission of an Indian Agent (i.e., the federal government), hire a lawyer to litigate a land claim without permission, sell produce to non-Indians without permission, attend university or join the armed forces without losing their Indian status, or wear traditional clothing or perform traditional ceremonies of any kind.

The Indian Act created a system of restrictions on the lives of Indigenous people. The system permeated all aspects of Canadian society and continues to do so even today. Prior to contact with Europeans and their infectious diseases (which were previously unknown in North America, and which included smallpox and even the common cold), Indigenous people enjoyed relatively good health. By 1885, the number of Indigenous people in Canada had declined to only 5 per cent of the pre-contact population. Layered on top of this biological catastrophe were the occasionally genocidal practices of the Canadian government, which withheld food rations from starving Plains Indians in order to force them to sign treaties and move onto reserves (this is something that Canada's first prime minister, Sir John A. Macdonald, boasted about in the House of Commons).

Canada's lack of empathy towards Indigenous people didn't reduce their numbers by 95 per cent from pre-contact levels (from two million in 1491 to one hundred thousand in 1885). It was a combination of infectious diseases and a legal system that ensured that Indigenous people would always live in poverty that did it. Today, Indigenous people have made a remarkable comeback, and there are now over 1.5 million living in Canada.

Perhaps there is a lesson here for Israel and Palestine: in Canada, the colonizer was unable to devise a system of oppression capable of eliminating the very last Indian—despite all the help received from some very nasty germs. After a century of Zionist effort, there are now more Palestinians in Palestine than ever before, and there is still no Jewish majority.

EXAMPLES OF ISRAELI-PALESTINIAN EMPATHY, CO-OPERATION, AND COORDINATION

The Baron-Cohen article discussed above mentions the Parents Circle-Family Forum as an example of a grassroots project that attempts to restore empathy between Israelis and Palestinians.[2] There are many such efforts underway, mostly in the health-care and education sectors. Each time I visit Israel, I'm astonished by the quantity and the quality of the projects aimed at building bridges and strengthening civil society (many with the quiet support of both the Israeli and Palestinian governments). Below are just a few examples.

St. John Eye Hospital

The St. John Eye Hospital was established in Jerusalem in 1882, under the patronage of Queen Victoria. Originally dedicated to the treatment of trachoma (an infection of the eye associated with poverty and poor sanitation), the hospital now treats mostly Palestinian patients with cataracts, diabetic retinopathy, and congenital eye diseases (which are especially common in the Palestinian population due to the high level of consanguinity). Today, the St. John of Jerusalem Eye Hospital Group is the only charitable provider of expert eye care in the West Bank, Gaza, and East Jerusalem, treating patients regardless of ethnicity, religion, or ability to pay.[3]

The main hospital, which was built in 1960 in the Sheikh Jarrah neighbourhood of East Jerusalem, maintains close working ties with Hadassah Medical Center, Tel Aviv University, and Soroka Hospital. In 2014, the St. John Eye Hospital saw over 124,000 patients and performed 5,200 sight-saving operations. Their mobile outreach program accounted for 10,500 of the total number of patients treated, and their community health-care program screened 14,700 patients for diabetic retinopathy.[4] In 2012,

4 per cent of the hospital's total expenditure was spent on manage-ment and administration. These costs included managing the hospital in Jerusalem and two static clinics, as well as coordinating two mobile outreach clinics and the medical and nursing training programs. The cost of generating funds represented only 6 per cent of the hospital's total expenditure.[5]

Until his death in 2012, Dr. Saul Merin, professor and head of ophthal-mology at Hadassah Medical Center, and himself a Holocaust survivor, worked closely with colleagues at the St. John Eye Hospital, consulting on difficult cases and training physicians who worked for the Palestinian Authority.

The St. John Eye Hospital opened a new clinic in the Gaza Strip in 2016. The clinic was built with the quiet co-operation and coordination of the Israeli government at a time when the Gaza Strip was under a com-plete land, sea, and air blockade, and when the importation of build-ing materials was strictly prohibited for fear that they would fall into the hands of Hamas. In 2017 alone, the Gaza clinic had seen more than 27,600 patients and performed almost nine hundred operations—cases that would otherwise not have been seen at the main St. John Eye Hospital in East Jerusalem. In 2018, the Gaza clinic treated over 30,200 patients and performed 1,200 major operations.

Augusta Victoria Hospital

Less than two kilometres from the St. John Eye Hospital in East Jerusalem is Augusta Victoria Hospital, currently the sole remaining specialized-care hospital in the Palestinian Territories. It's also the second-largest hospital in East Jerusalem. Completed in 1910 as a centre for the German Protestant community in Ottoman Palestine, the hospital is named for Augusta Viktoria of Schleswig-Holstein, the wife of Kaiser Wilhelm II. Its mission statement includes the provision of health care without regard to race, creed, gender, or national origin. The hospital is primarily financed by the Lutheran World Federation, and the United Nations Relief and Works Agency for Palestine Refugees in the Near East (UNRWA). The pediatric oncology ward of Augusta Victoria, however, was partially funded by the Peres Center for Peace,[6] various Italian foundations, and the Hadassah University Hospital, which also trained the oncologist and nursing staff.

Because they are both located in East Jerusalem, neither the St. John Eye Hospital nor Augusta Victoria Hospital receive a penny from the state of Israel. In August 2018, the Trump administration cut all American funding to a network of East Jerusalem hospitals, including the St. John Eye Hospital and Augusta Victoria Hospital, in order to pressure the Palestinian Authority into accepting the American peace deal for Israel and Palestine (the details of which had yet to be disclosed). If anyone may be accused of an extreme lack of empathy, it's the Trump administration.

Save a Child's Heart

The Save a Child's Heart organization receives funding from both the Palestinian and Israeli Ministry of Health, as well as the Israeli Ministry of Regional Cooperation.[7] According to their website:

> Save a Child's Heart (SACH) is one of the largest undertakings in the world, providing urgently needed pediatric heart surgery and follow-up care for indigent children from developing countries. Based in Israel, our mission is to improve the quality of pediatric cardiac care for children from countries where the heart surgery they need is unobtainable.
>
> Every 29 hours our doctors save a child's life in our medical facilities in Israel or on medical missions in partner countries around the world. Thousands of children are alive today because of a small group of medical professionals who volunteer their time and expertise to perform life-saving cardiac surgery and train local medical personnel.
>
> All children, regardless of race, religion, sex, color, or financial status receive the best possible care that modern medicine has to offer.

Save a Child's Heart, with an annual operating budget of some $4.5 million,[8] has treated more than 3,600 children from forty-eight countries, with 50 per cent from Iraq, Jordan, the Palestinian Authority, and Syria.

In co-operation with the Palestinian Authority, Save a Child's Heart has examined more than 6,000 children and treated 1,750 children, trained twenty-one medical personnel, and conducted seminars for Palestinian medical personnel. The "Heart of the Matter Project," funded by the European Union, US Agency for International Development, the Palestinian Ministry of Health, and the Israeli Ministry of Regional Cooperation, is currently training a team at the Wolfson Medical Center from the Palestine Medical Complex in Ramallah and provides funds for Palestinian children's care in Israel.[9] The average cost per child is $10,000, which includes transportation to and from Israel, the surgery, and follow-up visits. The program is among the finest examples of medical outreach in the world.

Project Rozana

Project Rozana was launched in 2013 by Hadassah Australia, a Jewish volunteer organization that's part of the worldwide Hadassah network. Inspired by the story of a young girl from Ramallah, Rozana Salawhi, who received life-saving care at the Hadassah Medical Center in Jerusalem, Project Rozana focuses on three areas: (1) the training of Palestinian health professionals in Israeli hospitals, (2) the transportation of Palestinian patients from checkpoints in the Gaza Strip and the West Bank to Israeli hospitals, and (3) financial assistance for critically ill Palestinian children in Israeli hospitals when funding from the Palestinian Authority reaches its limit.

Current projects within Project Rozana include the Road to Recovery (a volunteer transportation network mainly for Palestinian children), patient navigators (Arabic-speaking patient advocates), the Acre Women's Association, support for Palestinian patients undergoing gender reassignment surgery, the binational school of psychotherapy, an ocular genetic research project in partnership with the St. John Eye Hospital, and a project aimed at training Palestinian health professionals in the provision of peritoneal dialysis in the West Bank.

Hand in Hand: Center for Jewish-Arab Education in Israel

The Israeli education system has four official pedagogical tracks, but there is a fifth (unofficial) track, the Hand in Hand schools, whose goal is to "build a shared society—one school, *one community at a time.*"

According to a mission statement published on its website, Hand in Hand

> is building integration and equality in Israel through a growing network of Jewish-Arab public schools and shared communities. In six locations across the country, thousands of Arab and Jewish students, teachers, and families come together every day in multicultural, bilingual classrooms, and integrated communities. Hand in Hand is transforming fear and mistrust into friendship and cooperation, proving to all of Israeli society that Arabs and Jews can live together.
>
> Most schools in Israel are segregated. This results in ongoing hostility and misunderstanding between Arab and Jewish citizens. Hand in Hand's public schools, by contrast, build friendship and cultural understanding. We educate about 1,500 Jewish and Arab children—Muslims, Jews, Christians and Druze from 20 different communities—together in the same classrooms. Arab and Jewish students learn both Hebrew and Arabic from teachers speaking their native tongues. Differences in culture, religion and historical viewpoint are discussed openly. Arab and Jewish staff work together to teach tolerance, respect and coexistence. When Arab and Jewish children learn together, they break the cycle of negative stereotypes and learn to relate to one another with mutual understanding and respect. Hand in Hand's extraordinary model provides a clear and simple example that Jews and Arabs can study, work and live together in peace. Hand in Hand's community extends well beyond the walls of the classroom, to parents, extended families and neighbors. Thousands of individuals are taking steps every day to transform society and build lasting peace.

In November 2014, Jewish terrorists torched the Max Rayne Hand in Hand High School in Jerusalem, spray-painting the classrooms with graffiti celebrating extremist right-wing rabbi Meir Kahane. "Kahane was right" and "There's no coexisting with cancer" were two messages left by the arsonists on the walls of the country's largest bilingual school. The following day supporters carrying posters reading "Spread the light together against terror" gathered in front of the smouldering school.

The Jewish terrorists who torched the Hand in Hand school in Jerusalem obviously lacked any empathy for the lives and lifestyle of their victims, but lack of empathy was not the root cause of the violence. What lies at the root of the Israeli-Palestinian conflict are systemic and structural factors that enable such violence to arise in the first place.

SYSTEMIC AND STRUCTURAL FACTORS THAT PERPETUATE THE ISRAELI-PALESTINIAN CONFLICT

Systemic and structural factors are factors that are inherent in society as a whole. Most are so perniciously and deeply embedded that it's virtually impossible to uproot them.

- *International recognition of two separate nations in historic Palestine.* The international community has effectively recognized two separate nations in historic Palestine: Israeli and Palestinian. This is in direct conflict with Zionist interpretations of nationality, which recognize only a Jewish nation and an Arab nation. It has also created an impossible political scenario: both Israel and Palestine cannot be sovereign over the same physical territory at the same time (unless agreed upon by mutual consent).
- *The settler colonial nature of the Zionist project.* The Mandate for Palestine was established by the League of Nations in 1922. It was always meant to be a temporary legal instrument, but right-wing groups have taken the view that it is still in effect, thereby allowing for the continued colonization of historic Palestine by Jewish settlers. The Law of Return, which is an Israeli domestic law, also opens the door for an influx of Jewish immigrants to historic Palestine. Both

the Mandate for Palestine and the Law of Return are legal factors, of a structural nature, that perpetuate the conflict.

- *UNRWA and the Palestinian right of return.* The United Nations Relief and Works Agency for Palestine Refugees in the Near East, which was established in 1949, is unique in the world among NGOs that provide assistance to refugees. Dedicated exclusively to the refugees of the 1948 Arab-Israeli conflict in Palestine, and with no mandate to resettle them (unlike, for example, the United Nations High Commission for Refugees), UNRWA together with the Palestinian Right of Return may be regarded as structural factors that perpetuate the conflict.

- *The incentivization of poverty within the Haredi community.* The Jewish people are locked in a demographic battle with the Palestinian people. Rather than both coordinating their efforts and reducing the fertility rates in a win-win scenario for everyone, Israel has chosen to offer generous financial subsidies to the Haredi community, who seem content with having more than seven children per woman of childbearing age and living in a cycle of poverty. In economics, this is called a perverse incentive. The rapid growth of the Haredi community over the past two decades adds to the conflict because it creates a need for land, housing, and infrastructure.

- *Traditional Jewish and Palestinian attitudes that favour large families.* Even among religious/traditional non-Haredi Jews, there are cultural attitudes that favour large families. No doubt this has something to do with replacing the six million who were lost during the Holocaust. But what many fail to grasp is that these six million were spread out over the entire continent of Europe—an area more than 360 times the size of historic Palestine. Again, this adds to the conflict by creating a need for land, housing, and infrastructure. The same can be said for the population of the Gaza Strip, which continues to grow notwithstanding the horrendous overcrowding.

- *American/Russian need for strategic control of the Middle East.* Both powers are interested in spreading their influence throughout the region. To this list, we should also include Turkey, Iran, and Saudi Arabia.

- *The nature of Israeli democracy itself.* The Israeli multi-party system is an extension of the Assembly of Representatives (*Asefat HaNivharim*), which was the elected parliamentary assembly of the Jewish community in Mandatory Palestine. This system emphasized representation and freedom of expression over governability in order to enlist the widest possible support for the Zionist cause. When the state of Israel was founded in 1948, the multi-party system was simply transitioned to the Israeli Knesset, without giving much thought to how it would affect the governability of state institutions such as the military. As a result, every Israeli government has been a coalition government, with minority parties holding the balance of power. In a very real sense, the Israeli majority has always been ruled by the opinion of the minority. This system of governance desperately needs to change. As things currently stand, however, Israel permits a significant number of her citizens the right to reject the social contract of a modern welfare state while at the same time reaping all the benefits of a modern welfare state.

- *Messianic thinking.* Increasingly, this is becoming a systemic factor in the Israeli-Palestinian conflict. The idea that the state of Israel has a divine right to Eretz Yisrael HaShlema (the whole of the Land of Israel, or Greater Israel) is a politically dangerous concept, yet increasing numbers of Jewish Israelis and their Christian evangelical supporters and enablers take this idea for granted. As an example, Christians United for Israel (CUFI) played a bigger role in pushing the Trump administration to move the embassy from Tel Aviv to Jerusalem than the American Israel Public Affairs Committee (AIPAC).[10] Messianic thinking is difficult to reconcile with modern international relations.

UNDERSTANDING THE NATURE OF THE GAME

In this book, we've explored the Israeli-Palestinian conflict from a game theory perspective. Early on, we rejected the idea that the conflict can be represented as a Prisoner's Dilemma (PD). In a PD, there's a dilemma between co-operating with a co-operative opponent (in the hope of reaping a greater collective reward) or betraying them because you anticipate that they will ultimately betray you. The Nash equilibrium for a PD is for both sides to betray. Thus, if a one-state solution is synonymous with double co-operation, then a two-state solution (as exemplified by India and Pakistan) represents a double betrayal (or double autonomy). In the case of Israel and Palestine, however, any two-state solution would itself require such a high degree of co-operation and interdependence that it would constitute a double co-operation rather than a double autonomy. This creates an unresolvable political paradox.

Most Israelis no longer favour the two-state solution. This is because of how Jewish Israelis view the state of Israel herself. According to Zionist theory, there's no such thing as an Israeli nation or a Palestinian nation—there's only a Jewish nation and an Arab nation. This reduces the Israeli-Palestinian conflict to the Basic Dilemma illustrated in figure 9.4.

Arab nation

		co-operation	autonomy
Jewish nation	co-operation	nobody co-operates (1, 1)	an Arab state (1, 4)
	autonomy	a Jewish state (4, 1)	*nobody has autonomy* *(1, 1)*

Nash equilibrium in bold italics text

FIGURE 9.4

In this restrictive worldview, Jewish Israelis must either fight every day to retain their autonomy or get sucked into the black hole of non-autonomy. For a society that's only a couple of generations removed from the Holocaust (the ultimate example of human non-autonomy), the choice is pretty clear.

In practice, the Israeli-Palestinian conflict comes down to three separate games. Under a worst-case scenario (e.g., Israel and Hamas), it's an iterated game of Chicken. Under a best-case scenario (e.g., the Shin Bet and the Palestinian Security Services), it's a game of Coordination. And under the usual case scenario (e.g., Israel and the Palestinian Authority), it's a game of Bully.

Against this three-game backdrop is a fourth game, a game of demographic Deadlock that bodes ill for Jews and Palestinians alike. With the number of Jews and non-Jews in historic Palestine at almost equal levels since 2005, and with the average Israeli fertility rate well above 3 (and the average Palestinian fertility rate above 4), there's little chance that the Zionist dream of a sovereign Jewish state with a Jewish majority (in the whole of historic Palestine) will ever be fulfilled. Additionally, according to Israel's Central Bureau of Statistics, by 2059 Israel's population will hover around eighteen million, and half will be either be Haredi or Arab. The economic and political implications of this huge demographic shift have yet to hit home.

CONCLUSION

Traditional Zionist values (as embodied in Israel's Declaration of Independence) are laudable for their embrace of democracy, religious freedom, minority rights, and the two-state solution. But if Israel may be accused of anything, it must be accused of allowing her citizens *too much* freedom—including the freedom to *reject* traditional Zionist values. Sadly, the Zionist state has gradually become a Jewish nationalist state. What's equally disappointing is that after eight decades of effort, there's no Westphalian solution for historic Palestine. Instead of peace, there's an ersatz peace that takes the form of a game of Coordination. And even the latter is under constant threat as Israel continues to colonize historic Palestine and engage in all sorts of zero-sum games that benefit the Jewish nation at the expense of the Palestinian nation.

The state of Israel embodies many paradoxes: an OECD country with the life expectancy of a Western European country, the ultranationalist politics of an Eastern European country, the fertility rate of a sub-Saharan African country (at least among the Haredim), and the land base of Slovenia (one of the smaller republics of the former Yugoslavia, and now an independent state). In two generations or less, Israel will become one of the hottest, most horribly overcrowded places on earth, with basically no water and few natural resources to draw upon—unable to support herself at the same economic level as today. This is not some wild prophecy—it's just simple math—the inevitable downside of relentless compound growth and stubborn magical thinking. In a world that will be at least two degrees Celsius warmer than the pre-industrial era, the climate around the eastern Mediterranean will once again strike with biblical proportions.

Israel can't keep kicking the can down the road forever. 'No solution' is not an acceptable solution because in time, every young person (both Jewish and non-Jewish) who has the ability to do so, will pick up and leave. Instead of Aliyah there will be Yerida—the departure of Jewish talent and resources from Eretz Yisrael—much to the detriment of all.

If there's ever to be real peace in Eretz Yisrael, then the Palestinians must have the freedom that only full sovereignty can bring them. No less important is the need for creative and transcendent solutions to the many social dilemmas that plague Israeli society itself. So far, few if any have emerged.

By adopting a game theory approach to the Israeli-Palestinian conflict, we can learn to see it from a new perspective. The first-century BCE Jewish sage Hillel the Elder is quoted in *Ethics of the Fathers* as saying: "If I am not for myself, then who will be? And if I am for myself alone, then who am I?" At first glance, there would appear to be a conflict between the principles of self-advocacy and altruism. But from a game theory perspective, Hillel's words can be represented as a game of Deadlock that reminds us of the Four Sons of the Passover seder (see figure 9.5): the wicked son (who advocates only for himself), the simple son (whose actions are purely altruistic), the son who doesn't know to ask (and is thus incapable of either self-advocacy or altruism), and the wise son (who balances his self-interests with the needs of others). Like the wise son, the state of Israel must both stand up for herself and consider the needs of others—in particular the Palestinians.

Altruism

Self-advocacy		no	yes
	no	The son who does not know to ask (2, 2)	The simple son (1, 4)
	yes	The wicked son (4, 1)	***The wise son*** ***(3, 3)***

Nash equilibrium in bold italics text

FIGURE 9.5

History has taught us that what ultimately brings about peace between two nations is not so much the threat of superior firepower, as the opportunity to engage in meaningful commerce. But a necessary prerequisite for meaningful commerce is a political solution that's equitable and acceptable to all sides.

From a game theory perspective, two states for two peoples is not a viable solution for historic Palestine. But neither is an undemocratic, apartheid-like state dominated by Jewish ultranationalists. This leaves only two other choices: either an Arab state, or a state where Jews and Palestinians learn to set aside their differences and pursue a program of reconciliation and rational co-operation.

Nobody said this was going to be easy. Truth and reconciliation are never easy. Rational co-operation is never easy. But if Jews and Palestinians ever wish to move beyond the zero-sum game, both must begin by asking themselves: what kind of a one-state solution would I be prepared to accept?

Afterword

NO REGRETS

Regrets, both real and anticipated, play a central role in decision-making and game theory. In any non-zero-sum game, a Nash equilibrium is a set of 'no regrets' strategies that applies equally to all players. In other words, each player has no regrets about their choice given the choices of all the other players.

Regret can only arise in the context of what we believe to be either true, or potentially true. Prior to Israel's disengagement from the Gaza Strip in 2005, a number of prominent rabbis promised the Strip's eight thousand Jewish settlers—despite numerous warnings to the contrary from the Israeli government—that there would be a last-minute miracle and that the eviction order would be rescinded. When the disengagement finally occurred, it had a negative impact on the faith of the religious Zionist community that continues to resonate to this day.

In 1956, MIT social psychologist Leon Festinger and colleagues published *When Prophecy Fails: A Social and Psychological Study of a Modern Group that Predicted the Destruction of the World*, detailing the story of a UFO doomsday cult led by a Chicago housewife, Dorothy Martin. After receiving messages from the planet Clarion, Martin informed her circle of followers that the world would be destroyed by a flood, scheduled for dawn on December 21, 1954. The group made extensive preparations in anticipation of being rescued by a flying saucer from Clarion, but as the midnight rendezvous came and went—as did the time for the predicted flood the next morning at dawn—the group's leader announced that she had received another message from the aliens: the world would be spared from destruction. Their "little group, sitting all night long, had spread so much light that God had saved the world from destruction." Cleverly, Martin was able to insist that her prophecy had not been invalidated or exposed as an error; it had merely been modified at the last minute. The belief system of the cult remained intact. Festinger coined the term "cognitive dissonance" to explain the vast gulf that separated belief from reality in the minds of the cult followers.

Broadly speaking, there are two types of statistical error. A type I error results from falsely inferring the existence of something that is not there. This is otherwise known as a false positive error. A type II error results from falsely inferring the absence of something that is there. This is otherwise known as a false negative error.

According to many religious Zionists and those on the political right, there simply can't be as many Palestinians in Eretz Yisrael as the numbers would suggest because Eretz Yisrael belongs to the Jewish people by divine right. The Israeli Central Bureau of Statistics (CBS) doesn't report on the number of Palestinians living in the Palestinian Territories, and the Palestinian Central Bureau of Statistics (PCBS) must certainly be lying (or so the thinking goes). As for the United States Census Bureau (USCB), they're probably getting their numbers from the PCBS, and so they must be wrong as well.

But what if the USCB's numbers are correct? What if the non-Jewish population of historic Palestine will, in fact, overtake the Jewish population by the year 2021? Should Israel count on a flotilla of flying saucers to appear at the last minute and abduct as many Palestinians as necessary in order to ensure a Jewish majority in Eretz Yisrael? More significantly, what would be the consequences for Israel of a type II error (i.e., falsely inferring the absence of a significant Palestinian population)?

Many Jewish Israelis would naturally want to do everything they can to avoid becoming a minority in their own country (assuming they acknowledge that such a thing is even possible). There are, of course, a number of direct ways of achieving this goal (most involve gross violations of human rights, so there's no need to elaborate any further). But as it turns out, the easiest way to reduce the Palestinian fertility rate is through

MICHAEL DAN

the creation of economic prosperity. Prosperity is like kryptonite to fertility. Well-educated, financially successful women raise smaller families and provide better for their families. This is as true in historic Palestine as it is elsewhere in the world (even among the Haredim). But prosperity can't occur in a political vacuum, hence the dilemma of Palestinian prosperity.

Israel obviously has a big role to play when it comes to greasing the wheels of the Palestinian economy. As Palestine's main trading partner and supplier of electricity, Israel can literally turn the Palestinian economy on or off with the flick of a switch. This invites a chicken-and-egg debate over the relationship between peace and prosperity. Israel currently enjoys peace treaties with Jordan and Egypt, even though the trade that flows between Israel and these two countries has had a very modest impact on Israeli prosperity.

But asking if peace leads to prosperity, or the other way around, is asking the wrong question. A better question is this: given Israel's present set of circumstances, what is the no regrets strategy when it comes to the Palestinians? If the Jewish people are about to lose (or have already lost) the demographic war in historic Palestine, then what regret is there in doubling down on democracy, civil society, and social justice (all of which are values embodied in Israel's Declaration of Independence)? The two-state solution may no longer be viable, but there are still plenty of Zionist values worth fighting for (in particular, respect for minority rights). The alternative is to embrace a dark, racist, and xenophobic vision of humanity—a vision that will only lead to profound regret in the future. Sadly, such a vision is already embedded in the recently passed Basic Law: Israel–The Nation-State of the Jewish People.

According to this new law, which has the status of a constitutional norm and therefore cannot be overruled by subsequent laws, the state of Israel is the nation-state of the Jewish people (55 per cent of whom don't even live in Israel) and not the nation-state of all its citizens. Only the Jewish people have the right to national self-determination in Israel, notwithstanding the fact that more than a quarter of Israel's citizenry is non-Jewish. National self-determination may involve projects to Judaize physical spaces, encourage the construction of Jewish settlement projects, and exclude non-Jews from specific communities. The law conceptualizes Jewish-Arab relations as a zero-sum game, in which power and privilege reside exclusively with the Jewish people.

Even if portions of the nation-state law are eventually repealed, there remain on the books—according to the Israeli NGO Adalah (The Legal Center for Arab Minority Rights in Israel)—no less than sixty-five *other* domestic laws that discriminate either directly or indirectly against Palestinian citizens of Israel.[1] We need to look no further than these sixty-five discriminatory laws for a measure of how far Israel has strayed from both the spirit and the letter of her own Declaration of Independence.

With each passing day, there is a mounting risk that Israel and her children will journey even closer to the point of no return.

Appendix

DEMOGRAPHIC CALCULATIONS, INCLUDING PROJECTIONS

The number of Jews and non-Jews living in historic Palestine is challenging to ascertain. In 1922 and 1931, the British conducted two very thorough censuses. These remain the best sources of demographic data prior to August 1948, when the state of Israel undertook to register all her citizens.

From 1948 onward, Israel's Central Bureau of Statistics (CBS) has maintained a database that categorizes citizens and permanent residents according to their ethnic group (Jewish, Arab, and Other). The data are summarized every year in a publication called the *Statistical Abstract of Israel*.

In 1967, Israel annexed East Jerusalem, and since then all Jewish settlers living in East Jerusalem have been included in the Israeli census data. In 2014, they numbered around 201,200.

Israel annexed the Golan Heights in 1982, and since then all Jewish settlers living in the Golan Heights have been included in the Israeli census data. In 2016, they numbered around 22,000, which is a relatively small number.

The term "West Bank" is a source of confusion. Technically, East Jerusalem is part of the West Bank; however, most demographers understand the term "West Bank" to mean the territory that Israel captured from Jordan in 1967, *minus* East Jerusalem. For the sake of consistency, I use this more restrictive definition of West Bank when I refer to the West Bank.

For several years following the Six-Day War, the number of settlers living in the West Bank was negligible (the CBS reported only 1,182 in 1972). In 2016, the number of settlers was estimated at 391,000 (according to the CIA World Factbook). All West Bank settlers are included in the Israeli census data, even though they are living in "disputed territory." All non-Jewish residents of the Palestinian Territories (the West Bank and the Gaza Strip) are excluded from Israeli census data.

The total number of Jewish settlers in 2016 was around 605,000. This number includes all settlers living in East Jerusalem, the Golan Heights, and the West Bank.

The United States Census Bureau (USCB) maintains public records for Israel, the Gaza Strip, and the West Bank going back to 1950. These records also include projections going forward to 2050. The numbers in the USCB records are the same as in the CIA World Factbook.

In 2005, only eight thousand Jewish settlers were living in the Gaza Strip. All of them were expelled by the government of Israel. For demographic purposes, the Gaza Strip has always been a non-Jewish territory.

The USCB records for Israel *include* the Jewish settlers living in East Jerusalem, but *exclude* the Jewish settlers living in the West Bank. The USCB records for the West Bank *exclude* the Jewish settlers living in East Jerusalem, but *include* the Jewish settlers living in the West Bank. This way, nobody gets double-counted.

The organization B'Tselem maintains a detailed public record of the number of Jewish settlers living in the Palestinian Territories. If we compare, year by year, the CBS figures for the total population of Israel with USCB figures for Israel, the difference is typically the number of Jewish settlers living in the West Bank.

Using historical data from the British census of 1922 and 1931, the CBS, the USCB, and B'Tselem, it was possible to determine the number of Jews and non-Jews living in historic Palestine between 1920 and 2017. Since 1997, the Palestinian Central Bureau of Statistics (PCBS) has maintained a database of Palestinians living in East Jerusalem, the West Bank, and the Gaza Strip; however, I did not rely on any figures from the PCBS for this study. The PCBS figures are slightly higher than the USCB figures, but not by much.

PROJECTIONS TO 2050

The *Statistical Abstract of Israel 2018*, which is the most recent version, does not contain any population projections. The USCB data do however. In order to estimate the Jewish population of Israel out to 2050, it was first necessary to estimate the West Bank settler population out to 2050. By adding the latter to the USCB projections for Israel, we would have an estimate of the total population of Israel out to 2050, as reportable by the CBS.

The West Bank settler population out to 2050 was estimated using an exponential extrapolation of the B'Tselem data from 1996 to 2017, as indicated in figure A.1. The formula used was $y = 4.61522E{+}46{*}e^{\wedge}{-}0.05506x$.

From this graph, we can see that the annual growth rate of the West Bank settler population has been dropping quite substantially and is projected to be only 0.44 per cent by 2050. This makes sense. There is only so

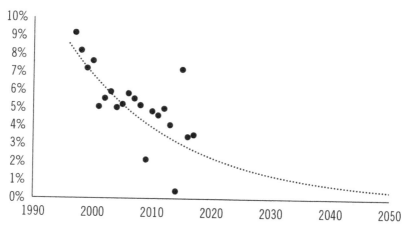

FIGURE A.1 WEST BANK SETTLER ANNUAL GROWTH RATE, 1996–2050, BASED ON B'TSELEM DATA, 1996–2017

SOURCE: Data from B'Tselem—The Israeli Information Center for Human Rights in the Occupied Territories.

much room in the West Bank for new settlement construction. The settler population in the West Bank in 2050 is estimated to be around 609,000, which is roughly 49 per cent higher than the 2017 population. Based on these figures, plus the USCB projections for Israel, the total population of Israel in 2050 is estimated to be around 13 million, which is also roughly 49 per cent higher than the 2017 population.

The annual growth rate of the Jewish population of Israel was also estimated using an exponential function, based on the CBS data from 1949 to 2017, as indicated in figure A.2. The formula used was y = 8.10305E+10* e^-0.01808x.

This graph shows that the annual growth rate of Israel's Jewish population has been declining steadily. It's projected to be only 0.71 per cent per year by 2050.

In order to estimate the non-Jewish population of Israel from 2018 to 2050, I took the USCB projections for Israel, added in the West Bank settler projections (as calculated above), then subtracted the Jewish population of Israel projections (as calculated above).

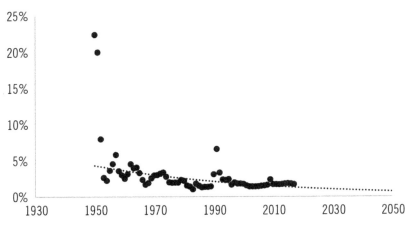

FIGURE A.2 ISRAEL JEWISH ANNUAL GROWTH RATE, 1949–2050, BASED ON CBS DATA, 1949–2017

SOURCE: Data from the Israeli Central Bureau of Statistics.

MICHAEL DAN

In order to estimate the non-Jewish population of historic Palestine from 2018 to 2050, I took the non-Jewish population of Israel projections (as calculated above), added in the USCB projections for the West Bank, plus the USCB projections for the Gaza Strip, then subtracted the West Bank settler projections (as calculated above).

To estimate the percentage of the Jewish population of Israel plus the West Bank, I took the Jewish population of Israel and divided it into the total population of Israel plus the non-Jewish population of the West Bank.

ACKNOWLEDGEMENTS

I've had the opportunity to meet and work with many accomplished individuals, but few as inspiring as Dr. Izzeldin Abuelaish. We are both doctors and, over the past decade, we've also become close friends. Together, we've spent countless hours sipping cardamom-spiced coffee and talking about our favourite patient: the Middle East. Those conversations eventually inspired me to write this book.

Izzeldin was born and raised in the Jabalia Refugee Camp in the Gaza Strip. He is a passionate and eloquent proponent of peace between Palestinians and Israelis, and has dedicated his life to that cause. He received his primary and secondary education in the refugee camp schools, followed by a scholarship to study medicine in Cairo, Egypt. He completed his residency in obstetrics and gynecology at the Soroka University hospital in Beer Sheva, Israel, followed by sub-specialty training in fetal medicine in Italy and Belgium, and a Master's in public health from Harvard. He speaks Hebrew fluently and is the first Palestinian doctor to receive an appointment in medicine at an Israeli hospital.

Following the death of his wife, Nadia, from acute leukemia in September 2008, Izzeldin became justifiably concerned about his ability to support his family, both from a logistical and an emotional viewpoint. His work at the Sheba Medical Center in Tel Hashomer, Israel, necessitated complicated border crossings and week-long absences from his home. Eventually, he made the difficult decision to circulate his CV among his network of friends and colleagues. By chance, a copy of his CV landed in my inbox on January 9th, 2009. The date is significant because at the time, the Gaza Strip was caught in the middle of a devastating war (Operation Cast Lead).

After reading Izzeldin's CV, I decided to act quickly. I contacted a former classmate of mine, Peter Singer, and his colleague, Abdallah Daar,

243

both professors of global health at the University of Toronto. Within days we had a job lined up for Izzeldin, unaware at the time that Harvard was also in the process of recruiting him. The truth is that Izzeldin could have found a job practically anywhere in the world, but under the circumstances, the last thing on his mind was to abandon his people and his extended family during a time of war.

Meanwhile, our small group in Toronto thought Izzeldin's recruitment was going quite well until suddenly, disaster struck: the IDF fired two tank shells into the Abuelaish apartment, exactly three months to the day after Nadia passed away.

The first shell instantly killed two of Izzeldin's daughters, Mayar and Aya, and their cousin, Noor. Another daughter, Shatha, and Izzeldin's brother, Naser, and a second niece, Ghaidaa, sustained non-life-threatening injuries. When Izzeldin's oldest daughter, Bissan, entered her sisters' bedroom to assess the damage, the second shell hit and she too was instantly killed. Izzeldin finally arrived on the scene and the devastation that he saw before him confirmed the worst fears of any father. But what he did next continues to amaze me to this day.

Moments after losing three daughters and a niece, Izzeldin picked up the phone and reached out to his Israeli journalist friend, Shlomi Eldar—a newscaster at Channel 10—unaware at the time that Eldar was in the middle of a live TV broadcast. After receiving a series of calls from Izzeldin, Eldar finally decided to answer his mobile phone, only to learn of the tragedy that had just befallen the Abuelaish family. Once Eldar understood what had happened—and breaking every rule of broadcast journalism—he simply walked off the set while continuing to talk with Izzeldin. Quickly, Eldar made arrangements for an ambulance to evacuate the injured Abuelaish family members to the Sheba Medical Center.

Izzeldin's cries, broadcast all over Israel on live TV, shook the nation and the world, and came to symbolize the war itself. Two days later Israel's prime minister, Ehud Olmert, declared a unilateral ceasefire. Operation Cast Lead was over. Camera crews converged on the Sheba Medical Center, and for a moment, every Israeli felt a sense of responsibility for Izzeldin's loss. At a hastily convened press conference (which was conducted in Hebrew), Izzeldin reaffirmed his unshakeable commitment to peace.

To this day, Izzeldin refuses to hate or to embrace violence in all forms.

"Let my daughters be the last price to pay," he said.

Soon afterwards, the Belgians nominated him for the Nobel Peace Prize. Others quickly followed.

Izzeldin eventually accepted the offer of employment from the University of Toronto, and moved to Toronto with his remaining children in July 2009. In 2011, he established a charitable foundation called the Daughters for Life Foundation, which offers educational bursaries and scholarships to girls and women from the Middle East regardless of race, nationality, or religion. To date, over four hundred of Daughters for Life bursaries have been awarded in the Middle East, and there are now over fifty Daughters for Life scholars who have attended, or are attending, universities all over the world. I am immensely proud to have played a small part in all the good work that Izzeldin has accomplished.

I also wish to thank friends and colleagues at the University of Toronto who helped to bring the Abuelaish family to Canada: Peter Singer, Abdallah Daar, Jack Mandel, David Naylor, and Cathy Whiteside. Today, the Abuelaish children are all models of strength and resilience, and I treasure my friendship with all of them: Shatha, Dalal, Mohammed, Raffah, and Abdallah. This book is also dedicated, in part, to the memory of their siblings and cousin who perished in Operation Cast Lead.

Other members of the University of Toronto community who have been helpful with either general discussions or reviewing my manuscript, or both, include Howard Hu, Adalsteinn Brown, Suzanne Stewart, David Palmer, Audrey Laporte, and Rahul Deb. A special thank you to Smadar Peretz for her very careful and meticulous review of the manuscript. Friends at the University of Haifa whom I wish to acknowledge include Aaron Ben Ze'ev, Ron Robin, Ami Ayalon, and Majid Al-Haj.

Literary and journalistic friends who helped me to write this book include Louise Dennys, Haroun Siddiqui, and Ken Alexander. I also wish to acknowledge the following friends who work tirelessly for peace in the

Middle East: Mohammad and Najla Al Zaibak, Shawky Fahel, Robert Massoud, Karen Mock, and Arie Raif.

I am grateful to the following individuals for their friendship and peace-building efforts: Nicholas Woolf, Fiona Woolf, Tom Ogilvie-Graham, Ahmad Ma'ali, and Isla Richards of the St. John of Jerusalem Eye Hospital; Ron Finkel and Mark Ansham of Project Rozana; Bernie Goldman of Save a Child's Heart; Shuli Dichter, Rebecca Bardach, and Mohamad Marzouk of Hand in Hand; Bill Graham, John English, and Michael Humeniuk of the Bill Graham Centre for Contemporary International History at the University of Toronto.

A special thank you to Bernie Farber, Mira Sucharov, Mamdouh Shoukri, Sarah Horowitz, Jonathan Richler, Rabbi Roy Tannenbaum, and David Zimmer.

No book is ever finished—especially one about the Middle East. And this book in particular would never have been finished were it not for the outstanding editorial efforts of Jonathan Schmidt. Thank you, Jonathan, for your patience, humour, thoughtful curiosity, and helpful insights. Thank you also to Sarah Scott of Barlow Books for indulging my countless revisions to the manuscript.

Most of all, thank you to my loving wife, Amira, for your critical thinking and for lighting the way for me in the humanities. Maia and Lana, thank you for tolerating your father's writing habits. Both your parents hope that you will always remember and uphold the Jewish principles of human dignity and universal justice.

NOTES

Introduction: Why Now?

[1] Aaron Kalman, "Supreme Court rules against 'Israeli' ethnicity on ID," *The Times of Israel*, October 3, 2013.

Chapter 1: The Game Theory Perspective

[1] Luce and Raiffa, see bibliography.

[2] Available at https://www.investopedia.com/terms/n/nash-equilibrium.asp.

Chapter 2: Three Zionist Dilemmas

[1] https://972mag.com/contradicting-its-own-ruling-israels-supreme-court-legalizes-segregated-communities/96817/.

[2] https://www.cjnews.com/news/perspectives-no-dogs-no-jews-no-evidence.

[3] Yoman (Diary) Ben-Gurion, July 13, 1922.

[4] Teveth, *Ben-Gurion and the Palestinian Arabs*, 84.

[5] Ibid., 39–40.

[6] Ibid., 43.

[7] Ibid., 44.

Chapter 3: An Unfinished Country

[1] Klein, *Lives in Common*, 30.

[2] Alexander Scholch, "The Demographic Development of Palestine 1850–1882." *International Journal of Middle East Studies* XII (1985): 485–505. JSTOR 00207438.

[3] Teveth, *Ben Gurion and the Palestinian Arabs*, 20.

[4] Prophetically, this was the first of many associations between Zionism and the modern arms industry.

[5] Christopher Simon Sykes, *The Man Who Created the Middle East: A Story of Empire, Conflict and the Sykes-Picot Agreement* (London: William Collins, 2006), 306.

[6] Ibid., 270.

7 Fromkin, *A Peace to End All Peace*.

8 Nir Hasson, "How the Fight Against Malaria Infected the Future Map of Israel," *Haartetz*, March 5, 2008.

9 Available at http://www.transferagreement.com/.

10 Available at https://www.haaretz.com/opinion/1.818186.

Chapter 4: The Epistemology of Identity

1 Available at https://www.history.com/news/history-lists/6-things-you-may-not-know-about-the-dead-sea-scrolls.

2 Available at https://web.archive.org/web/20131101012524/http://www.jpost.com/Magazine/Features/A-sound-in-silence.

3 Available at https://hermeneutics.stackexchange.com/questions/4325/was-n percentC3percentBBn-deleted-from-psalm-145-in-the-masoretic-text.

4 Available at http://www.ecmarsh.com/lxx/Psalms/index.htm.

5 Available at https://hermeneutics.stackexchange.com/questions/7862/what-is-the-original-text-of-deuteronomy-328-9.

6 Available at https://www.amazon.ca/Meme-Machine-Susan-Blackmore/dp/019286212X/ref=sr_1_1?ie=UTF8&qid=1549594658&sr=8-1&keywords=the+meme+machine.

7 Exodus 29:12, Leviticus 4:18.

8 Teveth, *Ben-Gurion and the Palestinian Arabs*, 30–1.

9 Available at http://en.hebron.org.il/news/491.

10 Available at http://www.jpost.com/Magazine/Features/This-is-a-conflict-between-brothers-its-all-a-big-misunderstanding.

11 Available at http://en.hebron.org.il/news/491.

12 Available at http://www.pnas.org/content/97/12/6769.full.

13 Available at http://www.pubmedcentral.nih.gov/articlerender.fcgi?tool=pubmed&pubmedid=11573163.

14 Dawkins, *The Selfish Gene*, Kindle e-book, location 1625-5.

Chapter 5: Not Quite Normal

1 From an address given to Technion University students (19 March 1969), a transcription of which appeared in *Haaretz* (April 4, 1969), quoted in Edward Said, *The Question of Palestine*, 14.

2 Peter Beaumont, "The $18 Billion Arms Race Helping to Fuel Middle East Conflict," *The Guardian*, April 23, 2015.

[3] Available at https://www.sipri.org/googlemaps/2015_of_at_top_20_exp_map.html.

[4] Available at http://www.jpost.com/Defense/Israel-among-top-arms-exporters-and-importers.

[5] Amos Harel, "Israel's Arms Exports Increased by 20 Percent in 2012," *Haaretz*, January 10, 2013.

[6] Yair Auron, "Shimon Peres, Apologize for Israel's Enablement of the Rwandan and Serbian Genocides," *Haaretz*, January 26, 2015.

[7] Steven Chase, "Canada Now the Second Biggest Arms Exporter to the Middle East, Data Show," *The Globe and Mail*, June 14, 2016.

[8] Available at http://site.jnf.ca/index.php/about-jnf/vision/.

[9] Zafir Rinat, "JNF Agrees Reluctantly to Limited Transparency," *Haaretz*, June 6, 2014.

[10] Adiv Sterman, "JNF Reports Finances, Holds Land Worth $2 Billion," *The Times of Israel*, July 8, 2015.

[11] Available at http://www.wzo.org.il/world-zionist-organization.

[12] Available at http://www.nbn.org.il/.

[13] Available at http://www.kkl-jnf.org/about-kkl-jnf/green-israel-news/december-2013/jnf-canada-negev-dinner-stephen-harper/.

[14] Available at https://www.adalah.org/uploads/oldfiles/eng/intl06/un-i6-jnf.pdf.

[15] Available at http://www.pewforum.org/2016/03/08/israels-religiously-divided-society/.

[16] Daniel Estrin, "The King's Torah: A Rabbinic Text or a Call to Terror?" *Haaretz*, January 22, 2017.

[17] Available at https://www.washingtonpost.com/news/worldviews/wp/2015/05/07/israels-new-justice-minister-considers-all-palestinians-to-be-the-enemy/?utm_term=.5d8d72c721fd.

[18] Available at https://www.israelnationalnews.com/News/News.aspx/230975.

[19] Available at https://www.politico.eu/article/how-yitzhak-rabins-assassin-won/.

[20] Ravit Hecht, "Muslims Are 'Culturally Murderous' and Israel Belongs to the Jews, Says Lawmaker Amir Ohana," *Haaretz*, October 17, 2017.

[21] Josh Breiner and Jonathan Lis, "Israeli President Accused of Treason after Refusing to Pardon Hebron Shooter Azaria," *Haaretz*, November 20, 2017.

[22] Bryan Randolph Bruns, "Names for Games: Locating 2 × 2 Games," *Games* 6 (2015): 495–520.

Chapter 6: An Iterated Game of Chicken

[1] Available at https://www.cia.gov/library/publications/the-world-factbook/geos/gz.html.

[2] Available at https://www.cia.gov/library/publications/the-world-factbook/geos/sn.html.

[3] Available at https://www.cia.gov/library/publications/the-world-factbook/geos/hk.html.

[4] Available at https://www.cia.gov/library/publications/the-world-factbook/geos/we.html.

[5] The ratio of population density to per capita GDP for the Gaza Strip is 1.173; for Bangladesh it's 0.314, based on the CIA World Factbook.

[6] Available at http://elderofziyon.blogspot.com/2010/07/how-much-agricultural-gaza-land-does.html.

[7] Available at http://atlismta.org/online-journals/0607-journal-development-challenges/the-environment-and-conflict-in-the-rwandan-genocide/.

[8] Available at http://www.unrwa.org/userfiles/2010011995652.pdf.

[9] Available at http://www.unrwa.org/where-we-work/gaza-strip/camp-profiles?field=1.

[10] David McDowall, *Palestine and Israel: The Uprising and Beyond* (London: I.B. Tauris, 1989), 84.

[11] Andrew Higgins, "How Israel Helped to Spawn Hamas," *The Wall Street Journal*, January 24, 2009.

[12] Available at http://www.shabak.gov.il/English/EnTerrorData/decade/Pages/default.aspx.

[13] Shahar Smooha, "All the Dreams We Had Are Now Gone," *Haaretz*, July 19, 2007.

[14] Peter Beinart, "Gaza Myths and Facts: What American Jewish Leaders Won't Tell You," *Haaretz*, July 30, 2014.

[15] Available at http://www.shabak.gov.il/English/EnTerrorData/decade/Pages/default.aspx.

[16] Available at http://www.vanityfair.com/news/2008/04/gaza200804.

[17] Available at http://www.shabak.gov.il/English/EnTerrorData/decade/Pages/default.aspx.

[18] Available at http://www.informationclearinghouse.info/article27196.htm.

[19] Available at http://www.shabak.gov.il/English/EnTerrorData/decade/Pages/default.aspx.

[20] Amos Harel, "IDF Rabbinate Publication during Gaza War: We Will Show No Mercy on the Cruel," *Haaretz*, January 26, 2009.

[21] Available at http://www2.ohchr.org/english/bodies/hrcouncil/docs/12session/A-HRC-12-48.pdf.

[22] Available at http://www.aljazeera.com/news/middleeast/2009/10/200910395820396287.html.

[23] Natasha Mozgovaya, "Goldstone to Attend Grandson's Bar Mitzvah as Zionist Groups End Feud," *Haaretz*, April 23, 2010.

[24] Available at https://www.ochaopt.org/documents/ocha_opt_gaza_blockade_factsheet_june_2012_english.pdf.

[25] Available at http://www.mfa.gov.il/mfa/pressroom/2012/pages/operation_pillar_of_defense-statements.aspx.

[26] Available at http://www.aljazeera.com/news/middleeast/2011/03/201132718224159699.html.

[27] Available at http://www.nbcnews.com/storyline/middle-east-unrest/how-realistic-are-hamas-cease-fire-terms-n157516.

[28] "Report of the Detailed Findings of the Commission of Inquiry on the 2014 Gaza Conflict," ohchr.org (United Nations A/HRC/29/CRP.4), 22 June 2015, 70–79, paragraphs 251–299.

[29] Available at http://www.telesurtv.net/english/analysis/The-No-Nonsense-Gaza-Crisis-2014-Timeline-20140804-0046.html.

[30] Yaakov Katz and Yaakov Lappin, "Iron Dome Ups Its Interception Rate to Over 90 Percent," *The Jerusalem Post*, March 10, 2012.

[31] Source: UN Independent Commission into 2014 Gaza Conflict.

[32] Jeremy Ashkenas, Archie Tse, et al., "Assessing the Damage and Destruction in Gaza," *The New York Times*, August 15, 2014.

Chapter 7: A Small House

[1] Ephron, *Killing a King*, 94.

[2] Off, *The Lion, the Fox, and the Eagle*, Kindle e-book, location 3207.

[3] Available at https://en.wikipedia.org/wiki/Geneva_Initiative_(2003).

[4] Available at http://www.haaretz.com/opinion/.premium-1.608008.

[5] Available at http://www.rand.org/pubs/research_reports/RR740-1.html.

[6] David Rosenberg, "The Fiction of the Israel-Palestine Peace Dividend," *Haaretz*, June 17, 2015.

[7] Available at http://www.wrmea.org/2006-july/a-conservative-estimate-of-total-direct-u.s.-aid-to-israel-$108-billion.html.

[8] Available at https://www.fas.org/sgp/crs/mideast/RL33222.pdf.

[9] US Bureau of the Census, Statistical Abstract of the United States: 1954 (1955), 899, table 1075.

[10] Available at https://www.timesofisrael.com/us-aid-to-palestinian-security-services-to-end-friday-at-pa-request/.

[11] Available at http://www.washingtoninstitute.org/policy-analysis/view/fixing-unrwa-repairing-the-uns-troubled-system-of-aid-to-palestinian-refuge.

[12] Available at http://www.unrwa.org/sites/default/files/2015_donors_ranking_overall.pdf.

[13] Available at https://www.washingtonpost.com/world/middle_east/us-aid-cuts-wont-end-the-right-of-return-palestinians-say/2018/08/31/8e3f25b4-ad0c-11e8-8a0c-70b618c98d3c_story.html?utm_term=.f0065b72cf4a.

[14] Available at http://www.unrwa.org/palestine-refugees.

[15] Yitzhak Gal and Bader Rock, "Israeli-Palestinian Trade: In-Depth Analysis," published by the Tony Blair Institute for Global Change, October 17, 2018.

[16] Barak Ravid, "Israeli Minister: Palestinian Authority Will Collapse, the Only Question Is When," *Haaretz*, February 29, 2016.

[17] Available at http://israelpolicyforum.org/wp-content/uploads/2015/05/Annexation-Summary-English-V1.pdf.

Chapter 8: The Demographic Deadlock

[1] Private testimony of Ben-Gurion to the Peel Commission.

[2] Public testimony of Ben-Gurion to the Peel Commission.

[3] Available at https://www.reuters.com/article/us-israel-palestinians-population/jews-arabs-nearing-population-parity-in-holy-land-israeli-officials-idUSKBN1H222T.

[4] Available at https://www.timesofisrael.com/expert-confirms-jews-and-arabs-nearing-population-parity/.

[5] As estimated by the Population Reference Bureau in 2018.

[6] Source: 1949–2006: available at https://israelipalestinian.procon.org/; 2018: CIA World FactBook.

[7] Ibid.

[8] Dan Ben-David, "Overpopulation and Demography in Israel: Directions, Perceptions, Illusions and Solutions," Shoresh Institution for Socioeconomic Research, November 2018.

[9] Available at http://www.president.gov.il/English/ThePresident/Speeches/Pages/news_070615_01.aspx.

MICHAEL DAN

[10] *Haaretz* correspondents, "Israel Votes to Effectively Cancel Core Curriculum for Ultra-Orthodox Schools," *Haaretz*, August 2, 2016.

[11] Gershom Gorenberg, "Faulty Education at Israeli Ultra-Orthodox Schools Is Tantamount to Child Abuse," *Haaretz*, April 26, 2016.

[12] Available at http://edu.gov.il/owlHeb/Tichon/BechinotVbagruyot/BechinotAbagrut/Pages/entitlement-data-2014.aspx.

[13] Yarden Skop, "Haredim, Arab Communities Have Lowest Matriculation Pass Rates," *Haaretz*, September 2, 2012.

[14] Available at http://www.ynetnews.com/articles/0,7340,L-4255183,00.html.

[15] Available at http://www.economist.com/news/middle-east-and-africa/21656207-israel-cannot-afford-keep-paying-ultra-orthodox-men-shun-employment-eat.

[16] See "Special Analysis of Central Bureau of Statistics, Labor Force Study, 2011," and "State of Israel, Second Progress Report on the Implementation of the OECD Recommendations: Labour Market and Social Policies" (August 2015).

[17] National Insurance Institute. Poverty Report 2014.

[18] Available at http://www.economist.com/news/middle-east-and-africa/21656207-israel-cannot-afford-keep-paying-ultra-orthodox-men-shun-employment-eat.

[19] Available at https://www.cia.gov/library/publications/the-world-factbook/geos/is.html.

[20] Dan Ben-David, "The Shoresh Handbook: Education and Its Impact in Israel," Shoresh Institution for Socioeconomic Research, 2017.

[21] Dan Ben-David, "Overpopulation and Demography in Israel: Directions, Perceptions, Illusions and Solutions," Shoresh Institution for Socioeconomic Research, November 2018.

[22] "Poll: Only 17 Percent of Israeli Ultra-Orthodox Celebrate Independence Day," *Times of Israel*, April 18, 2018.

[23] Available at http://jppi.org.il/new/en/article/israelijudaism-summary/#.XErq7FxKiUk.

[24] Available at https://www.cia.gov/library/publications/the-world-factbook/geos/is.html.

[25] Sources: 1914–2005: available at https://israelipalestinian.procon.org/ 2018: CIA World FactBook.

[26] Ruth Schuster, "Climate Change Is Slamming the Mediterranean, and Risks Are Being Underestimated, Scientists Warn," *Haaretz*, November 1, 2018.

[27] Available at https://www.jpost.com/Enviro-Tech/Climate-change-puts-5m-Israelis-at-risk-of-severe-flooding-events-330695.

[28] The Forward and Josh Nathan-Kazis, "26 Billion Bucks//Uncovering the US Jewish Charity Industry," *Haaretz*, March 26, 2014.

[29] Available at http://www.timesofisrael.com/half-of-israel-to-be-arab-ultra-orthodox-by-2059-projections/.

[30] Tom Persico, "There Is Somewhere Else Where Israelis Coud Go," *Haaretz*, May 15, 2019.

[31] Available at https://www.nobelprize.org/uploads/2018/06/aumann-lecture.pdf.

[32] Available at https://www.ynetnews.com/articles/0,7340,L-3205817,00.html.

Chapter 9: An Ersatz Peace

[1] Available at https://www.theguardian.com/commentisfree/2019/jan/22/empathy-cycle-violence-israel-palestine.

[2] Available at http://theparentscircle.org/en/about_eng/.

[3] Available at http://www.stjohneyehospital.org.

[4] St. John of Jerusalem Eye Hospital Group, Trustees Annual Report, 2014.

[5] Available at http://www.stjohneyehospital.org/frequently-asked-questions#a004.

[6] Available at http://www.peres-center.org/pediatric_hemato-oncology.

[7] Available at http://www.saveachildsheartus.org/.

[8] Dr. Bernie Goldman, personal communication.

[9] L. Sasson, A. Tamir, S. Houri, et al., "Mending Hearts and Building Bridges: The Save a Child's Heart Foundation," *J Public Health Management Practice* 22, 1 (2016): 89–98.

[10] Available at https://forward.com/news/israel/389233/evangelicals-led-drive-to-name-jerusalem-as-capital-aipac-stayed-on-sidelin/.

Afterword: No Regrets

[1] Available at https://www.adalah.org/en/content/view/7771.

BIBLIOGRAPHY

Abuelaish, Izzeldin. *I Shall Not Hate: A Gaza Doctor's Journey.* Toronto: Random House Canada, 2010.

Abunimah, Ali. *One Country: A Bold Proposal to End the Israeli-Palestinian Impasse.* New York: Holt, 2006.

Acemoglu, Daron, and James A. Robinson. *Why Nations Fail: The Origins of Power, Prosperity, and Poverty.* New York: Crown Business, 2012.

Adelson, Roger. *Mark Sykes: Portrait of an Amateur.* London: Jonathan Cape, 1975.

Anderson, Scott. *Lawrence in Arabia: War, Deceit, Imperial Folly and the Making of the Modern Middle East.* New York: Signal, 2013.

Axelrod, Robert. *The Evolution of Cooperation.* Cambridge: Basic Books, 1984.

Beinart, Peter. *The Crisis of Zionism.* New York: Times Books, 2012.

Bergman, Ronen. *Rise and Kill First: The Secret History of Israel's Targeted Assassinations.* New York: Random House, 2018.

Binmore, Ken. *Game Theory: A Very Short Introduction.* Oxford, UK: Oxford University Press, 2006.

Blackmore, Susan. *The Meme Machine.* Oxford, UK: Oxford University Press, 1999.

Carlstrom, Gregg. *How Long Will Israel Survive? The Threat from Within.* Oxford, UK: Oxford University Press, 2017.

Carter, Jimmy. *Palestine: Peace Not Apartheid.* New York: Simon & Schuster, 2006.

Dawkins, Richard. *The Selfish Gene.* Oxford, UK: Oxford University Press, 1989.

Eban, Abba. *My Country: The Story of Modern Israel.* New York: Random House, 1972.

Elizur, Yuval, and Lawrence Malkin. *The War Within: Israel's Ultra-Orthodox Threat to Democracy and the Nation.* New York: Overlook Duckworth, 2013.

Ephron, Dan. *Killing a King: The Assassination of Yitzhak Rabin and the Remaking of Israel.* New York: Norton, 2015.

Finkelstein, Israel, and Neil Asher Silberman. *The Bible Unearthed: Archaeology's New Vision of Ancient Israel and the Origin of Its Sacred Texts.* New York: Touchstone, 2001.

Fromkin, David. *A Peace to End All Peace: The Fall of the Ottoman Empire and the Creation of the Modern Middle East.* New York: Holt, 1989.

Gilbert, Martin. *Israel, a History.* Toronto: Turner Books, 1998.

Glick, Caroline B. *The Israeli Solution: A One State Plan for Peace in the Middle East.* New York: Crown Forum, 2014.

Goodman, Micah. *Catch-67: The Left, the Right, and the Legacy of the Six-Day War.* New Haven: Yale University Press, 2018.

Gorenberg, Gershom. *The Unmaking of Israel.* New York: Harper, 2011.

Halevi, Yossi Klein. *Letters to My Palestinian Neighbor.* Toronto: HarperCollins, 2018.

Herzl, Theodor. *The Jewish State: An Attempt at a Modern Solution of the Jewish Question.* Newton Stewart: Anodos Books, 2018.

Khalidi, Rashid. *The Iron Cage: The Story of the Palestinian Struggle for Statehood.* Boston: Beacon Press, 2006.

Klein, Menachem. *Lives in Common: Arabs and Jews in Jerusalem, Jaffa and Hebron.* Oxford, UK: Oxford University Press, 2014.

Levy, Gideon. *The Punishment of Gaza.* London: Verso, 2010.

Luce, R. Duncan, and Howard Raiffa. *Games and Decisions: Introduction and Critical Survey.* Mineola, NY: Dover Publications, 1989.

MacMillan, Margaret. *Paris 1919: Six Months That Changed the World.* New York: Random House, 2001.

—. *The War That Ended Peace.* Toronto: Allen Lane, 2013.

Morris, Benny. *One State, Two States: Resolving the Israel/Palestine Conflict.* New Haven: Yale University Press, 2009.

Nusseibeh, Sari. *What Is a Palestinian State Worth?* Cambridge: Harvard University Press, 2011.

Nusseibeh, Sari, and Anthony David. *Once upon a Country: A Palestinian Life.* New York: Picador, 2007.

Off, Carol. *The Lion, the Fox, and the Eagle: A Story of Generals and Justice in Rwanda and Yugoslavia.* Toronto: Vintage Canada, 2000.

O'Malley, Padraig. *The Two-State Delusion: Israel and Palestine—A Tale of Two Narratives.* New York: Penguin, 2015.

Ong, Walter J. *Orality and Literacy.* New York: Methuen & Co. Ltd., 2002.

Pappe, Ilan. *The Ethnic Cleansing of Palestine.* Oxford, UK: Oneworld, 2006.

—. *Ten Myths about Israel.* London: Verso, 2017.

Poundstone, William. *Prisoner's Dilemma: John von Neumann, Game Theory, and the Puzzle of the Bomb.* New York: Anchor Books, 1992.

Said, Edward. *The Question of Palestine.* New York: Vintage Books, 1992.

Sand, Shlomo. *The Invention of the Jewish People.* London: Verso, 2009.

Schama, Simon. *The Story of the Jews: Finding the Words, 1000 bce-1492 ce.* Toronto: Allen Lane, 2013.

Senor, Dan, and Saul Singer. *Start-Up Nation: The Story of Israel's Economic Miracle.* Toronto: McLelland & Stewart, 2009.

Shavit, Ari. *My Promised Land: The Triumph and Tragedy of Israel.* New York: Spiegel & Grau, 2013.

Shlaim, Avi. *The Iron Wall: Israel and the Arab World.* New York: Penguin Books, 2014.

Stoddard, John L. *John L. Stoddard's Lectures, Complete in Ten Volumes, Volume Two: Constantinople, Jerusalem, Egypt.* Boston: Balch Brothers Co., 1905.

Straffin, Philip D. *Game Theory and Strategy.* Washington, DC: The Mathematical Association of America, 1993.

Sykes, Christopher Simon. *The Man Who Created the Middle East: A Story of Empire, Conflict and the Sykes-Picot Agreement.* London: William Collins, 2006.

Tal, Alon. *The Land Is Full: Addressing Overpopulation in Israel.* New Haven: Yale University Press, 2016.

Teveth, Shabtai. *Ben-Gurion and the Palestinian Arabs: From Peace to War.* Oxford, UK: Oxford University Press, 1985.

Thrall, Nathan. *The Only Language They Understand: Forcing Compromise in Israel and Palestine.* New York: Metropolitan Books, 2017.

Tilley, Virginia. *The One-State Solution: A Breakthrough for Peace in the Israeli-Palestinian Deadlock.* Ann Arbor: The University of Michigan Press, 2005.

Twain, Mark (Samuel L. Clemens). *The Innocents Abroad, or The New Pilgrims' Progress.* Hartford: American Publishing Company, 1869.

INDEX

and Israeli borders, 119, 120
ownership of, 122
Trump recognizes Israeli sovereignty, 5
Goldstein, Baruch, 9, 143, 164
Goldstone, Richard, 152–53
Goldstone Report, 152–53
Gore, Al, 115
Great Britain
    aftermath of 1936 riots, 68–70
    attitude to Middle Eastern people, 66
    Balfour Declaration, 59
    erosion of trust with Jews and Arabs, 62
    shifting allegiances, 39
    support for Jewish homeland, 59–60
    and Sykes-Picot Agreement, 57–58
    and UN Resolution 181, 72
    value of Zionism to, 67
    withdraws from Palestine, 73
Grinevitsky, Ignaty, 45
GRUDGER, 56
Grün, David, 53. *See also* Ben-Gurion, David

H
Hadassah massacre, 73
Hamas
    bombings and shellings, 143
    ceasefire conditions, 155–56
    ceasefire with Israel, 157
    creation of, 141–43
    election results for, 145, 147–48
    kidnappings, 155
    objections to Annapolis conference, 4
    relationship with Israel, 142, 144–45, 158–59
    status of, 150
    suicide car bomb attack, 142–43
    takeover of Gaza Strip, xiv
    truce with Israel, 154–55
    use of civilians as shields, 156, 157
Hammer, Michael, 98
Hand in Hand schools, 225–26
Haniyeh, Ismail, 150
Hardin, Garrett, 115
Haredi community, 192, 193–97, 198–99, 200, 201–2, 227
Harper, Stephen, 127
Hawk and Dove, 102–3
Herzl, Theodor, 25, 27, 47–51, 54, 63, 122, 201
Heston, Charlton, 82
Hillel the Elder, 231

Hobbesian Trap, 62
Hovevei Zion, 46
Huseini, Faisal, 163

I
Iliad (Homer), 80
immigration
    Herzl's view of, 49
    illegal to Palestine, 69–70
    Jewish, 37–38, 39, 53, 57, 68
    and One Million Plan, 71
Immovable Ladder, 214–15, 217
An Inconvenient Truth (Gore), 115
India, 23, 74, 176–77, 229
Indian Act (1876), 219–20
Indigenous people (Canadian), 42, 218–21
Irgun, 37–38
Iron Dome, 154, 156
The Iron Wall (Jabotinsky), 65–66, 120
Islam, influence of Judaism and Christianity on, 94
Israel. *See also specific topics*
    admitted to United Nations, 106
    armistice agreements, 106–7
    attacks into and from, 148–49, 150–52, 154–55
    barrier erection, 167
    breakdown of civil society, 129–32
    constitution of, 75
    defence industry in, 124–25
    democracy in, 117–18, 228
    description of, 31–32
    disengagement from Gaza Strip, 145–47
    economy of, 171, 198
    education system in, 194–95, 198–201, 202, 225–26
    Egypt peace treaty, 166
    enabled by U.S., 172–73
    as ethocracy, 23
    fertility rates, 6, 204–5, 209–11, 227, 230
    food production in, 204
    future conditions in, 231
    and Goldstone Report, 152–53
    and Hamas, 142, 144–45, 154–55, 157, 158–59
    health care in, 223–24
    impact of annexation on, 134–35
    and Jewish Diaspora, 132–34
    Jordan peace treaty, 166
    kidnappings, 155
    and Law of Return, 123
    natural resources in, 6, 231

necessary accommodations by, 116
nuclear weapons program, 111
and Palestine dilemma, 39–41
and Palestinian conflict, 226–28
Palestinians' rights in, 34
Palestinians treatment after indepen-
    dence, 74
political system, 117–18, 228
population growth, 191–93, 202–4, 205,
    227
and Prisoner's Dilemma, 19–21
recognition of, 105
recognition of Palestinian sovereignty,
    129–30
religious tradition in, 201
rights of citizens, 130
secular and Haredi co-operation, 114
self-sufficiency of, 204
support for two-state solution, 74–75
Israeli Defence Forces (IDF), 54, 116, 119,
    130, 131, 141, 144, 145, 148, 149, 150, 151,
    152, 154, 155, 156, 157, 169, 183, 202, 244
"Israeli solution," 180–83
Iterated Prisoner's Dilemma, 55–56

J
Jabari, Ahmed, 154
Jabotinsky, Ze'ev, 27, 33, 37, 42, 43, 55, 62,
    63, 65–66, 69, 70, 75, 120, 187, 188, 193,
    202
Jerusalem, 5, 7, 52, 78, 96, 99, 165, 168, 169,
    214, 228
Jesus, 86
Jewish Diaspora, 132–34, 204
Jewish National Fund, 126–28
Jewish War (Josephus), 78
The Jewish Wars (Josephus), 97
Jews, similarities to Palestinians, 98–99
Jordan, 8, 32, 33, 41, 63, 81, 121, 164, 165,
    166–67, 235, 237
Judaism, texts of and Christian texts,
    94–95
Judea, 11–13

K
Kahane, Meir, 226
Kant, Immanuel, 51
Kerry, John, 4
Khalil, Izz El-Deen Sheikh, 144
Khdeir, Mohammed Abu, 155
kibbutz, first, 53, 63
The King's Torah (Shapira and Elitzur), 130,
    131
Klein, Menachem, 52

Kook, Abraham Isaac, 55

L
Law of Return, 123, 226–27
Lawrence, T. E., 59
League of Nations Mandate for Palestine,
    37
Lilienblum, Moshe Leib, 54
*Lives in Common: Arabs and Jews in
    Jerusalem, Jaffa, and Hebron* (Klein), 52
Lloyd, William Forster, 115
Low Battle, 132–33
LXX, 85–87

M
MacDonald, Ramsay, 39
Macdonald, Sir John A., 220
Madrid Conference (1991), 169
Magnes, Judah L., 70, 73
Malthus, Thomas Robert, 191
Mandatory Palestine, 33, 38, 39, 65, 68, 72,
    74, 139, 161, 163, 176, 178, 187, 226–27,
    228, xi
Martin, Dorothy, 233–35
Mashal, Khaled, 142
Masoretic Text (MT), 78–79, 81–84, 86–87
McMahon-Hussein correspondence, 59,
    63, 66
Meir, Golda, 35, 163, 209
The Meme Machine (Blackmore), 91–92
memes, 91–96
Merin, Dr. Saul, 222
messianic thinking, 228
Middle East
    division of (1916), 57–58
    strategic control of, 227–28
    strategic importance of, 67
minimax principle, 165–67
Mitchell, George, 4
Moses, 79, 80, 82, 83
Motzkin, Leo, 54
MT. *See* Masoretic Text (MT)
Muhammad, 94
Muslim Brotherhood, 139, 141–42

N
Nakba, 107–8
Nash, John, 21
Nash equilibrium, 21–22, 30, 103, 110, 111,
    112, 114, 132, 134, 135, 159, 176, 179, 180,
    210, 212, 214, 216, 229, 233
Nasser, Gamal Abdel, 121, 140
Nebel, Almut, 98
Nebi Musa Riots, 62

MICHAEL DAN

state of democracy in, 130
terminology to describe, 121
Pareto, Vilfredo, 22
Pareto principle, 22, 23
Paris Peace Conference (1919), 60
partition
of British Raj, 23, 74, 176–78, 229
compared to King Solomon ruling,
178–79
dilemma of, 29, 36–37, 41
game theory applied to, 176–80
of Mandatory Palestine, 72
and Resolution 181, 72, 107, 161, 175–
76
UN plan for, 72, 75, 140, 161, 163, 177
Passfield White Paper, 38–39
Paul VI, Pope, 214, 216
Peace (game), 213–14, 215–16
A Peace to End All Peace (Fromkin), 66
Peace to Prosperity, 5
Peel Commission, 39, 68–69, 161, 177, 202
Peres, Shimon, 3, 4, 124, 146, 170
Pinsker, Leon, 54
Pittsburgh Platform, 133
Pontiac, Chief, 219
Population Registry Law (1965), 7
Price, George, 101, 102, 212
Principles of Biology (Spencer), 90
Prisoner's Dilemma, 13–21, 22, 47,
55–56, 104, 109, 110, 176, 229. *See also*
GRUDGER; TIT FOR TAT
Project Rozana, 224–25
Psalm 145, 84–87
Ptolemy II Philadelphus of Egypt, 85

Q
Qassam Brigade, 142, 143
Qur'an, creation of, 94

R
Rabin, Yitzhak, 2, 3, 36, 128, 131, 140, 143,
163, 164, 165
RAND Corporation, 170–71
Rapoport, Anatol, 56
refugees, 138–39, 141, 161–62, 173, 174
Reines, Yizchak Yaakov, 55
replication, of sacred texts, 95–96
replicators, 89
Resolution 181, 72, 75, 107, 122, 130, 161,
175–76
Resolution 194, 106, 173, 174, 175, 176
Revisionist Zionism, 27, 37–38
Rice, Condoleeza, 149
ritual slaughter, 93–94

Rivlin, Reuven, 131–32, 193–94, 195, 196–
97, 201, 210
Roadmap (for peace), 3, 4, 147
Rogers, William, 1
Rogers Plan, 1–2
Rontzki, Avichai, 151–52
Rosenberg, David, 171, 197
Rosner, Shmuel, 201
Rousseau, Jean-Jacques, 113
Russell, Bertrand, 109

S
Sadat, Anwar, 2
Salawhi, Rozana, 224
Samhadana, Jamal Abu, 148
Save a Child's Heart, 223–24
Schelling, Thomas, 211
Schelling's Dilemma, 62, 149
Schwimmer, Al, 124
The Selfish Gene (Dawkins), 89, 101
Septuagint, 85–87
settler colonialism, 41–43, 120–21, 122, 226
settlers/settlements, 4, 5, 34, 37, 53, 54–55,
63, 65, 68, 70, 81, 145, 162, 167, 168–69,
171, 172, 233, xi
Shaer, Gilad, 155
Shaked, Ayelet, 131
Shalit, Gilad, 149, 154
Shamir, Yitzhak, 72
Shapira, Yitzhak, 130, 131
Sharett, Moshe, 122
Sharon, Ariel, 141, 145, 146–47, 167, 169
Shehade, Salah, 144
Shlaim, Avi, 6
Six-Day War, 1, 43, 74, 118–20, 121–22
Smith, John Maynard, 101, 102, 212
social dilemmas and game theory, 108–15
Sokolow, Nahum, 54
Solomon, King, 178, 179
Spencer, Herbert, 90
spontaneous mutations, 84, 87, 102
St. John Eye Hospital, 221–22, 223
Stag Hunt (game), 113–14
suicide bombings, 142, 143, 144, 167
Sykes, Christopher Simon, 58
Sykes, Sir Mark, 58, 60, 66–67
Sykes-Picot Agreement, 57–58, 59, 63, 66
Szold, Henrietta, 70

T
taking turns, 30
tefillin, 92–93
The Ten Commandments (movie), 82
Teveth, Shabtai, 35–36

Theodosius I, 96, 97
TIT FOR TAT, 56
Torah, 79–80, 81, 84, 85–86, 87
tragedy of the commons, 115
Transfer *(Ha'avara)* Agreement, 68
Transjordania, 41, 62, 63, 65, 66
Treaty of Paris (1763), 219
Trimbobler, Larissa, 131
Trump, Donald, 1, 4–5
Trumpeldor, Joseph, 62
Turkey, 153
Twain, Mark, 27
Two-Nation Theory, 176
two-state solution. *See also* Peel
  Commission
  advantages of, 20, 170–71
  British opinion of, 39
  disadvantages of, 171
  failures of, 161–62
  in India and Pakistan, 23, 74, 176–78,
    229
  interdependent *vs.* independent, 177–
    78
  Israel support for, 74–75
  lack of support for, 39
  mention at UN Security Council, 168
  as Nash equilibrium, 21–22
  in Prisoner's Dilemma example, 20
  proposal by Israel, 162

U
United Nations High Commissioner for
  Refugees (UNHCR), 174, 175, 227
United Nations Relief and Works Agency
  (UNRWA), 128, 138, 139, 174–75, 222,
  227
United States, 172–73
UN Resolution 242, 1–2, 119–20

V
Victoria, Queen of England, 221
Volunteer's Dilemma, 111, 115, 201
von Neumann, John, 109

W
Weisglass, Dov, 168
Weizmann, Chaim, 39, 53–54, 60, 63, 70,
  122
West Bank
  division of, 166–67
  freezing of settlements in, 4
  health care in, 222

and Israel barrier erection, 167
Israel seizes, 121, 122
Palestinian Authority in, xi
Palestinian sovereignty over, 129
and recognition of state of Israel, 162
Westphalian system of government, 105,
  xiv–xv
When Prophecy Fails (Festinger), 233
White Paper (1939), 69, 70
Wilson, Woodrow, 58
Wolfensohn, James, 147, 148
Woodhead Commission, 39, 68–69, 161,
  177

Y
Yassin, Ahmed, 141, 142, 144
Yom Kippur War, 2, 141
Young Turk Revolution, 55

Z
Zangwill, Israel, 28–29
zero-sum game
  and Israel, 172
  minimax strategy, 167
  of Netanyahu, 169
  and Prisoner's Dilemma, 47
Zionism
  attitude to Palestine, 67
  birth of political, 25–29
  core dilemmas, 31
  dilemmas facing, 39–41
  dilution of term, 76
  effect of annexation on, 134–35
  expansion of, 46
  goals of, 206–7
  and Great Britain, 67
  and Jewish National Fund policies,
    127–28
  Jewish opposition to, 71
  leadership in British Empire, 53–54
  and One Million Plan, 71
  political, defined, 29
  post-Zionism, 43, 208–9
  purpose of, 7
  quest for sovereign state, 70–72
  and religious observance, 200–201
  and settler colonialism, 41–43
  streams of, 54–55
  and terrorist undertakings, 72
  view of nationality, 8
Zionist Organization, 25–29. *See also*
  Zionism

MICHAEL DAN